AN INVITATION TO *Feast*

AN INVITATION TO *Feast*

A deep dive into India's culinary treasures

SONA BAHADUR

With every good wish,
Sona

ALEPH

ALEPH BOOK COMPANY
An independent publishing firm
promoted by ***Rupa Publications India***

First published in India in 2025
by Aleph Book Company
7/16 Ansari Road, Daryaganj
New Delhi 110 002

Cover photograph: Shutterstock/Indian Food Images

ISBN: 978-93-6523-653-8

1 3 5 7 9 10 8 6 4 2

Printed in India

To the ten-year-old

Contents

Introduction

A LOT ON MY PLATE

I was wafting about at home in my PJs when the offer to write this book surfaced.

It was not a fabulous time in my life. The food monthly I helmed had been shuttered a few years ago, and I was loath to move on. Deeply saddened by the decline of magazine journalism in front of my eyes, I had taken up a stint designing food tours for Cox & Kings. It enabled me to combine my two great loves—food and travel—but I yearned to write. Completely unsure of what I wanted to do with my life, I felt useless, irritable, numb.

When David Davidar from Aleph Book Company reached out and proposed an immersive look at the most beloved dishes of India, it seemed almost providential, and immediately got my creative juices flowing. Pondering his proposal, it occurred to me how little I actually knew about India's signature foods.

I adored the classics I grew up with. Yet years of eating them had not automatically led to an increase in knowledge. Very often, I hadn't savoured them with conscious intent or taken time to concentrate on what makes them great and special. Then there were the regional gems I was less familiar with but which I knew needed to feature more prominently in India's culinary iconography. From a writer's perspective, the idea of penning a culinary memoir seemed exciting. Although the past decade has seen a flowering of narrative food writing within the country and the diaspora—Anoothi Vishal's *Mrs LC's Table;* Padma Lakshmi's *Love, Loss, and What We Ate*; Sadia Dehlvi's *Jasmine & Jinns*; Saee Koranne-Khandekar's *Pangat, a Feast*; Tarana Husain Khan's *Degh to Dastarkhwan*; and Tabinda Jalil Burney's *Fabulous Feasts, Fables and Family*, to name a few—many of these 'foodoirs' focus on particular cuisines, or family lore and recipes. We lacked an intimate pan-India account of our defining dishes.

It also seemed like the perfect *moment* to write this book. A region can be defined 'by its superlative dishes,' writes American restaurant critic and author Robert Sietsema in his book *New York in a Dozen Dishes*, 'the ones that induce pride among the citizenry and excitement among visitors and speak eloquently of its history and current condition.'

This couldn't be truer for India. Globally, there is a bigger appetite than ever to understand Indian food. Celebrating our classics can become a big part of tapping into our strength as a nation and promoting the appreciation of Indian culinary culture around the world.

I thought to myself, that's it! That's what I need to do next—go on a gastronomic tour of India, sampling its treasures at source. The food would be its own delicious reward, and the stories of those who know and make it best my focus. This India-trotting spree, however, turned out to be more challenging than I had imagined. Designed as a one-year sprint, my quest became more of a marathon as the pandemic played spoilsport.

Six years on, what has emerged is a patchwork of facts, stories, impressions, recollections, epiphanies, opinions, revelations, recipes, and photos. This book presents eleven dishes that shaped my investigations into Indian food. Each chapter is dedicated to a classic, presenting vignettes of my time spent with experts who have aced it—as well as recipes (traditional, and where possible, modern riffs too) for those who feel tempted to cook after reading it. The order in which the chapters appear is random, and follows the chronology of my research.

I chose these dishes because of their profound significance to Indian cuisine. With their winning mix of familiarity, continuity, and comfort, they are pillars of our culinary culture. Most have innumerable regional variations, constituting more of a class of dishes than a single, perfect recipe.

A balance had to be struck between including the most recognized—dosai, butter chicken, biryani, chhole, rasgulla, dhansak—and those that aren't talked about as much, but contribute to a fuller appreciation of Indian cuisine—smoked pork, undhiyu, and the now-out-of-fashion shami kebab. I have included vada pav, too, to represent the bustling universe of our street food.

Tracing the trajectory of each dish, I have tried to piece together its past, present, and future into a larger culinary picture. Though I've touched upon foodways to give some context to each dish, there's a plurality of versions when it comes to origins. I'd like to celebrate that. The information presented here is based upon the views and opinions of the people I interviewed.

Let history remain contested. This book is about *living* history—the intersection of food, culture, people, identity, and places. What we have here are honest snapshots of the many luminous meals I ate during my jaunts, seasoned with moments of bonding, sharing, learning, and fun.

I chose to write this book through stories as their pull is eternal. They show rather than tell, triggering the same neurological regions that are activated when we experience something in real life. It's the next best thing to physically taking my readers there.

The questions I expect to be asked the most, of course, are, 'Why did you not write about lal maas, or rogan josh, or dal makhani, or payasam? Why did you choose undhiyu over dhokla? And dosai over idli.' Fair questions.

Curation is always personal. I freely admit that the criteria I used to pick the dishes are capricious. For instance, I chose undhiyu over dhokla as I found the seasonality and ritualism of the winter harvest feast associated with the former more interesting. This doesn't mean dhokla is any less iconic. Likewise, Goan fish curry, an everyday food eaten by all communities in Goa seemed more representative of the state to me than the equally famous, and worthy, pork vindaloo.

And it's not just the dishes—I have left out entire regions and states. To atone for these sins of omission, I hope to write a second volume to this book devoted to the foods and places I couldn't include here—and there are many.

Again, there's bound to be a fusillade of contradictory opinions about who makes a dish best. I have included the people who wowed me with their passion, authenticity, and uncompromising quality. But there are many other geniuses out there.

This book is neither exhaustive, nor entirely objective. I can't pretend to have brushed more than the surface of our cuisine. But it was an endlessly rewarding brush. The more I roamed India, the more I realized how delicious it is. My travels took off my blinders and enabled me to see each classic for what it truly is—a category of dishes with a sprawling scope and shifting ingredients. Not only did I have the privilege to relish some of the finest in the land, I got to witness the extraordinary love that goes into making them.

Savouring these gems in their traditional habitats enabled me to appreciate how tenacious they are. Persisting over centuries, they are our intangible cultural heritage, heirlooms that need to be protected and preserved for posterity.

But a classic is not a museum. It's a dynamic work in progress. As creativity, globalization, sustainability, tech, and AI rewrite the culinary landscape, these foods are becoming more vivid and variegated. Take, for example, the baked rasgulla. A genius play on the original, it's now a modern classic in its own right.

One of my key takeaways from my peregrinations was how misrepresented Indian food still is. Chef Manish Mehrotra, formerly with the iconic Indian Accent restaurant, had vented at length about this during one of our meetings. 'Indian food is not things just randomly mixed up in a bowl. We have a well-researched cuisine. Everything we do has a reason. The world needs to understand this,' he fumed.

The import of his words was apparent everywhere I went. For instance, the idea of pairing teflam with mackerel in a vivacious Hindu Goan fish curry has an underlying logic. The native Goan pepper is a digestive and helps make the oily, heavy fish more palatable.

Indians have perfected the art of complexity and balance, of flavour combinations and interactions. The meticulousness of our cuisine is reflected most beautifully in our spice blends. Be it the Parsi dhansak masala, the vatap (a wet paste that forms the base of Goan curries) or the eight-spice Mappila garam masala used to season a Thalassery biryani, each mix is a masterpiece of measured precision. And it's not always about spice mixes. Herbs take over plates in the northeast, where simplicity shines and every ingredient tastes luminously of itself.

I've often wondered why we don't radiate a greater sense of joy and pride in our cuisine. We have more culinary diversity and traditions than anywhere else in the world. We have thousands of interpretations of the same dish. Yet we underplay our staggering wealth of culinary heritage.

Masters of alchemy, we can turn curdled milk into an ambrosial sweet (rasgulla) and ferment batter naturally to make our own version of crêpes (dosai). We know a thing or two about olfactory stimulation (biryanis and pulaos) and layering fat with savouriness (butter chicken) to deliver knock-your-socks-off deliciousness. Why, then, are we not smitten with our food like we are with our cinema, our cricket, and our monuments?

France woke up early in the game to the potency (and marketability) of its cuisine by projecting gastronomy as being at the very heart of its national identity. In more recent times, Italy, Spain, Japan, and others have topped global culinary rankings. While the food of these nations is undoubtedly great, they have also taken it to that level by portraying it as a vital element of their soft power. Indians haven't fully harnessed this potential yet.

There are reasons for this. The enormity of India's size poses a challenge. As every Indian state has its own cuisine and sub-cuisines, gastronomic pride in India has existed more in a regional rather than national sense. Add to that the colonial hangover induced by nearly 200 years of British rule, which significantly impacted the way we think and talk about our food.

Also, our culinary culture has been historically based upon the oral transfer of recipes. The anthropologist Arjun Appadurai points out, 'Recipes, the elementary forms of culinary life, are missing in the great tradition of Hinduism.... Food is principally either a moral or medical matter in traditional Hindu thought.'[1]

To fully honour and successfully leverage our exceptional legacy, we need to elevate our culinary discourse. Finding new relevance in the midst of our growing global stature, we ought to become a lot more nuanced in the depiction of our foodscape. The brilliance of our classics hides in plain sight. To uncover this magic, we need to tell the unique stories of the fantastic dishes we have and verbalize their appeal.

This book is a tiny step in this direction. More than anything else, it is about belief in the greatness of our cuisine and the conviction that we can be world champions in gastronomy. I hope reading it will jumpstart a fresh way of thinking about Indian food.

At a personal level, writing this book also restored my faith in myself, and in journalism. Feasting through India tided me over a bittersweet period in my life tinged with uncertainty and self-doubt.

People who cook are among my favourite people. During my sojourn, I met many of them—chefs, home-cooks, restaurateurs, street-food vendors, caterers, bloggers, YouTubers, and others. The very personification of the Indian dictum 'atithi devo bhava', they welcomed me into their worlds with great kindness and warmth. I couldn't help but be touched to the core by their generosity, and their infectious enthusiasm to educate, feed, and indulge me.

These meals created an environment of convivial eating, which not only provided a major source of pleasure, but also nourished me spiritually and emotionally. Strewn all around me were stories of courage, hope, conviction, and adversity turning into triumph. Among the many lively conversations, and between all that eating, I also got my mojo back.

My cross-country adventure changed me. Not only did it leave me edified, it made me a kinder, happier, and less insular person. Though the many ups and downs of life remained, a door had been kicked open. I took a leap of faith from beleaguered magazine editor to independent author.

I hope the pages that follow inspire you with their stories and recipes and immerse you in the joy of Indian classics. But even more than that, I hope they lure you to travel in the pursuit of these potent flavours.

The journey begins here.

Biryani

MAKING RICE DANCE

'Butter chicken? That's just for you north Indians. But biryani is for *everyone*,' intoned Calicut-based chef Abida Rasheed when I asked her what ought to be the country's national dish.

Although there are several other worthy contenders for this distinction, she had a point.

Biryani is everywhere, but *everywhere* in India.

It virtually exceeds any other dish in pan-India popularity, a small miracle given the diversity of our palates—and even more remarkable when one considers that the dish originated in Central Asia and Persia.

By all accounts, the very first meat-and-rice mergers were simple meals—basic one-pots cooked to feed an army on the march. This workhorse morphed into the more nuanced pilau or pilaf. When, as food historian Lizzie Collingham notes in *Curry: A Tale of Cooks and Conquerors*, the 'delicately-flavoured Persian pilau met the pungent and spicy rice dishes of Hindustan' in the kitchen of emperor Akbar, the biryani was born.

It is in India that the classic reached its dazzling zenith, taking a myriad delectable forms. From the elegant, fluffy pulaos of Lucknow and Rampur to the big, bold biryanis of Dindigul, the range is endless. This plenitude has always intrigued me. How has the trifecta of meat, rice, and spices managed to win so many hearts? How has it conquered such diverse culinary environments?

Delving into these questions, I decided to cover the length and breadth of our great nation, tasting biryanis and pulaos in their traditional enclaves and uncovering the stories of the people who create and cherish their many versions.

This is easier said than done. A good meat-and-rice dish happens around every corner in our country. To enjoy them in all their mutations would have become the mother and father of all gastronomic trips.

I decided, therefore, to limit my culinary romp to seven hotspots.

LUCKNOW

Idrees Biryani with Abubakar

To many, the pulao–biryani distinction might seem entirely arbitrary. But as any true-blue pulao fan will tell you, there is a canyon-sized gap between the two.

While a pulao is cooked in a base of yakhni or spiced meat stock, a biryani is made by layering meat curry and almost-cooked rice, and relies on the technique of dum pukht or slow-fire cooking, generally in a dough-sealed pot.

Lucknowites have always been underwhelmed by biryani. For them, the dish is neither delicate nor sophisticated. It is the pulao, closer in essence to the Persian pilaf, that they regard as the OG.

Author Abdul Halim Sharar states this quite plainly in his book. 'In the view of gourmets, a biryani is a clumsy and ill-conceived meal in comparison with a really good pulao, and for that reason the latter was more popular in Lucknow,' he writes in *Lucknow: The Last phase of an Oriental Culture.*[1] Mirza Jafar Hussain says much the same thing in his memoir, *The Classic Cuisine of Lucknow*. 'When biryani came to Lucknow from Delhi, it was compared to a mash. The refined tastes of our forefathers corrected this and had a variety of pulaos prepared... gulzar pulao, noor pulao, coco pulao, moti pulao and chameli pulao.'[2]

Interestingly, this water-tight distinction seems to fall apart in the case of Lucknow's favourite biryani haunt, Idrees Biryani. The layered, orange-flecked dish of meat and rice served at the revered roadside joint has always reminded me more of a biryani than a pulao.

To quell my confusion, I decided to visit Idrees and meet its owner Abubakar, who runs the beloved shop with his younger brother Abu Hamza. As always, the ramshackle place in Chowk was bursting at the seams with devout locals lining up to gorge on some damn fine

Awadhi fare: ultra-tender nihari, ulte tawe ke parathe (parathas made on an inverted griddle) and a ravishing mutton korma.

Clad in a chequered lungi and a Madras cotton shirt, the fifty-something greeted me with a broad smile, his teeth very white against his rugged, tanned face. 'Anyone can throw meat korma and boiled rice together. But only a karigar (skilled artisan) can make a pulao,' Abubakar declared, when I presented my query. I pressed him to elaborate. 'Madam, zabaan yeh kissa batayegi (The tongue will tell this tale),' he replied enigmatically, inviting me to a demo and a taste.

I was just in time to watch his 'pulao' being made. Stretching over four hours, it warranted unwavering concentration and involved many lengthy procedures. First, the yakhni was made by cooking mutton with ghee, powdered and whole spices, curd, and khushbu ke masale (aromatics) like saffron, khus (vetiver), and mushk attar made from musk.

When the meat was done, the botis (pieces of mutton) were separated and the stock strained through a fine muslin cloth. The yakhni was then refined into a jhol by cooking in milk, with a tiny amount of malai (cream) for additional decadence. To give the pulao extra fragrance, a slew of aromatics—meetha attar (an essential oil used to perfume Awadhi dishes), rose essence, sandalwood powder, saffron—were again added to the jhol. In the end, layers of meat and partially cooked arwa rice were drenched with the stock in a copper degh (large, deep vessel), lavished with more saffron, and cooked on dum.

The triumphant ensemble of rice, meat, and spices that emerged at the end left no doubt that I was in the presence of greatness. The kernels of rice, having soaked up the umaminess of the yakhni, nevertheless remained light and distinct. The moist loveliness of every mouthful mingled with a potent aroma.

At ₹160 per portion (half-plate), Idrees Biryani is truly one of life's less expensive luxuries. When I complimented Abubakar on the sophistication of the dish, he heaped praises on his late father. 'My father Mohammad Idrees devoted twenty long years to learning the art of cooking from his mentor. He would always say, "Beta, handi ka pet kabhi mat katna (Son, never skimp on using good ingredients)."'

It's this moral zeal, inherited from his father, that had prevented the veteran from getting on delivery apps or exploring franchises. 'I don't want to be rich or famous. I just want to serve the food of my forefathers to one and all,' he said simply.

At the end of our session, I remained unconvinced that the elaborate masterpiece I had partaken in was a mere pulao. But I didn't really care. What stood out was the idealism, the extraordinary work ethic, and the endearing romanticism of its maker.

The tongue, *and* nose, had told this tale. Abubakar is serving the food of kings to the common man.

To me, he is one of the last great dreamers.

RAMPUR

Rampuri Yakhni Pulao with Peeli Mirch ki Chutney at Noor Mahal

Pulao is as much of an emotion in Rampur as in Lucknow.

Indeed, to people in this former princely state in western Uttar Pradesh, their version is *the* version, stealing a march over the more famous Awadhi pulao. 'That's because we Rampuris love real food, not fluff,' scoffed Nawab Kazim Ali Khan, summarily dismissing Lucknow's obsession with aromatics.

The grandson of Rampur's last ruling nawab Raza Ali Khan, fondly known as Nawed Miyan, had invited me for a meal at his palatial home Noor Mahal. Joining us were his mother Begum Noor Bano, his wife Yaseen Bano, and some family friends who were visiting from London.

Watching Chef Mehfooz Qureshi, a fourth-generation royal khansama (cook), make the dish in their kitchen, enabled me to nail the key differences between the Rampuri and the Awadhi versions. The use of khushbu ke masale like kewra (screwpine) and meetha attar is omitted in Rampur. The yakhni for the pulao is cooked with nalli ka gosht (mutton shanks). Also, in a nod to the local terroir, the pulao is spiced with Rampur's peeli mirch, a piquant yellow chilli that grows abundantly in these parts.

Mehfooz had dished out a menu of Rampur's greatest hits for lunch—yakhni pulao; dahi bade (fried lentil dumplings soaked in curd); white urad dal; and the pièce de résistance, Rampur's legendary taar gosht. The pulao, escorted by a bowl of peeli mirch ki chutney, was enchantingly light. But it was the taar, a ghee-laden mutton stunner, that had me in raptures.

At the table, Begum Noor Bano waxed nostalgic about Rampur's lost rice treasures. 'Today, we only talk about yakhni pulao and biryani. But when I got married in 1956, there were dozens of pulaos on the royal table. The pulao khansama, a specialist in rice dishes, would make murg dumpukht (in which the stomach of a whole chicken was filled with pulao and dry fruits), dum turti (quail pulao), and mutanjan (a pulao made from sweetened rice),' she recounted.

This grand repertoire, Kazim explained, emerged from the gentrification of Rampuri cuisine carried out by his forefathers.[3] 'The erstwhile nawabs of Rampur were descendants of the Rohilla Afghan Pathans. During the Indian mutiny of 1857, the Rampur royals sided with the British, attracting the cream of chefs from the besieged regions of Awadh and Delhi. The resulting culinary churn led to the emergence of a refined "haute" Rampuri cuisine that broke away from the tribal roots of the Rohillas,' he elaborated.

'We took the best of Delhi and Lucknow,' the begum said, beaming, a naughty gleam lighting up her kohl-rimmed eyes. 'And for a while, we were better than both.' Woefully, Rampur's glory days didn't last. The refusal of the royal chefs to share their recipes coupled with the abolition of the privy purses led to much of the royal cuisine dying out.

Though the tradition of stellar royal cooking continues in their kitchen, Noor Bano rued the extinction of many Rampuri delicacies. Confined to the zenana (women's quarters) during her youth, she regretted not having direct access to the royal kitchens. 'The khansamas worked in the mardana (men's quarters) and never let anyone enter their domains. They took their secrets to their graves. Ab toh bas naam reh gaya Rampur ke khane ka (Only the name of Rampuri cuisine remains now),' sighed the matriarch, as Mehfooz laid out bowls of chawal ki kheer, an utterly sinful rice pudding from the royal dastarkhwan, to conclude the feast.

Made languid by the spread, I stepped into food historian Tarana Husain Khan's home for a jolt of black coffee. The author of *Degh to Dastarkhwan,* who spent years decoding the trove of recipe books buried in Rampur's Raza library, added more lost gems to Noor Bano's list: ananas (pineapple) pulao, tamarind pulao, pulao sheer shakkar (a type of sweet pulao), and do gosht pulao. The last was made with two different meats—mutton on bone and chicken meatballs. 'When you bit into the chicken balls, you actually found pieces of mutton,' she explained.

It's not merely these pulaos that are now extinct, Tarana revealed, but the local hansraj rice that channelled the delicacy of the Rampuri yakhni pulao in an entirely unique way is gone too. 'Hansraj had a shorter grain than basmati, and its wonderful aroma could be smelled throughout the mohalla. In the 1990s, it was the rice of choice to make pulao, but over time it has been edged out by basmati. Now it has vanished from the mandis,' she lamented.

Thankfully, there is a silver lining to this dark cloud. As part of the high-impact Forgotten Foods Project, Tarana has actively worked to revive these lost dishes and rice varieties.[4] She had successfully recreated the do gosht pulao for two food festivals[5] and promised to make some for me on my next visit. A return trip to Rampur is due. Who could resist the lure of pleasures past?

HYDERABAD

Zaffrani Kacche Gosht ki Biryani with Mehboob Alam Khan

'What's all the fuss about Hyderabadi biryani?'

When I posed the question to Mir Mazharuddin, the founder of the iconic Hyderabad House sounded half-miffed, half-puzzled. 'Madam, how could you even *ask* such a thing?' he asked, cringing. Hyderabad evidently takes its role as India's biryani capital very seriously.

Realizing my education was lacking, having visited the city just once, he promptly offered to fill in the gaps. 'You need to eat the best biryani in town. I'll take you to the master,' he said, a sagely figure running his hands through his flowing white beard.

When he uttered the name Mehboob Alam Khan, my ears perked up. Most food lovers would kill for an invitation to the Shah Alam family. The son of the late industrialist Nawab Shah Alam Khan is highly regarded for his culinary prowess, having fed and hosted princes, movie stars, even the revered Aga Khan himself.

I was first introduced to Mehboob's brother Ahmed Alam Khan, himself a keen epicure known for his lavish shindigs. 'What shall we cook for you?' That was his first question as we connected over the phone.

'Biryani!' I replied with the enthusiasm of a fifth-grader.

'Yes, of course, Mehboob will do a zaffrani (saffron) biryani. You can watch it being made. He'll make mirchi ka salan (curried chilli peppers) too, and bagare baingan (a tart and spicy eggplant dish), and some dahi ki chutney. What else? Oh okay, just leave it up to me,' he drawled.

Ahmed himself drove me to Mehboob's place the following day. Set in a beautiful old house with art deco elements, the sprawling Barkatpura residence evoked an older Hyderabad. As we entered the spacious courtyard, Mehboob's daughter-in-law Nimra, an almond-eyed beauty, came out to welcome us. 'Baba's waiting for you,' she smiled, pointing me to an elderly, silver-haired gent immaculately clad in whites. 'Adab. So you're the journalist. Aaiye, aaiye,' he greeted warmly.

Mehboob lucidly put the Hyderabadi biryani into context. The world of biryani, he explained, is sliced into two camps: those who make pake gosht ki biryani and those who make kacche gosht ki biryani. In the former, the meat curry is prepared beforehand and layered with cooked rice, while in the latter, marinated raw meat is used. 'The charm of the Hyderabadi kacche gosht ki biryani is that the raw lamb cooks along with the rice. So the flavours and juices of the meat are not lost.'

An elaborate mise en place had been laid out in the lawn. Under Mehboob's gentle tutelage, Nimrah marinated the lamb with astonishingly nimble fingers. A massage of raw papaya (to tenderize the meat) was followed by slatherings of whole spices like cardamom, cloves, and cinnamon; ginger-garlic paste; red chilli powder; green chillies; and garam masala. Next came sprinklings of lemon juice, fried onions, chopped mint and coriander, and curd. Pours of oil, ghee, milk, and saffron soaked in water finished the procedure.

For the assembly, the meat was spread at the bottom of the degh followed by a layer of half-cooked basmati rice. More milk, ghee, and saffron were added. The pot was then sealed and nestled over glowing coals. 'I think it's going to be a good biryani,' Mehboob said quietly.

An hour-and-a-half later, the glistening, orange-tinted biryani was held up for the first reveal. Eyes half-closed, I took a sniff. For a moment, I was floating amid a fragrant fog of spices. I wanted to remain there, but the degh was promptly whisked off to the dining room.

As the day's labour was ladled out, the room filled up with more dishes than I could count. Tandoori chicken, seekh kebabs, dal makhani (creamy urad lentils), mutton korma (goat meat braised with curd and spices), kali mirch ka gosht (pepper-flavoured mutton), chaap (spiced mutton chops), Hyderabadi naan, mirchi ka salan, and kishmish (raisin) ki chutney.

Seated at the head of the table, Mehboob held court over the gathering like a pasha. Amiable chaos prevailed amid a barrage of wah wahs, jokes being cracked, naan platters being refilled, and Mehboob's wife beseeching everyone to eat more.

I devoured the biryani plain without a single dunk in the accompanying raita or mirchi ka salan. Defying the popular notion of Hyderabadi biryani as being chatpati, the taste was gently spicy, with a vivacious note injected by the herbs and lemon juice. The lamb was rendered bone tender by the long slow bake—and there was *lots* of it.

To Mehboob, the single most alluring part of the biryani was the last crusty layer called tehdehri (teh means bottom, and deh derives from degh). As the biryani cooks, the ghee and flavours of the biryani settle at the bottom. 'You get the whole essence of the biryani [in the tehdehri],' he said with childlike wonder, signalling the domestic helper to get some for me. It was a lovely study in contrasts—the delicately crisp rice setting off the ultra-soft, almost-melting lamb.

Chatting with my hosts, I discovered Hyderabad's biryani creds are not limited to zaffrani biryani. The real connoisseur's biryani is the sufiani, made without the use of saffron, red chillies, or turmeric. Apparently, the omission of these spices tests a cook's skills to the hilt.

The meal wended around ambrosial caramel custard and sheer kurma. I left to effusive goodbyes and promised to return for Ramzan. 'Come soon. I'll make sufiani biryani for you. And my special haleem,' Mehboob said affectionately.

There was a particular pleasure in savouring this slow-cooked biryani after watching it being made. Mehboob's passion, knowledge and warmth that afternoon had moved me deeply. Now, every time I eat biryani, he will be by my side, urging me to savour the crusty beauty of the tehdehri.

The following morning, Mazharuddin called to enquire whether my doubts had been quelled. 'Okay, you win,' I said. 'It *was* the best biryani in the world.'

KOLKATA

Kolkata-style Mutton Biryani with Manzilat Fatima

All that stuff you hear about Kolkata's passion for potatoes in their biryani is true—and I love them for it. But how the spuds got there in the first place elicits vastly different opinions.

The common story goes that they were added as a thrifty hack in the nineteenth century. In 1857, Nawab Wajid Ali Shah, the last ruler of Awadh, was dethroned by the East India Company. He eventually settled in Matia Burj near Kolkata, where a sizeable population followed him from Lucknow. With so many mouths to feed, his khansamas took to adding potatoes to scale down the meat and 'add bulk' to the biryani.[6]

To test the truth of this chestnut, I met up with Manzilat Fatima aka Manzie. A scion of Nawab Wajid Ali Shah from his son Birjis Qadr, the chef serves up her family's heirlooms at her rooftop home diner in east Kolkata. She looked elegant in a simple chevron-print salwar kameez, a diamond nose pin accentuating her dainty features.

'I get mad. Very mad,' Manzie fumed, as I gently broached the topic. 'No, Wajid Ali Shah was not one to skimp on food. And no, his cooks would not have substituted potatoes for meat,' she said sharply.

'But how could you know for sure?' I persisted.

'Wajid Ali Shah was a great connoisseur of food,' she said. 'How could a king who was used to food coming from seven kitchens in Lucknow resort to such desperate measures?'

The cook argued that though potatoes were introduced by the Portuguese to India during the sixteenth century, they were still considered relatively exotic during the nineteenth century.[7]

The likeliest theory, according to her, was that the nawab's cooks experimented with the tuber out of curiosity. 'Potato tasted good, was mild enough not to disturb the flavours of the biryani, and became popular,' she surmised.

Spending time with Manzie in her kitchen, I discovered that though adapted from the Awadhi style, the ingredients for the Kolkata biryani are different. She used mustard oil to cook the korma. The garam masala blend featured spices like shahi zeera (caraway seeds), kababchini (allspice), and white pepper. 'So you see, there is more to Kolkata biryani than potatoes,' the cook said, smiling.

The biryani she fed me bore this out amply. Served with a creamy raita of curd, mint leaves, and rock salt, it was an enchanting creation in its own right. As I tucked in the fragrant mound of rice, Manzilat marvelled at the twist of fate that brought her relationship with the dish full-circle.

'The Kolkata biryani evolved in my great-great-grandfather's kitchen and became popular across the city after his cooks started restaurants of their own,' she explained 'When I began my pop-ups, the dish came back to its original home.'

Eating at Shiraz, the iconic Kolkata restaurant dating back to 1941, the following day, added another layer of understanding to my appreciation of this biryani. Served with a boiled egg, it had the most alluring aroma. My favourite part was the accompanying chaap, a ghee-drenched, gravy-laden piece of fried mutton with tiny bones.

I was, however, still curious about the potatoes. Like Manzilat, the MD of Shiraz Hotels, Ishtiaque Ahmad, held the view that they elevate a simple biryani to a more interesting dish. 'Potatoes impart both texture and flavour. They turn the biryani into its best version,' he said. However, he did not entirely rule out the thrift theory.

The tubers, Ishtiaque believed, would always be a hot potato among culinary debates. 'And that's a good thing. It only adds more spice to things,' he said, smirking.

CHENNAI

Long-grain Ambur Biryani with Khatta Baingan at The Ambur Canteen

In Ambur, you might step out to buy shoes and return with a box of biryani.

I learnt this startling fact while hanging out with Zeeshan Anees at The Ambur Canteen in Chennai. The genial owner of the restaurant was telling me about his hometown. The mecca for stock-lot footwear became renowned for its biryani, thanks to the large Muslim population employed in the city's tanneries. 'Many shops sell both,' he said, laughing as I tried to picture the surreal scenario.

Growing up, this sleepy Tamil Nadu town is where Zeeshan and his restaurant partners, Mohamed Samee and Mohammed Faraaz, spent their summer holidays. The cousins, who were schooled at Chennai's Don Bosco, would eagerly look forward to the sumptuous Muslim-style Ambur dishes made by their family cook Mohideen at their ancestral home. Mohideen would feed them chawal rotis, ghee rice and kurma (coconut-based chicken gravy), a peppery curry known as phaal, and of course, biryani.

As elsewhere in India, biryani is staple wedding fare in Ambur. What sets it apart, Mohammed pointed out, is its minimalism. 'The greatest taste comes from humble ingredients. The base of the biryani is a light yakhni of tomatoes and meat with the barest hint of masalas. It's milder in terms of spices and oil. There are no strong flavours, just the juices of the meat soaking into the rice.'

The desire to take these culinary heirlooms outside their native city led the trio to launch The Ambur Canteen in Chennai in 2023. It was my friend Ashwin Rajagopalan, a seasoned food and travel writer, who told me about this gem in the heart of T. Nagar. 'You *have* to go there. The owners are my ex-classmates. They serve kickass Ambur biryani,' he raved, promising to join in.

Ashwin was late. The authentic aromas wafting in from the kitchen had caused the rumble in my stomach to rise to a crescendo. Having swiped off way too much chicken 65, I was afraid I wouldn't do justice to the main course.

The biryani, happily, was the very definition of simple. Light-textured, with a subtle tomato-ey twang, it reminded me a lot of a North Indian pulao. The flavour whack came from the sweet-sour khatta baingan, or mashed eggplants simmered in a gravy of tamarind, jaggery, fried mustard seeds, and spices.

The buddy reunion was a boisterous affair, with Don Bosco stories, jokes, and gossip being exchanged. Ashwin had an interesting biryani story from school. Growing up in a staunchly vegetarian TamBrahm (Tamil Brahmin) family, his introduction to biryani was through his Muslim classmates' tiffins. 'When these three would open their lunchboxes, the entire classroom would fill up with that amazing smell. I fell hard for Ambur biryani,' he reminisced.

Those early flavours and aromas got lodged in his memory, making the 'tiffin biryani' of his childhood the benchmark against which all others must be measured.

'That's the thing about first tastes, right? They always win,' he said.

Dindigul Biryani with Nagasamy 'Satish' Naidu at Dindigul Thalappakatti

A punchy counterpoint to the delicate Ambur style, Dindigul biryani satisfies the Tamil's desire for more assertive flavours. It's by no means a shy biryani, and announces itself to the palate with a powerful taste.

Although several restaurants serve it in Chennai, the godfather of them all is Dindigul Thalappakatti. A household name in south Indian biryanis, the chain has prospered for decades, spanning a swath of countries across the globe including Sri Lanka, UAE, Dubai, Singapore, Malaysia, and the US.

I stepped into Chennai's Guindy outlet to meet the owner, Nagasamy Dhanabalan. A tall, purposeful figure in his early forties, he bounded into the diner wearing a crisp white shirt and a navy suit. 'Call me Satish,' he said, shaking my hand as we sat down to chat over tall glasses of cool jigarthanda (a local milk drink seasoned with sarasaparilla syrup and chia seeds).

The first DT, he shared, was founded in 1957 in Dindigul and got its name because of the thalapa (turban) his bald grandfather Nagasamy Naidu would wear as he sat in the tiny shop, selling his wife Kannamma's rustic Naidu-style mutton biryani.

Though Satish's grandparents passed away before he was born, their formidable biryani skills were handed down to him by his father and uncles. The celebrated taste is his signature, coursing through every meal served at Dindigul Thalappakatti.

The recipe calls for marinating mutton (specially sourced from a network of artisanal goat suppliers in Kannivadi) overnight with curd and lemon juice and cooking it with the secret Dindigul masala made of spices like cardamom, cinnamon, and cloves. 'Dry spices are cooked along with shallots, ginger-garlic, coriander, and mint leaves to make the masala paste, which is used to season the meat and short-grain seeraga samba rice. The biryani is then cooked for forty-five minutes on dum and served with boiled eggs,' Satish detailed.

I tried some. Set off with an onion raita, it packed a mouthful of fiery, tangy flavour. The full-bodied spiciness took some getting used to, but I relished it with a side dish of slow-cooked lentils called dalcha.

The earthy taste is now a global tour de force. Inspired by KFC—where Satish also did a short stint—the Hotel Management graduate was on a blitzkrieg. After setting up a jaw-dropping 101 outlets across the world, he is now experimenting with automation and chef-less kitchens. 'We want to be a factory and not a restaurant. My plan is to expand pan-India with centralized commissary kitchens that can cater to ten to fifteen restaurants each in the metros. In the next five years, we will expand to 250 outlets and become a unicorn of the F&B space,' he said grandly.

Despite his plans of global domination, Satish is never far from his humble Dindigul roots. His dark eyes softened as he recalled his first biryani lessons. 'In those days, biryani would only be cooked on charcoal. The workers, bare-backed and clad in thin cotton dhotis, would be sweating it out in 50°C, amid smoke. To date, I marvel at how they survived that heat. They were my heroes,' he said wistfully.

A funny childhood story lightened the moment. Every day pots of biryani along with boiled eggs would be transported from the kitchen to the nearby restaurant in a truck. A ravenous Satish would sneak in and polish off about a dozen eggs. When his father would take the inventory, he would demand to know where the missing eggs were, and all hell would break loose.

'A hundred-and-one outlets and counting. I think you've made up for all those boiled eggs you stole,' I teased him as we said goodbye.

'I think I have,' he said, grinning proudly.

CALICUT

Thalassery Mutton Biriyani with Faiza and Chovakaran Moosa

North Kerala's Thalassery biriyani is a kind of Malabar-and-Middle East union that reflects the region's Arab influence.

To me, everything about the Mappila Muslim biriyani is exceptional. The short-grain kaima rice sourced from hilly Wayanad, the unique eight-spice Mappila masala blend, the garnish of jewel-like golden raisins, and the one-of-a-kind accompaniments. It's even spelt differently—biriyani, and not biryani.

In my opinion, no one makes it better than Faiza Moosa, the author of *Classic Malabar Recipes.* For over three decades, Faiza and her husband Chovakaran Moosa have crisscrossed the globe, spreading the gospel of Mappila cuisine to places as far-flung as Lyon and New York.

I first met the Moosas at Ayisha Manzil, their imposing, colonial-style Thalassery bungalow. Perched dramatically on a cliff, it offered the most dazzlingly cinematic view of the Arabian Sea. Faiza had produced a succession of extraordinary Mappila dishes—a meat porridge called alisa, tart tamarind prawns, and golden lakottaappams, or crêpes wrapped around sweet egg-coconut filling. It was the start of an enduring fascination with Malabari food.

The couple has since moved to Calicut due to Moosa's failing health. When I connected with him about my biryani odyssey, he promptly invited me to fly down for a meal.

The day I did, it was raining on a Biblical scale in Calicut. The septuagenarian picked me up from my hotel in his bright orange Mini Cooper. 'It's the late-October rain of Calicut. We call it thula,' he said, clearly enjoying the downpour, as we drove down to their characterful 200-year-old Calicut home.

Welcoming me to her kitchen with her trademark warmth, a shy, sari-clad Faiza demonstrated the path to a perfect Mappila biriyani. Dreamy layers of kaima rice and mutton curry were infused with sprinklings of rose water and saffron, slathered with garam masala and fried onions, studded with raisins and cashews, and slow-cooked. The layered loveliness was served with a date pickle, raita, papadums, and a zesty chutney of curry leaves, mint, coriander, and lemon.

As biryanis go, the taste was very subtle, which I found interesting, given that spices run riot in Kerala. Faiza attributed the nuanced flavour to her Mappila garam masala, a perfectly balanced mix of cardamom, cinnamon, cloves, cumin, caraway seeds, nutmeg, mace, and the defining spice of Mappila cuisine, aniseed.

We passed a convivial hour at the table. Liberated from his diet for the afternoon, Mr Moosa was determined to extract the last ounce of pleasure from his cheat day. 'Tomorrow, Faiza and I complete forty-five years of marriage. We are putting today's biriyani on my celebration account,' he trilled.

An old hand at entertaining, he held forth on the central role played by biriyani at a Mappila wedding. The wedding feast includes three dishes: muttamala or egg garlands, alisa, and mutton biriyani. 'We call it MAB,' he said in his lilting Malayali accent.

Their wedding in 1979 was among the last to host the traditional Mappila supra—the traditional communal spread—before table service became the norm. 'Everyone ate from a common platter. It was amazing,' he said. Faiza had less happy memories from the event. Her two favourite goats were butchered for the wedding feast. 'I was so sad that I didn't eat anything,' she said.

After lunch, we descended into the living room, where the couple showed me photos from their wedding album. Faiza, then a twenty-something with henna-dyed palms, made a gorgeous bride. Not to be outdone, Moosa looked debonair in Aviators and a fine three-piece suit. 'Wait, you wore sunglasses at your wedding, Mr Moosa?' I ribbed.

'Don't blame me. It was the fashion that time,' he said with an eye-roll.

As I prepared to leave, one gastronomic oddity about the Thalassery biriyani was still boggling my mind. While eating lunch, I had noted that the mutton masala was served separately from the biriyani, in a different bowl.

'Oh *that*. That's how we like it here,' Moosa said. 'The meat is cooked, then combined with rice, then separated again. Just like first you're single, then you get married, and then you separate.'

The analogy evoked the most withering of looks from the wife. 'Not the best story to tell on the eve of your anniversary, Mr Moosa,' I teased. Moosa looked uneasy. Faiza blushed furiously.

It was an adorable moment. The love story of meat and rice might not always end happily ever after, but the Moosas are undoubtedly a match made in heaven.

Fish Biriyani with Abida Rasheed

The Mappila meen (fish) biriyani has a certain je ne sais quoi that sets it apart from its mutton counterpart. I couldn't imagine leaving Calicut without a taste and dropped in at YouTuber and food consultant Abida Rasheed's home in the sylvan suburb of Calicut's Vengeri.

'Meeeen biriyani has to be a meeeal by itself. Nothing should interfere with it,' she said emphatically. 'You need to smell it, touch it, feel it. All your senses should hunger for it. Now *that's* what I call a fish biriyani,' she gushed in her lyrical, full-throated voice.

'And I'm going to eat that today,' I said, grinning.

'Inshallah!' said she. 'By God's grace you shall.'

The tradition of making seafood biriyanis is unique to north Kerala. Living in the midst of such marine abundance, it's not surprising that the Malabaris take full advantage of this plenitude. The Arab influence might be at play, too. 'A lot of Yemenis, known to combine rice with fish, came to the Malabar as traders and influenced our cuisine,' Abida pondered.

Though associated with the region, Abida pointed out, fish biriyani isn't a common dish in these parts. 'Only certain upper-class families make it. The common man cannot afford to buy seer fish. And since fish breaks easily, this biriyani is more suited to parties than weddings.'

The recipe she recreated for me dated back generations. Reflecting on the flavourful dish of her grandmother, Abida recounted the care with which she would make fish biriyani. 'Meen biriyani was like a festival in our house. My grandmother would make the spice powder herself using produce from our own plantations. Because Mappila women didn't go out of the home during those days, she would instruct my dad or grandfather on which fish to buy. After the fish was bought, she would complain it had not been cut properly. The drama would just go on and on,' she said, smiling at the memory.

Watching Abida cook, I noted that the key differentiator in her fish biriyani was a wet masala made from coriander leaves, onions, ginger-garlic, and green chillies. Darne-cut pieces of seer fish were marinated with this thick paste before being shallow-fried. The fish was layered with cooked kaima rice, seasoned with Mappila garam masala, and left to cook on dum.

Even before we sat down to eat, I could sense this was unlike any other biryani I had eaten before. It smelled tantalizingly exotic, carrying with it the faintest whiff of the sea. The taste was extraordinary. The kaima rice, having perfectly absorbed the taste of the fish and masala, hummed with a piscine soulfulness. It was hard to imagine fish and rice could marry so perfectly.

I ate ravenously. 'How come Thalassery biriyani isn't more famous?' I asked, genuinely astonished that something so fabulous had not been cemented on the culinary map. Abida blamed the under-promotion of the Malabar by the tourism ministry.

She also attributed it to ethnicity. 'Us Mappilas are a matrilineal society. The brides stay back in their family. It's the grooms who leave their homes to stay with their wives. So our recipes have remained in the homes.'

But she didn't seem to mind too much. 'We don't really want too many tourists around here. We want to keep this part of the country to ourselves,' she confessed, flashing me a mischievous smile.

MUMBAI

Chicken Biryani with Mazhar Mansuri at Jaffer Bhai's Delhi Darbar

My friend Sheeba Iqbal Jairajpuri, a home chef from Lucknow, considers Bombay biryani a stodgy horror, utterly lacking in finesse or charm. But those of us who have acquired the taste for it tend to be pretty passionate about it. Chi-chi it isn't. But juicy? Satisfying? Fun? Yes, yes, and yes!

To me the road to Mumbai's biryani heaven leads directly to Jaffer Bhai's Delhi Darbar where they know how to layer on the flavours to create the signature dish that is now a beloved classic.

The time-honoured taste has remained the same since 1973, when its charismatic founder Jafferbhai Mansuri first introduced his masterpiece to the City of Dreams. Distinct from Delhi and Hyderabadi biryani, the fluffy kacchi-style biryani draws its charm from its unique spice mix, and a treasure of fried onions and aloo bukhara (dried plums).

I knew the taste well. What sparked my curiosity was the future of the brand after Jafferbhai's death. With the virtuoso's empire split between his four sons, what new directions would his biryani take? Would the famous Jafferbhai formula be tweaked, or *gasp*, changed?

To investigate, I schlepped down to the Grant Road outlet to meet his eldest son. A middle-aged man with a mop of soft-brown curls, Mazhar greeted me with a cheery hello seeped in a strong British accent.

As always, the iconic eatery was full of families and couples tucking into platefuls of biryani and dabba gosht (boneless mutton in a white gravy). 'They're all regulars,' he smiled, ushering me to his den—a small room behind the restaurant.

'Are you going to change the taste of your biryani?' I demanded to know right away, too impatient for pleasantries. He looked nonplussed.

'What? No. Never,' he cried. 'This is the 100 per cent tried-and-tested formula for Bombay biryani. It will never change.'

The restaurateur's voice was hushed and reverential as he spoke about his late father. 'I spent thirty years of my life working with dad. He put extraordinary care into preparing biryani. He always told me to follow the formula. And that's what I intend to do.'

'So what's the formula?' I asked.

'Oh, that's top-secret. But I'll tell you the basics. We make a dum pukht biryani. Raw meat is marinated for half an hour, layered with rice, potatoes, and masala, and slow-cooked on coals. We use more of fried onions or birista and aloo bukhara, and there's more juicy masala in there.'

It's a taste, Mazhar said, that holds sway across Mumbai. 'Everyone eats our biryani—the UP guys, the Maharashtrians, the Parsis. Eighty per cent of the crowd coming here is non-Muslim. That says a lot.'

He didn't deny that times are changing when it comes to biryani, with globalization unleashing a slow process of culinary osmosis. 'People want new. They get bored,' he admitted, pointing to the recent popularity of Arabic rice-and-meat dishes like kepsa and mandi as proof of this. Though he keeps abreast of food trends, Mazhar abhors fads and constant change. Millet biryanis are not for him, neither is lab-grown meat.

Later, when we stepped into the restaurant for a bite, the familiar mound of saffron-tinted rice embedded with chicken arrived on the table with a side of dahi kachumber (onion, cucumber and tomato raita). The subtle tang of the plums and the sweet, soft fried onions in the mix made it difficult to stop eating.

As I licked my fingers, Mazhar broke into a smile. 'Don't you just love that masala? Sometimes the best thing you can do for a dish is to not mess with it,' he said.

There was more than a kernel of truth to that.

Dark Kitchen Biryani with Farhat Navlakhi Saxena

Eating biryani out of a box is the kind of thing that normally breaks me out in hives. The travesties that pass for the dish these days are light years away from the original I grew up eating (and worshipping).

Yet there is no denying that tech is singularly responsible for catapulting the classic to its current superstar status. Year after year, chicken biryani emerges as the immediate bestseller on the annual reports published by food delivery apps like Swiggy and Zomato.[8]

The explosion of dark kitchens (delivery-only commercial kitchens) fuelled by the arrival of delivery apps, has taken the biryani world by storm, drawing new generations to the classic, and spawning a surge in variety.

When I asked Farhat Navlakhi Saxena, the co-founder of Mumbai-based Go! Biryan, the reason for biryani's mega success online, she pinned it down to three words. 'Evolution, evolution, evolution.' The meal-in-a-box format is easy, casual, convenient. 'Plus, it offers a dish for all tastes and budgets,' she said.

An excitingly experimental approach and hybrid flavour combinations underpin the line-up at Go! Biryan. Among the fifteen-plus biryanis squeezed into the delivery-only menu, classics like chicken tikka biryani and Bohri-style mutton biryani are top-sellers. But the unabashedly 'fusion' line-up also features the likes of Schezwan tikka biryani, butter chicken biryani, and mutton rogan josh biryani.

The popular picture of the biryani is of an old-world dish, she argued, but it's precisely this liberation from a hidebound past that has enabled the classic to realize its full potential. 'Biryani needn't always be a gourmet dish. It's also a wholesome meal,' she observed.

Farhat did, however, admit to a less savoury side of biryani's digital glory. Tradition dictates that a biryani should be cooked on dum. But today most cloud kitchens are selling pan biryani—just masala, rice, and meat or veggies tossed together in a pan (often due to the high commissions that the brand-owner has to pay to food-delivery players). 'There are no layers, no slow cooking, no dum in its pure form,' she lamented.

Scaling up also often means using pre-prepared frozen masalas, reducing the amount of meat in the biryani, and replacing basmati with cheaper rice varieties. 'Biryani has lost some of its grandeur. And we are to blame,' she admitted.

Though Farhat doesn't plead guilty to these crimes, she does prioritize wooing Gen-Z customers. 'I've tried to push the classic in more exciting directions. Every new avatar is an evolutionary experiment. Some—like butter chicken biryani—worked, while others—like brown rice biryani—sank without a trace,' she shared.

'So, what's the next hot biryani?' I asked.

'Oh, we're planning to introduce a make-it-yourself biryani,' she whispered, leaning forward as though to share a state secret. 'We want to personalize biryani like pizza or a noodle bowl. So you can choose the meat, the spice levels, decide if you want extra potatoes or eggs, and that sort of thing.'

I urged her to imagine something a bit more space age-y.

'Hmm. Let's see,' she said. 'I see a biryani ATM. Tap the screen and a box of biryani comes out. Oh, and you have the option of getting it hot or otherwise, depending on whether you wish to eat it on the spot or take away. And...let's see....'

◆

At the end of my forays, biryani and pulao had been well and truly celebrated.

These rice wonders are gateways to worlds of flavour. They're maddeningly sensual, yet linger on at a spiritual level. They make for blissful comfort food, yet feel luxurious. They wow at weddings, and also show up at birthday parties, funerals, remembrance meetings, baby showers, and graduations.

And that, to me, is the key to their magic—*everyone* gets them. Anyone can find one that's right for them.

Crisscrossing through India helped me uncover how these rice dishes have managed to thrive in such different contexts. The versatility of the one-pot format deserves credit. Because the combination of meat and rice is so universally accessible, it offers the perfect playground for personalization.

But it's how ingeniously Indians evolved a standard plate of meat and rice into endlessly delicious directions that is groundbreaking. Biryani and pulao are multifaceted gems in the realm of food. More than edibles, they are art forms. This speaks to India's culinary dynamism, and its unmatched flair with ingredients, techniques, and seasoning.

Juxtaposing so many different styles and tastes made me appreciate how polarized the flavours of biryani are. Set apart by foodways, terroir, rice types, spice blends, techniques, and a constellation of side dishes, every version I tried basked resolutely in its distinctiveness.

Yet, in each variant, the balance of the whole dish was outstanding. Each layered aroma and flavours with total mastery and was firmly anchored in its own community and traditions.

With virtually every region having its own version, there are strong opinions as to which one is the best. But why choose when each has something unique to woo the senses?

I can't wait to add more to my repertoire—Bhatkal biryani, Memoni biryani, Amroha pulao, Sufiani Hyderabadi biryani, donne biryani, and so many others.

I know each will tell its own story, and be its own kind of delicious.

Recipes from My Travels

MEHFOOZ QURESHI'S RAMPURI YAKHNI PULAO

SERVES: 4 TIME TAKEN: 1 HOUR 30 MINUTES

INGREDIENTS

Mutton	500 gms, curry-cut
Ghee	4 tbsp
Yellow/ red chillies, whole	2
Green chillies	2, slit
Cinnamon sticks	2
Green cardamom	4–5
Cloves	8–10
Black peppercorn	1 tsp
Bay leaves	2
Cumin seeds	1 tsp
Coriander seeds	1 tsp
Fennel seeds	1 tsp
Ginger-garlic paste	2 tbsp
Water	500 ml
Onion	1, sliced
Basmati rice	250 gms
Curd	100 gms
Saffron	a pinch, soaked in warm water

Orange food colour	a few drops, optional
Cardamom powder	½ tsp
Fried onions	2 tbsp
Salt	to taste

METHOD

Heat ghee in a pot and add mutton pieces to it. Sauté well for 5 minutes.

Add whole yellow/red chillies, green chillies, cinnamon sticks, cardamom, cloves, black peppercorns, bay leaves, cumin seeds, coriander seeds, fennel seeds, and ginger-garlic paste. Mix well.

Add 500 ml water and bring to a boil.

Cover and cook for 1 hour or until the mutton pieces are tender, or, pressure-cook for 4 whistles.

Once the mutton is tender, drain the pieces along with the spices and reserve the liquid. This liquid is the yakhni.

Wash and soak the Basmati rice in water for 30 minutes.

Heat 1 tbsp ghee in a pan and add sliced onions to it. Fry till golden brown.

Add the cooked mutton pieces along with the spices. Mix well.

Add curd to the mutton pieces. Mix well.

Add the soaked rice, 500 ml of yakhni, and salt.

Cover and cook for 10 minutes. Once the rice is cooked, switch off the flame and let it rest for 10 minutes.

Remove the lid and add 1 tbsp ghee. Sprinkle saffron soaked in water on top, fried onions, cardamom powder, and a few drops of orange food colour, if desired.

Mix gently and serve hot.

THE AMBUR CANTEEN'S MUTTON BIRYANI WITH KHATTA BAINGAN

For mutton biryani,

SERVES: 4

TIME TAKEN: 1 HOUR 30 MINUTES PLUS OVERNIGHT MARINATION

INGREDIENTS

Mutton	1 kg, cut into medium-sized pieces
Basmati rice	500 gms, pre-soaked for 30 minutes
Onions	4 medium, thinly sliced
Green chillies	6–8, slit
Ginger–garlic paste	2 tbsp
Mint leaves	1 cup, chopped
Coriander leaves	1 cup, chopped
Curd	200 gms
Lemon juice	2 tbsp
Bay leaves	2
Cinnamon	2-inch stick
Cloves	6
Green cardamom	4
Turmeric powder	½ tsp
Red chilli powder	1 tbsp
Biryani masala	1 tbsp
Salt	to taste
Oil	4 tbsp
Ghee	2 tbsp
Water	2 litres

METHOD

Take a large bowl and put mutton pieces in it along with curd, half of the ginger-garlic paste, turmeric powder, red chilli powder, half of the chopped mint and coriander leaves, lemon juice and salt.

Mix well and let the mutton marinate for at least 2 hours, or preferably overnight in a refrigerator.

For cooking the rice, bring 2 litres of water to a boil. Add half of the bay leaves, cinnamon, cloves, and cardamom along with 1 tbsp oil and salt.

Add the pre-soaked rice and cook until it's about 70 per cent done.

Drain the water and set the rice aside.

To prepare the biryani, heat oil and ghee in a large heavy-bottomed pot. Add the remaining whole spices.

Add the sliced onions and fry until golden brown. Add the remaining ginger-garlic paste and sauté until the raw smell disappears.

Add chopped tomatoes, green chillies, and the remaining mint and coriander leaves. Cook until the tomatoes are soft.

Add the marinated mutton and cook on high heat for 5 minutes. Then, reduce the heat, cover and cook until the mutton is tender (add a little water if needed), for around 1 hour, or 4–5 whistles in a pressure cooker.

Once the mutton is cooked, layer the cooked rice over it. Sprinkle 1 tbsp biryani masala and drizzle some ghee on top.

Cover the pot with a tight-fitting lid and cook on a very low flame for about 20–25 minutes. This process is called 'dum', where the flavours are sealed in.

Gently mix the biryani to avoid breaking the rice grains. Serve hot with raita and khatta baingan.

For khatta baingan,

SERVES: 4 TIME TAKEN: 30 MINUTES

INGREDIENTS

Eggplants (baingan)	250 gms, slit into quarters
Oil	4 tbsp
Mustard seeds	1 tsp
Fenugreek seeds	¼ tsp
Asafoetida (hing)	a pinch
Curry leaves	10
Ginger-garlic paste	1 tbsp
Turmeric powder	1 tsp

Red chilli powder	1 tsp
Coriander powder	1 tsp
Cumin powder	1 tsp
Tamarind paste	2 tbsp
Water	400 ml
Jaggery or sugar	1 tsp
Salt	to taste
Fresh coriander	a handful, chopped

METHOD

Heat oil in a kadhai, add mustard seeds, fenugreek seeds, asafoetida, and curry leaves, and let them splutter.

Add ginger-garlic paste and sauté for 30 seconds.

Add the eggplants, turmeric powder, and salt.

Cook covered for 10 minutes on a slow flame until soft.

Add red chilli powder, coriander powder, and cumin powder and mix well.

Add the tamarind paste and water. Bring it to a boil and let it simmer for 10 minutes.

Stir in jaggery or sugar and check for seasoning.

Once ready, sprinkle chopped coriander leaves and serve with Ambur mutton biryani.

Tip: You could add 1 cup fresh tomato purée along with water and tamarind paste to give more body to the gravy.

ABIDA RASHEED'S FISH BIRIYANI

SERVES: 4 TIME TAKEN: 1 HOUR

INGREDIENTS

King fish	500 gms, darne-cut
Turmeric powder	1 tsp
Salt	to apply on fish
Coconut oil	3 tbsp
Ghee	1 tbsp

Onions	2 cups
Ginger	3 tbsp
Garlic	3 tbsp
Green chillies	8, crushed
Tomatoes	1 cup, crushed
Curd	250 gms
Salt, crystallized	to taste
Fried onion	1 cup
Green coriander ground into a paste with a little water	1 cup
Garam masala	1 tbsp
Lemon juice	2 tbsp
Oil	2 tbsp

For the ghee rice,

Kaima rice	500 gms
Ghee	2 tbsp
Oil	2 tbsp
Green cardamom	2
Cinnamon	1-inch piece
Cloves	3
Onion	½, sliced
Hot water	1 l
Mappila garam masala	1 tbsp
Green coriander	a handful, chopped
Salt	to taste

METHOD

Coat the fish slices lightly with salt and turmeric powder and keep them aside for 10 minutes.

Crush the garlic on the grinding stone, followed by ginger. Grind the green chillies with this mixture.

Crush onions on the stone or coarse-grind them in a mixer.

Take a wide deep pan and heat 3 tbsp coconut oil in it.

Shallow-fry the marinated fish on both sides until golden and cooked, making sure the fish slices don't break.

Once the fish is fried, keep aside.

Add ghee to the same pan, followed by oil, and add the crushed onions to it and sauté for 5-6 minutes until the raw smell of onion disappears.

Add the crushed ginger, garlic, and green chillies. Sauté for a minute.

Add the chopped tomatoes and sauté for 10 minutes until they are soft.

Add the curd, followed by crystallized salt. Mix well.

Add half the fried onions and green coriander paste. Mix well.

Cook for 5 minutes until the gravy becomes saucy.

Check for seasoning and add salt.

Add 1 tsp of Abida Rasheed's Mappila Garam Masala, or that spice blend from any other brand.

Remove half of the gravy from the pan and keep aside.

Arrange half the fish slices over the remaining gravy in the pan.

Pour the reserved gravy over the fish and arrange the leftover fish on top.

Add the lemon juice over the gravy and keep aside.

To make the ghee rice, heat oil and ghee in a separate pan and add whole cinnamon, cardamom, and cloves till fragrant.

Add onion, hot water, and salt as required.

Once the water starts boiling, add the rinsed rice (no need to pre-soak) to it.

Cover and cook for 10 minutes.

Heat the masala gravy gently and sprinkle some garam masala on it.

Add the hot rice on top of the wet masala, followed by a sprinkle of garam masala, chopped coriander leaves, and the remaining fried onions.

Cover the pan with a lid and place on a hot tawa and let it cook for 5–10 minutes on a low flame.

Fish biriyani is ready.

Tip: If you can't find king fish, you could use any firm-fleshed variety of fish like singhara or rawas.

Dosai

LOVE (AND A LITTLE CHEMISTRY)

It was Chef N. Sheetharam Prasaad, corporate chef, GRT Group of Hotels, who suggested making Chennai the focus of my dosai spree. 'Why not explore Chennai first? You can taste almost every type of dosai from the south right here?' he said over the phone as I struggled to plot a worthy itinerary.

His advice made sense. From the rustic simplicity of the masala dosais served at Mylapore's stalwart old messes to glam iterations served at spiffy fine diners, the metro delivers an exceptional array of dosai options.

Besides, I love Chennai. For years, I've carried a torch for this characterful city, visiting it every chance I get. I adore the fragrance of jasmine lingering in the air, the long lines of flower-bearing faithfuls outside temples, the local women in their Kanjeevarams, the foamy waves lapping at my ankles at Marina Beach.

But this trip was about dosais. Though I grew up loving the classic, I was guilty of being stuck in a dosai rut, always having the same old dosais—rava, masala, Mysore masala—the same old way. The idea was to look afresh at the ones I already knew and throw in as many new ones as I could.

Chennai was perfect for this deep dive.

BATTER BASICS WITH CHEF NAT

Dosai batter is unique. And very clever.

It takes minimal ingredients—just rice and urad dal (black lentils)—to deliver extraordinary taste and texture, and manages to rise without the addition of yeast or artificial additives. This sets it apart from French crêpes and pancakes.

The action of beneficial microorganisms during fermentation, aided by warm climate, allows dosai's complex, slightly tangy flavours to develop. You don't taste sour; you taste sourdough perfection.

The magic doesn't end there. This wondrous mix continues to evolve over four to five days, and can be used to make idli and uttapam over the course of a week. The result: three iconic southern foods, each with a totally distinct taste and form.

To understand the nuances of dosai batter, I sought the help of Chef Natarajan Kulandai, known affectionately as Chef Nat in hospitality circles. Now retired, the former Taj group stalwart helped launch several iconic south Indian restaurants including Southern Spice at Taj Coromandel. He also consulted for Raintree in Taj Connemara, where we met over a Chettinad meal.

Stripping the formulation to its core, the stalwart broke down the role of its twin ingredients. Rice facilitates fermentation, while urad's unique structure helps lock in air when ground slowly with a little water. 'It's like beating an egg white to trap air molecules,' Chef Nat explained. Fenugreek seeds, used in most recipes, impart a golden-brown colour and a pleasantly bitter edge.

The blend is flexible and changes with region, budget, and pantry. Variations abound with regard to the types of rice used, the proportion of dal to rice, the soaking period, and the grinding technique.

Although each southern state has its own take on the dish, absolute regional specificity is hard to pin down. As Chef Nat sees it, there are just two kinds of dosais in the world—those made in restaurants and those made at home. 'Spend your time understanding these two, and you'll be fine,' he said, laying down a surprisingly simple method to navigate the knotty labyrinth of dosais.

The veteran recalled how, growing up in his native village, soaked rice and lentils would be pounded on a massive grinding stone or quern known as attu kal, operated singlehandedly by an experienced homemaker.

The practice of soaking the dal with its skin intact made the process even more cumbersome. The lentils had to be lightly, artfully squeezed to make the skin float. In the end, the glory was in the grind.

The continuous motion from slow pounding with minimal friction created a softer, fluffier dosai.

As a child, Nat loved standing close to his mother in the kitchen as she spread out the satiny blend on her cast-iron griddle. 'She would cover the dosai with a lid to let the top get cooked by steam while the bottom remained crisp. When done, she would feed it to me hot with some molaga or milagai podi (a condiment made with powdered lentils and chillies, also known as gunpowder) and homemade gingelly oil,' he recalled wistfully.

That pillowy dosai, permeated with his mother's warmth, still shows up in his dreams. He cherished it as much for its deliciousness as for the one-on-one time it guaranteed him with his mother.

'Remember, *that*, my dear, is the real intention behind making a dosai. It's an emotional connection,' he said softly.

HOME-STYLE DOSAIS

Dosai Tutorial with Kamalika Krishmy

Should a dosai be soft or crisp?

This question polarizes lovers of the savoury crêpe like no other.

A shatteringly crisp, verging-on-charred paper dosai might be a north Indian's idea of perfection, but the same texture would be decried as overdone by most Tamils.

It certainly chafed my friend Kamalika Krishmy, who believed I had eaten at way too many restaurants for my own good. 'It's time to get your basics right,' chided the Chennai-based baker and culinary artist, inviting me to her place for an introduction to real-deal Tamil dosais.

As I entered her home in Ashok Nagar, her little boy Adhitya had his head tucked into his father's shoulder. A moment later, a shriek: 'Appaaa!'

'Never mind him. He's just shy,' said Sudhakar, Kamalika's husband.

The warmth of her home was apparent in the mellow, peach sofa upholstery; the light-coloured furniture; and the serene balcony full of plants, where Kamalika takes most of her food photos.

More than half a dozen batters of varying colours and consistencies were arranged on a low table, along with chutneys, side dishes, and fillings. The regular dosai batter, made by grinding rice and urad dal in a 4:1 ratio, was for making masala dosai, podi dosai, ghee-roast, and onion uttapam.

There were separate batters for adai (a mixed lentil crêpe native to Tamil Nadu) and pesarattu (an Andhra specialty made from ground green moong dal).

First up was a plain dosai. Kamalika heated the dosai tawa for a minute and applied a thin layer of oil on it. Using a ladle, she spread the batter very evenly on the tawa and drizzled a little oil on the side.

As the batter sizzled, she explained that dosais in Tamil homes were never crisp, but thick and soft and more fermented. 'We use the word "padham" or "correct consistency" to describe the texture. Nowadays, because of the restaurant influence, kids are asking their mothers to make crisp dosais. But if you ask the old generation to make paper-thin dosais, they'll call you crazy!' she said.

Tearing into the piping hot edible, I experienced the difference. It was smaller, spongier, and allowed me to fully appreciate the diversified flavours of the fermented rice and lentils . 'You will never get this taste and texture at a restaurant,' Kamalika said proudly.

Each of the dosais that followed required a different cooking technique. Podi dosai called for sprinkling gunpowder on the half-cooked batter and allowing enough time for the granules to permeate the dosai. Masala dosai was not flipped, but covered and cooked in steam before potato mash was spooned over the crêpe. Uttapam, spread thicker on the tawa and sprinkled with sliced onions and gunpowder, was steamed and then flipped. For the ghee-roast, the batter was spread very thin on the hotplate and given an extra glug of ghee before being flipped. The last two, adai and pesarattu, were made from unfermented batter and sat the longest on low flame for optimal doneness.

We ate each hot off the tawa, and with a different relish—pesarattu was paired with ginger chutney, adai with ghee and molaga podi, and the rest with sambar and coconut chutney.

After the session, Kamalika described the key differences between home-style and commercial dosais. Homemade dosais are softer as the batter is ground in a wet grinder. Restaurants, on the other hand, use idli rice rava and freshly ground urad batter (or both in powder form) to save time. Not only is the dosai crisper, but the powder is also easier to preserve and minimizes wastage. The technique of spreading the dosai differs as well. Home-cooks use a ladle, which ensures the dosai has the right amount of batter to get the classic thin layers of crisp and soft texture. Restaurants tend to use a katori or steel bowl to spread the batter, leading to a texturally flat dosai.

Kamalika believes that the homemade versions, with their small size and true-blue taste, are the pinnacle of dosai perfection. 'Restaurant dosais are overrated,' she said. I couldn't agree more.

When I left, Adi blew me a shy kiss. Which restaurant could match that?

Masala Dosai and Ragi Dosai with Shri Bala

Mystery surrounds the birth and evolution of the dosai.

According to food historian K. T. Achaya, dosai is first noted in Tamil Sangam literature of the sixth century CE. 'It was then perhaps a pure rice product, shallow-fried in a pan....'[1] Ulundu (urad), which is 'so vital an ingredient in making dosai, adai, and idli does not appear in literature' of the first few centuries CE, he writes.[2]

In contrast, the recipe for dhosaka (dosai) and idarika (idli), mentioned in Manasollasa, a twelfth-century Sanskrit encyclopaedia compiled by King Someshvara III, calls for using only pulses and no rice.

I was puzzled. Was dhosaka the same as dosai? And how did dosai remain a rice-only and lentil-only food for so long?

Chef and food historian Shri Bala, whose pop-ups recreate bygone dishes from the Chola, Kakatiya, and Vijaynagara dynasties, allowed me to pick her brain about these questions at her beautiful home. 'I might not have all the answers, but I'll try to give you a taste of what the first dosais were like,' she promised.

Her apartment complex, Keshav Dugar, evokes a sense of grandeur with its majestic iron gates and gazebos. 'It's right out of *Ponniyin Selvan*,' I joked.

'Funny you should say that. The Cholas are my favourite. People say I'm obsessed with them!' she said, giggling.

A plate of mini red-rice idlis and vadai (crispy lentil doughnuts) along with chow chow bath, a combination of rava upma (savoury semolina) and rava kesari (sweet semolina), got us off to a fine start. Between mouthfuls, my hostess revealed the etymology of dosai, also known as dosa. It comes from the Tamil word osai, which means sound, and refers to the sizzling sound the batter makes as it lands in the pan. 'That makes dosai our very own Indian sizzler,' she said, underlining the crêpe's multisensory appeal.

Her carefully curated dosai line-up represented the two timelines often evoked to talk about the roots of the dish.[3] The most recent wave is traceable to about 100 years ago when Udupi restaurants first opened across India. The older one, more difficult to pin down, points to a progenitor that existed in ancient Tamil country.

The masala dosai and Mysore masala dosai Shri Bala had made were representative of the newer wave. Though both drew a direct lineage from the Udupi repertoire, she paired them with a Tamil-style potato masala, a sauté of mashed potatoes, green chillies, and cashews.

The unfermented ragi (finger millet) dosai that followed was inspired by the primordial Tamil dosai made from millets and ancient rice varieties. The soft, deep-brown dosai had a satisfying chew and earthy taste.

As we ate, Shri Bala pointed out that kal dosai was likely the first one to evolve. The airy, spongy dosai, which gets its name from the uneven black stone or kal on which it was made, was served as prasadam or devotional offering at various temples. As fermented foods were deemed unfit for religious offerings, the batter would be made fresh each morning. 'Even today, in places like the Azhagar Kovil temple in Madurai district, they make a thick, pizza-like, unfermented dosai seasoned with black pepper, dry ginger powder, and curry leaves, as prasadam,' said Shri Bala.

Although unable to pinpoint the exact century when south Indians began to combine rice and lentils to make the familiar fermented dosai,[4] she believes that the shift marked a turning point as it extended the life of the batter by several days. Likening the ageing of dosai batter to the stages of a butterfly's metamorphosis, Shri Bala recalled how the blend, which would take on new flavour dimensions over the course of a week, would be constantly repurposed at her home.

On the first day, her mother would use the blend to make a pristine white vella dosai. The flavour of fenugreek would be dominant in this as-yet-unfermented dosai, which tasted divine with molaga podi. For the next two days, the batter would be used to make idlis. On the fourth day, it would deliver a classic Bangalore-style dosai, crisp on the outside and spongy-soft inside. On day five, uttapam, an ideal outlet for using leftover batter, would be made with a topping of onions and a tempering of ginger and green chillies to tone down its sourness. Whatever would be left in the end would be fried into bondas (dosai batter snack with coconut slivers and green chillies).

The reminiscence, coupled with the aroma of ghee wafting around, had my hostess in a spell. Swaying on the large swing suspended from the ceiling, sipping kaapi from a dabara (traditional filter coffee tumbler set), she recalled how she and her brother would sit on the kitchen slab with folded legs as their mother made dosais. 'Amma would serve us in turns. She poured all her knowledge and love into those dosais.'

Later, when she was studying to be a chartered accountant, these dosai sessions helped Shri Bala counter the anxiety of exam results. When she would get a disappointing score, her mother would comfort her. '"Life has to keep moving. Hakuna matata," Amma would say, gently placing a vella dosai on my plate.'

The memories seemed to catch my hostess off guard. 'I miss Amma!' she said tearfully, overcome by a sudden torrent of feelings.

Brunch with Viji Varadarajan

Although different communities in Tamil Nadu—Chettiars, Mudaliars, Nadars, and others—put their own spins on the dosai, it is the side dishes that truly inspire the fiercest loyalties and let each group's personality shine through.

Cookbook writer Viji Varadarajan rubbished the notion that dosais must be eaten with sambar. Instead, she likes to pair them with thuvaiyals, an array of chutney-like pastes integral to her native Tamil Brahmin cooking.

Made without garlic or onions, thuvaiyals are typical of the 'satvik' TamBrahm repertoire. Often relished as a quick-fix main course mixed with steamed rice, they also team fabulously with dosais and other tiffin items. 'Who needs sambar?' Viji intoned in her musical voice, as we connected over the phone.

As thuvaiyals are rarely served in restaurants, the Gourmand Award-winning author agreed to have me over for a meal of dosais with traditional accompaniments at her home. Her only condition: I would do most of the cooking.

'Shall I come over for lunch?' I asked.

'Dosais are eaten for brunch or tiffin, my dear. Be there at 8.30 a.m. sharp,' she chided, leaving no room for negotiation.[5]

Viji's home in Uthandi, about 12 kilometres from Marundeeswarar Temple in Thiruvanmiyur, has an atmosphere of calm spirituality. As she pulled me into the pantry, her domestic helper Shanti was already busy whirring up a trifecta of thuvaiyals—kathirikkai thuvaiyal made with grilled, deskinned eggplants; kariveppillai thuvaiyal starring curry leaves; and peerkangai thuvaiyal featuring ridge gourds.

I watched as Shanti lightly sautéed each vegetable with roasted red chillies, asafoetida, and tamarind paste, and finished with a tempering of mustard seeds and urad dal. 'She's making a Tamil-style sambar, too, to give you a taste,' Viji said.

Spending time in Viji's kitchen allowed me to appreciate her flair for making an array of items from scratch—everything from dairy products to sambar powder. As we started our session, she held a teaspoon of homemade ghee under my nose for me to take in the dreamy, homey aroma. 'Smells great, right? This ghee is what sets my masala dosai apart!' she said, beaming.

Over the next hour or so, I made four types of dosais under Viji's tutelage—pillowy mendhiya (fenugreek) dosais with a network of tiny holes; masala dosais filled with a deliciously tangy potato stuffing; and pockmarked rava dosais made from a thin, unfermented batter of semolina, rice flour, maida, and curry leaves.

Each required deft manipulations of the flame, but Viji made it easy, giving detailed directions on everything from heat-control to wiping the tawa. To my surprise, I churned out perfectly golden dosais.

'See, it just needs patience,' my teacher said encouragingly.

Tutorial complete, we carried our plates across the foyer to her breezy living room to enjoy the fruits of our labour. As I plucked off pieces of dosai to mix and match with the thuvaiyals, I appreciated how each brought a new flavour dimension to the meal. The curry-leaf one resonated with a pungent, citrusy zest; the mashed-eggplant one had a charred, smoky flavour; and the ridge-gourd one held its own with its slightly astringent, vegetal taste. I barely touched the sambar.

When I complimented Viji on her culinary skills, she blushingly confessed she had never entered a kitchen until she was in her twenties. 'As a child, I would play with marbles and fly kites all day long. Cooking was never my thing. I was spoilt rotten,' she said.

That changed when she married into a family with a razor-sharp focus on food. 'There's a certain paranoia a young bride faces when she enters a Thanjavur Brahmin home. If you don't know how to cook, your mother-in-law will just pack your things and send you back home!'

Fortunately, hers didn't. Instead, she tutored her patiently, honing her into the brilliant cook that she is. 'My mother-in-law taught me wonderful cooking. Everything was very precise and measured. But it was hard in the beginning. I messed up a lot, and quietly threw it all away!' she recalled, chuckling.

Today, she promotes this underrated cuisine with an almost evangelical zeal. 'No other cuisine has contributed more to a healthier way of eating. It's easy on spices, uses very little oil, and still tastes great.'

There is also a deeper, spiritual dimension to the cuisine she reveres. 'Food or annam is sustenance, worship, passion, and incredible energy. It is a form of the almighty,' she said in a soft voice.

RESTAURANT DOSAIS

Millet Dosais at Prems Graama Bhojanam with N. S. Krishnamoorthi

Prems Graama Bhojanam is a portal to a different world.

Every element here—from the water served from matkas, inspired by the teertham, or holy water served in temples, to the tribal Madhubani art and hand-painted coconut shells hanging on the walls—is imbued with owner N. S. Krishnamoorthi's love for ancient Indian food and knowledge.

'We serve village food with love,' he said warmly, welcoming me to his quaint Adyar eatery, which is both simple and unique. The menu, a celebration of India's millet bounty, features varieties such as foxtail; barnyard; sorghum; proso, kodo, and pearl millet; as well as grains like red and black rice. 'I don't use a gram of white rice,' Krishnamoorthi said, sitting me down to a feast of his ruggedly charming dosais.

The delicacies arrived in quick succession. The wafer-thin ghee-roast, made with jowar flour, was finished with a blob of organic cow ghee. The thin green pesarattu, made from kodo millet and green gram, came with ginger chutney sweetened with jaggery. There was also an assorted platter of mini uttapams, crafted from jowar (sorghum), ragi (finger millet), and green gram. Faintly sour, the diminutive pancakes had a bouncy, almost focaccia-like texture. My favourite was the red-rice dosai, which gets its deep colour from healthy anthocyanins. Shallow-fried to a golden crisp, it had a nutty, earthy flavour.

Loath to describe his creations as 'trendy', Krishnamoorthi sees them as harkening back to India's past. Thousands of years ago, before terms like 'probiotic' and multigrain' became mega-trendy, he pointed out, our ancestors were already singing praises of millets.[6] 'Varieties like varagu, thinai, and samai were staples during the Sangam period and even find mention in *Tolkappiyam*, the oldest surviving work of Sangam literature compiled by Tolkappiyar.'

Krishnamoorthi rued the ignorance with which we often judge our past. 'Instead of laughing at our traditions, we should try to understand them. By building upon the deep knowledge of the ancients, we would ensure a great future not just for dosais, but Indian food culture as a whole,' he said ardently.

Millet dosais, which possibly predate their white-rice counterparts, are a testament to the potency of this centuries-old culinary wisdom. Compared to white rice or wheat, millets are high in fibre, protein, and calcium; have a lower glycaemic index; and control blood sugar. 'Besides checking all the health boxes, they are less water-intensive to grow than rice, more farmer-friendly, and taste better,' Krishnamoorthi said.

The side dishes around the dosais are equally healthy. 'Coconut chutney is made with raw coconut because our ancestors realized it's healthier than the cooked version. Today, raw coconut is hailed as one of the only sources of lauric fatty acids apart from mother's milk,'[8] he enthused.

It was impossible not to be infected by my host's passion. By the time I finished, I was in love with his complex-textured creations. Not only do they deliver a hefty dose of nutritional goodness, but each bite is also like tasting a vestige of India's rich, resilient ancient past.

Karnataka-style Dosais at Eating Circles with Chef Damu

While talking about dosai types, the Tamil Nadu–Karnataka binary is often held up as absolute, almost as though the two versions should have their own Geographical Indication. But the two traditions constantly overlap at Udupi joints in Chennai, making it difficult to find authentic Karnataka-style dosais in the city.

Eating Circles is a notable exception. The Alwarpet restaurant, which opened in 2019, serves typical Karnataka fare like maddur vadai (a deep-fried snack made from mixed flours), bisi bele bath (a spicy rice and lentil dish), and 'Bangalore' dosais. I stepped into the no-fuss eatery along with Chef K. Damodaran, aka Chef Damu, a leading authority on south Indian cuisine. As a Guinness World Record holder who has written twenty-six books and taught cooking for twenty-three years, the legend knows a thing or two about the nuances of dosais from the two states and what sets them apart.

We ordered a trio of dosais typically associated with the neighbouring state—golden-brown benne dosais, downy set dosais, and light-as-air neer dosais. 'Coffee, da?' Damu asked congenially as we waited for the food. Of course, I said yes.

The classic Bangalore dosai, he pointed out over sips of the strong brew, is typically crisp on the outside and spongy within. That gives it a unique mouthfeel and texture—the crispiness, together with the softness. 'It's the best of both worlds,' remarked Damu, 'which is why people call it the king of dosais.'

The batter usually includes rice flour; beaten rice or poha; and a little sugar, which gives the dosai its trademark deep brown colour and a hint of sweetness. 'In Tamil Nadu, we don't add sugar, poha, or rice flour. We just use raw rice, urad dal, and methi, so the dosais here are spongier and softer,' Damu pointed out, as our order arrived.

The luscious benne dosai, which traces its origins to the city of Davanagere in Karnataka, was fluffy yet crispy from being cooked in copious amounts of butter. The additional dollop of butter it came with disappeared in moments, seeping into every sinful bite. (Thankfully, the accompanying peanut chutney cut through some of the richness.) The sambar, with a hint of sweetness from jaggery, was typical of the Udupi version. 'You won't find a sweet sambar in all of Tamil Nadu,' Damu said.

The set dosais, so called because they come stacked like pancakes in sets of twos or threes, were smaller and spongier (from the addition of more fenugreek in the batter) than regular dosais. They reminded me of the homemade dosais I had eaten at Kamalika's. Damu placed them in the family of kal dosais and likened them to the thattukada (roadside cart) dosais sold across Kerala.

The star of the tasting was the neer dosai, native to the Tulu Nadu region of Karnataka. The barely-there delicacy, made from a batter of only rice and no lentils, paired divinely with the sweet crunchiness of the jaggery-and-coconut mixture that accompanied it. It was a simple yet disarmingly perfect combination. I couldn't resist a second round.

'Don't worry. They're low on calories,' Damu encouraged, sharing his own fondness for neer dosais with non-veg curries. 'In Mangalore, neer dosais are typically served with ghee-roast prawns or chicken and various fish curries. They're the perfect sponge to soak up a curry.'

Although Damu believes dosai was birthed in Udupi, he refuses to get pulled into a turf war. Wherever the origin of the golden wonder, he stressed, it transcended its roots long ago. 'Neither Tamil Nadu nor Karnataka can solely claim the dosai as its own. It belongs equally to Kerala and Andhra Pradesh as well. It's a dish that brings all south Indians, and ultimately all Indians, together,' he said.

Despite his vast gastronomic experience, the legend remains a sucker for the fresh, rugged fare of the countryside. 'In the villages of Tamil Nadu, eighty-year-old ladies still make a dosai on firewood and slather it with a coarse chutney made of coconut, fried gram flour, and green chillies. When you eat that dosai, you taste the flare of the chillies. You taste those hands. It's dynamite,' he said, virtually salivating at the sensory memory.

Podi Dosai, Ghee-roast Dosai, and Adai-avial at Sangeetha's

Over the years, a few defining restaurant chains in Chennai have become a barometer for south Indian vegetarian fare in the city—Saravana Bhavan, Murugan Idli Shop, New Woodlands, and Ratna Cafe, not to mention the messes of Mylapore.

Having tried them during earlier visits, I decided to step into Sangeetha, another icon, famed for its unrivalled variety of tiffin items and rotating list of daily specials.

The dosais, in particular, are hot sellers. Suresh Padmanabhan, the owner of Sangeetha, who joined me at their Parry's Corner outlet, told me they sell up to a whopping 50,000 to 60,000 dosais across their thirty Chennai branches on weekends.

A soft-spoken man with a professorial look, he promptly ordered a podi dosai when I voiced a desire to eat Tamil Nadu-style dosais. The cult popularity of the dosai derives not just from the supreme love Tamils have for molaga podi, but also from the overall combination. The dosai's mild notes contrast beautifully with the fiery, spicy notes of the dry chutney powder.

The one at Sangeetha didn't disappoint. As always, the simple act of sprinkling gunpowder on a dosai created greatness. I loved how the fiery, grainy condiment clung to the dosai. Though served with sambar and chutney, the dosai stood on its own, needing no accompaniment.

The pyramid-shaped ghee-roast, which arrived next, was as much a delight as the butter-soaked benne dosai I ate at Eating Circles. Although made with regular dosai batter, its crackly edges and rich flavour came from a generous basting of ghee. Rolling it into a cone gave it a new and eye-catching personality. 'It's the Rolls-Royce of dosais,' Suresh said with a grin. As I took a bite of the rich treat, I found no reason to disagree.

I also tried adai-avial, a welcome change from the dosai-sambar routine. More of a fusion dish in Tamil Nadu, the creaminess of the coconut-and-vegetable mash complemented the crispy, dense lentil flatbread. Served with a pinch of jaggery and a knob of vennai or white butter, the veggie-forward snack hit different flavour notes—sweet, spicy and salty—in every bite.

After the meal, Suresh drove me to his office at Adyar to introduce me to his daughter Sanjana, who has been gradually taking over the company's domestic operations. The close bond between the two was apparent as Sanjana proudly shared how her rockstar father left the family restaurant business in his early twenties to carve out his own path, working eighteen hours a day at small restaurants across Kerala before launching Sangeetha in 1985. 'Appa got here through sheer grit. He even taught himself English,' she said.

The collaboration between father and daughter had resulted in a broader approach to the restaurant business. No longer confining the menu at Sangeetha to traditional fare, the duo has recently introduced a range of healthy items, including a variety of multi-millet dosais and salads.

The additions, though novel, have been a bit of a slow-burn, Sanjana admitted. At the end of the day, Gen Z, too, roots for old-school dosais. 'At its heart, the dosai will always be comfort food,' she said, sharing how her father's masala dosais, which he made for her every Sunday morning, always made her melt. 'That taste. It's like coming home.'

Non-veg Dosais at J. Hind and Junior Kuppanna

Chennai is a magnet for carnivores (all those smoky chicken 65s and lip-singeing Chettinad curries), but its non-veg dosai scene often goes under the radar. Chef Sheetharam vouches for the city's love for meat-laden dosais. 'Meat and egg dosais are huge here, and even more so in southern Tamil Nadu.'

'How come the world doesn't hear more about them?' I asked, digging into the succulent keema dosai he had whipped up for me at

J. Hind, Grand by GRT Hotel's fine dining restaurant. 'Because we've been too busy eating them to make a noise,' he quipped.

Chatting with the veteran, I was even more surprised to learn about the antiquity of meat-dosais. 'A large population of ancient Tamils were avid non-vegetarians, so these dosais go back a long way. Even today, in places like Virudhunagar and Thoothukudi, many people still use pork fat to temper dishes,' he shared.

At his recommendation, I stepped into Junior Kuppanna, an Erode-origin restaurant chain famed for its robust Kongu fare, and the best place to eat Madurai-style kari (meat) dosais in Chennai.

Murthy Anna, who currently owns the chain, traces the family-run chain's origins to the launch of the original Kuppanna restaurant in 1960 by his father Thiru Kuppusamy. The restaurant was rebranded Junior Kuppanna when Murthy took over operations in 1983.

From its inception, the owners were sticklers for authentic taste and high quality. 'My mother Rukmini Amma would personally oversee the selection and combination of the fifteen to twenty spices that went into the masala blend until she was alive,' Murthy shared.

At his suggestion, I ordered two of JK's bestsellers—mutta (egg) dosai and kari dosai. The base of both, Murthy revealed, was the traditional kal dosai, their bestseller since 1960. 'We serve the *original.* It soaks the juices of meat curries beautifully.'

I stepped inside the eatery's spotless kitchen to watch the dosais being made. For the mutta dosai, a thickish layer of batter was spread on a greased tawa with a ladle and cooked for a bit. Then an egg was broken in the centre, and the yolk spread evenly around the dosai. When done, the dosai was flipped and allowed to cook on the other side.

The kari dosai was akin to a non-veg uttapam, with minced mutton masala layered onto a half-cooked kal dosai. After a pour of an egg, the crêpe was allowed to cook completely before being flipped. Thick and meaty, the reddish-brown creation was intensely spicy.

The dosais came with a side of sambar and salna, a paya-like soup made with mutton bones. I enjoyed both. In the end, though, it was the foundational kal dosai that left the biggest impression on me. The Plain Jane doesn't grab anyone's attention while it sits on a table. But as a blank canvas, it transforms anything that sits atop it, is paired with it, or is nestled into it, into something delicious.

Thousands of years later, this primitive wonder continues to quietly rock the dosai world.

Masala Dosai at Mangalambiga Coffee and Tiffin Center

Notwithstanding the cult status of masala dosais, I've always found them stodgy and overrated, much preferring a plain or rava dosai with a variety of chutneys and sambar instead.

'That's because you haven't eaten a masala dosai in Kumbakonam. It's the best in the world,' Shri Bala told me, clearly smitten by these dosais native to the Temple City. Her go-to place is Mangalambiga, a family-run eatery that's been cranking out legendary masala dosais for over a century. 'I'm a sucker for that homely taste,' she said dreamily.

I had planned to limit my trip to Chennai. But when some friends happened to mention they were headed on a road trip to the old delta, I couldn't resist an impromptu two-day visit to the city, which once served as the capital of the medieval Cholas.

We arrived around one in the afternoon after immersing ourselves in the grandeur of the Great Living Chola Temples at Thanjavur and Darasuram the previous day. The manic sightseeing had resulted in broken footwear, leading to a wild goose chase around town for a cobbler. Later, we ate like kings at Venkataraman, relishing a thali of potato poriyal (sautéed spiced potatoes); pumpkin kootu (pumpkin stew); cucumber pachadi (a side dish of curd, cucumbers and coconut); sambar; rasam; pickle; and sugar-studded dry gulab jamun, a local specialty. The rest of the day was spent trooping in and out of temples and shops selling oil lamps and brassware.

A stone's throw away from the famous Adi Kumbeswarar Temple, Mangalambiga was easy to find. When we arrived at around six in the evening, the typical Iyer mess was packed with locals and a few tourists contentedly chowing down tiffin items like rice upma served with sambar and tomato sevai.

I did a double take when Vignesh, the fourth-generation owner, told me they were not serving masala dosais. 'Sorry, madam, we've dropped them due to the rise in onion prices,' he said. After I whined and moaned about having driven all the way from Chennai for a taste, he relented and got a batch made for us.

The dosai was paired with coconut chutney and kadappa, a mild side dish typical to these parts, made with moong dal, cashew and poppy seed paste, and chunky bits of potatoes. The meal was served on a banana leaf.

Slightly thick yet crusty, the exterior was charred just enough here and there to give it a real rustic feel. It was the potato stuffing that blew my mind. There was something enjoyably old-fashioned about the velvety mash. I let it sit in my mouth, admiring the way the soft blandness of the potatoes was emphasized by the crunch of the vegetables.

Vignesh revealed that the magic lay in a century-old secret family recipe. 'The Tamil Brahmin community's potato masala is different from that of communities like the Chettiars. In addition to potatoes, we add green peas, chillies, grated carrots, and coriander to the filling. Our dosai batter is different too, which is why the crust is spongier.'

Vignesh admitted that nostalgia is a key draw. 'People often come here when they're missing the tastes of their childhood. The recipes taste the same as they did when we started in 1914.'

The tiffin, perfectly set off with Kumbakonam's famed 'degree kaapi'—so called because it's made from forty 'degrees' of pure cow's milk measured in a lactometer before being mixed with coffee decoction—got high marks for old-school appeal.

There was a certain warmth to embracing tradition in an ancient town dating back to the Sangam period. It felt like I had stepped into another era.

The lengthy detour to Kumbakonam had been worth it. I had tasted a masala dosai so nakedly honest, it was like eating the classic for the very first time

In the days to come, I would dream about this humble, potato-laden wonder, true to its Tamil roots, and oozing comfort with every bite.

DOSAI INNOVATIONS

Chef Nat's Dosai Wrap

Fusion dosais are everywhere in Chennai. With street kiosks and eateries like Dosai Plaza offering kitschy hybrids like pav bhaji dosai and 'chipotle spicy delight' dosai, snappier fast-food versions of the classic have also garnered fans.

But as the crêpe gets diversified into increasingly interesting directions, even bolder new benchmarks are being set. Back in Chennai, Chef Nat told me about one such genre-bending dosai experiment he worked on a few years ago.

The 'dosai wrap' was the brainchild of a food connoisseur who wanted to create a 100 per cent automated dosai, he shared. The idea was to have a dosai made by a machine. Once ready, a person standing near the counter would put the desired stuffing inside it, roll it like a frankie, wrap it up, and give it to the customer. 'Instead of sticking to classic dosais, we wanted to create four to five different batters and lots of international fillings,' Nat said. 'We also wanted to do away with the ritual of sitting and eating a dosai with messy accompaniments; instead, we would have a sprinkling of dehydrated sambar and chutney on the wrap. So, that, in a nutshell, was our dosai on the go.'

After much trial and error—which included altering the proportions of rice and urad in the batter—Nat and team cracked the recipe for making classic and multigrain dosais as well as pesarattu in the machine format. The accompaniments came together, too, after they approached a factory that was already making dehydrated sambar-rice for an airline.

Although the project ultimately fizzled out (the idea wasn't profitable enough), Nat is convinced we will continue to see daring, boundary-pushing versions that surprise and delight us. 'But some things are out of bounds,' he said.

'Such as?' I asked.

'We should not mess with the fundamentals. It's *not* a good idea to inject vodka into a dosai,' he said, scowling.

Dosai Tacos and Kaapi Waffle at ITC Grand Chola

There are plenty of chef-driven dosais to be tasted in Chennai. Arguably, the finest renditions are to be found at ITC Grand Chola's modernist diner Avartana, famed for its chic reimagining of south Indian spices, flavours, and textures.

I tried two of their innovations. The chicken Chettinad tacos were mini dosais wrapped around spicy chicken Chettinad and topped with crunchy kachumber. A genius marriage of flavours and textures, they had a moreish, pick-me-up appeal, and had all the makings of a modern party classic.

Next, I had the kaapi waffle. Made with dosai batter, it was a piece of Tamil sophistication. An ingenious riff on Chennai's favourite brew, it came with a generous sprinkling of roasted filter coffee and demerara sugar, and a side of black jaggery syrup with coconut milk.

Both were uber-stylish presentations that managed to break from tradition and reinvent the classic in a way that was playful and compelling. They were proof that when executed well, haute dosais could be just as delightful as the venerable old ones.

◆

It was time to head back.

My short visit to Tamil Nadu was memorable, revelatory, and delicious. It enabled me to shrug off my usual dosai routine and eat more eclectically. It challenged several notions I held about a dosai's taste and texture, and the array of accompaniments it can be paired with. It also gave me unforgettable moments and a peek into the fantastic worlds that shape dosai history.

Although I had barely scratched the surface—round two would be in Karnataka followed by Kerala and Andhra Pradesh—I was grateful and happy to have savoured the classic in some of its most delectable guises.

Waiting to board my flight back at Chennai Airport, I pondered the greatness of the staple. It's economical, delicious, and supremely satisfying. It's a near-perfect health food, delivering the ideal combination of carbohydrates and proteins, with probiotic enzymes to boot. It's light, yet manages to feel sumptuous with a dash of ghee. (Notice how idli can be polarizing, but a golden, marbled dosai is almost always a slam dunk?) It's quintessentially Indian, yet its luscious taste and endless versatility have won it the world's attention.[8]

But as familiar as we are with it, there's something unusual and remarkable about the south Indian icon. Thinking about the meals I had enjoyed over the past few days, it suddenly occurred to me that the edible's greatest pleasure isn't tangible at all.

For many I spoke to, eating a dosai was a way of time-travelling back to their childhoods. It was bonding time with their mothers (or fathers or grandmothers) in the kitchen. As Chef Nat observed, 'A ghee-laden dosai is full of a mother's affection for her child. The dish becomes a vehicle for conveying a feeling.'

Listening to these extraordinary stories, it became evident to me that at its best, dosai ceases to be food. It's an act of filial love.

Unlike idli or upma, which can be made and kept, dosai is most enjoyable eaten hot off the pan. This affirms a primary bond between the maker and the eater, giving the crêpe a more immediate emotional flavour.

That, to me, makes it one of India's most intimate dishes.

Recipes from My Travels

SANGEETHA'S GHEE-ROAST DOSAI

MAKES: 10 DOSAIS

TIME TAKEN: 20 MINUTES PLUS SOAKING AND FERMENTING

INGREDIENTS

Idli rice	250 gms
White urad dal, skinless	65 gms
Methi seeds	7 gms
Water	350 ml approximately
Salt	to taste
Ghee	10 tbsp, to cook dosais

METHOD

Wash and soak the rice, dal, and methi seeds for 3 hours.

Rinse and clean. Blend everything together with approximately 350 ml water, to a smooth batter. The batter should not be too thick or too thin.

Add salt and set aside for 6–8 hours to ferment.

Heat a dosai tawa and brush with 1 tbsp ghee.

Put a spoonful of the batter on the tawa and spread using a swirling motion with the spoon.

Drizzle a liberal dose of ghee on top, and let it cook for a minute or two on medium flame.

Carefully slide a flat spoon under the dosai to remove from the tawa.

Roll the dosai or shape into a cone. Serve hot with sambar and coconut chutney.

SANGEETHA'S ADAI-AVIAL

SERVES: 4 TIME TAKEN: 30 MINUTES PLUS SOAKING AND RESTING

INGREDIENTS

For adai batter,

Green gram dal	40 gms
Yellow moong dal	75 gms
Urad dal	75 gms
Idli rice	75 gms
Toor dal	50 gms
Guntur chillies	4–5
Cumin seeds	1 tbsp
Black pepper	10–12
Fennel seeds	1 tbsp
Oil or ghee	3–4 tbsp
Curry leaves	6–8 pieces
Onion	1 medium-sized, chopped

For avial,

Carrots	1, cut into 2-inch pieces
French beans	5, cut into 2-inch pieces
White pumpkin	100 gms, cut into 2-inch pieces
Yam	75 gms, cut into 2-inch pieces
Snake gourd	100 gms, cut into 2-inch pieces
Drumsticks	2, cut into 2-inch pieces
Green chillies	3
Curd	200 gms
Turmeric	1 tsp
Coconut	100 gms, grated
Cumin seeds	1 tsp
Salt	as required

For tempering,

Coconut oil	2 tbsp
Curry leaves	10–12
Green chillies	2, slit

METHOD

For adai,

Wash and soak the dals and rice for 2–3 hours.

Drain, rinse, and blend the dal and rice along with chillies, cumin seeds, black peppercorns, fennel, and 2 cups of water to form a smooth, fairly coarse-textured batter.

Mix with chopped curry leaves, onion, and salt, and let it rest for 15–20 minutes.

Heat a tawa and brush it with 1 tbsp oil or ghee.

Spread around 100 gms of batter with a spoon in a swirling motion. Sprinkle ghee or oil.

Let the adai cook for 2 minutes.

Carefully slide a flat spoon under the adai. Flip it and let it cook on the other side for 1 minute.

Remove the adai from the tawa.

For avial,

Blend the coconut, cumin seeds, and green chillies in a mixer with 50 ml water to make chutney.

Set aside.

Put carrots, beans, white pumpkin, drumstick, yam, and snake gourd in a vessel with 2 cups of water, turmeric, and salt.

Bring to a boil. Let it cook for 7-8 minutes. Add the coconut chutney and cook for 5 minutes.

Add 200 gms of curd, mix well, and switch off the flame.

Heat 2 tbsp coconut oil in a pan, add curry leaves and slit green chillies, and pour it over the avial.

Serve adai and avial together.

N. S. KRISHNAMOORTHI'S RED-RICE DOSAI

MAKES: 12 DOSAIS

TIME TAKEN: 5 HOURS SOAKING PLUS 8 HOURS FERMENTING

INGREDIENTS

Unpolished red rice	400 gms
Urad dal	100 gms
Fenugreek seeds	1 tsp
Red-rice poha	1 tbsp
Salt	to taste
Oil	2 tbsp

METHOD

Wash and soak the urad dal in water for 3 hours.

Wash and soak the unpolished red rice along with fenugreek seeds in a separate vessel for 5 hours.

Wash and soak the red-rice poha just half an hour before you are ready to grind the red rice.

Drain and grind the soaked urad dal, adding a little water at regular intervals until smooth.

Drain and grind the soaked red rice, fenugreek seeds, and red-rice poha with some water into a smooth paste. Don't use too much water.

Mix the urad dal paste and rice paste together, adding a little water at a time till you get a smooth pouring consistency.

Add salt and let the batter ferment for 8 hours or overnight.

To make the dosais, heat an iron dosai tawa with a little oil. Pour one ladle of batter on the tawa and spread it thinly using a swirling motion.

Drizzle a few drops of oil on the dosai edges and let it cook for a minute or until it starts leaving the sides.

Carefully slide a flat spoon below the dosai and flip it over, and let it cook on the other side for a minute. Remove from tawa.

Serve hot with coconut chutney.

JUNIOR KUPPANNA'S EGG DOSAI

MAKES: 4 DOSAIS

TIME TAKEN: 10 MINUTES PLUS SOAKING AND FERMENTING

INGREDIENTS

Dosai batter	400 gms
Eggs	4, beaten
Oil	for brushing the dosai

For dosai batter,

Raw rice	125 gms
Idli rice	280 gms
Urad dal	50 gms
Bengal gram dal	25 gms
Salt	to taste

METHOD

For batter,

Wash and soak the raw rice, idli rice, and Bengal gram dal together for 3 hours.

Wash and soak the urad dal for 3 hours.

Drain and grind the urad dal with ½ cup water until fine.

Drain and grind the rice mixture with 2 cups water until smooth.

Mix both the batters together, add salt, and let it ferment for 6 hours. Add more water if required for a smooth pouring consistency.

For dosai,

Heat a tawa and brush it with a little oil. Pour 100 gms of dosai batter and swirl it to the size of a side plate.

Once the base is cooked, pour one egg all over the dosai. Flip the side and cook till it's done.

Serve hot.

JUNIOR KUPPANNA'S MUTTON KARI DOSAI

MAKES: 10 DOSAIS

TIME TAKEN: 45 MINUTES

INGREDIENTS

Mutton mince	500 gms
Turmeric powder	1 tsp
Oil	150 ml
Onion	200 gms, chopped
Ginger-garlic paste	60 gms
Green chillies	5–6, chopped
Tomato	50 gms, chopped
Mutton masala/keema masala	3 tbsp
Coconut milk	½ cup
Salt	to taste
Dosai batter	1 kg
Eggs	10

METHOD

Put the mutton mince in a pressure cooker along with 1 tsp turmeric powder, 1 tsp salt, and ¼ cup water.

Let it cook for 2 whistles and switch off the flame.

Heat oil in a pan, add the chopped onions, and fry till golden brown.

Add green chillies, ginger-garlic paste, and cook for a minute.

Add chopped tomatoes and cook for 10 minutes until the tomatoes are mashed.

Add the keema masala along with the cooked mutton keema and mix well.

Continue cooking for another 10 minutes.

Add coconut milk and let it cook for another 5 minutes.

Check for seasoning and switch off the flame. Use the keema as required.

For dosai,

Spread 100 ml of dosai batter on a hot tawa to make a dosai the size of a side plate.

Add 100 gms of cooked keema and spread on top of the dosai.

Cover it with a lid for a minute, then pour one raw beaten egg. Cook for a minute and then flip the dosai.

Cook for a minute or two until the egg sets.

Kari dosai is ready. Serve hot.

Tip: Instead of mutton masala, you could use garam masala powder.

Butter Chicken

THE BURDEN OF THE BIRD

As a school kid growing up in the 1980s, two words would set my mouth watering and heart racing—butter chicken. The buttery, creamy, tomato-ey melange of tandoori chicken tossed in rich gravy seemed like the height of luxury in those simple days.

Come Saturday evening, my brother and I would drop everything and head straight to Delhi's Pandara Road Market to pick up our weekend dinner treat. Driving back, the tantalizing aromas from the takeaway would torment us in the car, causing us to tear into the tangy, smoky mess the moment we hit home. Finally, our rumbling stomachs would be quieted by its rib-sticking deliciousness.

Then sometime around the late 1990s, there was trouble in paradise. Terrible crimes began to be committed in the name of butter chicken. Menus became virtual minefields of gloppy, bland, khoa-filled[1] butter chicken versions.

Things got worse when I moved to Mumbai to work a few years later. The astonishingly sweet butter chickens of the city were downright unbearable to me. Something inside me snapped. I stopped eating the dish altogether.

Apparently, I wasn't the only one. In the years that followed, India seemed to be slowly falling out of love with butter chicken. Chefs and diners alike had begun looking down upon the dish as a bit of a cliché. The common refrain: why worship at the altar of butter chicken when Indian cuisine is suffused with worthier regional dishes?

But as new versions flooded the marketplace, I grew curious about my old love. The idea of rediscovering it simultaneously fascinated and intimidated me. The butter chicken scene had matured exponentially. I needed a guide who was at home in both the classic and nontraditional worlds. Chef and F&B consultant Ashish Bhasin, famed for his encyclopaedic knowledge of north Indian cuisine, was kind enough to mentor me through this journey.

Over a long telecon from Mumbai, I spoke without reservation of my previous disappointments to Ashish. Though sympathetic towards my disenchantment, he assured me that there was still a lot of incredible butter chicken around. 'Honestly, the problem with butter chicken is not that its overrated,' he said, 'but that every restaurant makes its own version.'

With such a plethora of options, defining a 'good' butter chicken was subjective, varying greatly with individual taste and preference. There was only one way to find *the* one. 'You gotta try them all!' Ashish said, urging me to take up the gauntlet and fly down to Delhi.

So what happens when you return to a beloved dish after not eating it for nearly two decades? I was about to find out.

CLASSIC

Butter Chicken with Monish Gujral at Moti Mahal in Greater Kailash 1

The origin story of butter chicken invites fierce clashes, contrasting claims and opinions.

One narrative about butter chicken goes that it was invented by Kundan Lal Gujral, a refugee from Peshawar, who came to Delhi during the Partition and set up the cult restaurant Moti Mahal in 1947. As per Monish Gujral, Kundan Lal's grandson, in the absence of proper refrigeration in those days, tandoori chicken used to become dry hanging over the hot tandoors. To be able to serve it and to avoid food wastage, his grandfather decided to cook it in a humble and simple butter-and-cream-laden tomato gravy which led to the invention of the butter chicken, also known as murgh makhani

Raghav Jaggi and Amit Bagga, the founders of Daryaganj Restaurant, challenged this by declaring that the dish was actually created by Kundan Lal Jaggi,[2] Gujral's erstwhile partner at Moti Mahal. (It didn't help that both 'inventors' shared the same first name and sported handlebar moustaches!)

According to Raghav and Amit, when a group of people unexpectedly arrived at the Delhi eatery and requested to be fed, Jaggi improvised by taking leftover tandoori chicken and tossing it in a tangy sauce of tomatoes, butter, and cream.[3]

A third view posits that though the dish is most commonly associated with Delhi, prototypes of butter chicken existed in Punjab well before it was served at Moti Mahal. The late food historian and gourmet Ashish Chopra,[4] who held this opinion, went as far as to claim that a Punjabi farmer first cooked up the dish in his kitchen in Ludhiana.

So was the dish invented by Jaggi or Gujral? Did it come from Punjab or Delhi? What was the exact year? It seemed appropriate to pose these questions to Monish Gujral, the presiding spirit of Moti Mahal for over twenty years.

Clad in an aquamarine button-down shirt, Monish blithely dismissed any other claim to the dish's pedigree as heresy. 'Moti Mahal was and remains the original butter chicken,' declared the scion as we chatted over coffee at his Okhla office in south Delhi. 'Everyone knows Kundan Lal Gujral invented it. The rest are just trying to piggyback on our fame.'

To Monish, butter chicken is a dish about legacy. The classic, which started as a means of rehydrating leftover tandoori chicken, spoke to the towering genius of his grandfather. 'With butter chicken, he created the first superstar of Indian food. Not only did it become a mainstay of Indian cuisine, it exported our food to the world. The British appropriated it as chicken tikka masala. But who are we kidding? It is just butter chicken made with canned tomato soup,' he said.

His face was equal parts tenderness, awe, and reverence as he reminisced about his larger-than-life grandfather. 'He was like a character from the movies—very humble, yet so charismatic. Our Civil Lines home was massive, nearly an acre in size, and there was always a sea of people to meet him. He would help all selflessly without expecting anything in return.'

The gentle giant proved to be a tough boss when a just-out-of-college Monish joined Moti Mahal as an intern. 'I was made to slog with the khansamas in the blazing heat, wash pots and pans, and sent off to the market to buy ingredients at 4 a.m. Only then did I earn my internship,' he said, beaming.

Honing his skills under the master's tutelage, Monish learnt the three guiding principles of turning out the perfect juicy bird. One, a small chicken of about 700 grams is optimal. Two, the spices must be freshly ground and correctly proportioned. Three, juicy, pulpy red tomatoes work best and ought to be ground in a way so as to retain some seeds and skin to add texture to the gravy.

The process of making butter chicken detailed in his book, *On the Butter Chicken Trail: A Moti Mahal Cookbook*, stands out for its minimalism. 'It's a no-nonsense recipe with barely any spices. Cumin and red chillies are the only masalas used,' Monish said.

It is this simplicity, the restaurateur explained, that underpins the universal popularity of the dish. 'Done right, the timeless combination of tomatoes, cream, and butter is more than the sum of its parts. It's like arrabbiata sauce, very simple, with just the taste of tomatoes and a little garlic. Everyone can relate to it. That's why butter chicken is a global icon,' he opined.

Eschewing the corruption of the classic at the hands of overzealous practitioners, the tycoon urged me to hop into their flagship outlet in Greater Kailash 1 for the real deal. Walking into the M Block Market outlet the next day, I felt a frisson of recognition (my aunt, Rani Bua, who lives in GK, would often order from Moti Mahal when my brother and I visited her as kids).

Free of the additions—khoya, fenugreek, honey—too often integral to the versions today, I relished its uncomplicated, tangy-sweet taste. Evocative of an older, simpler era, the dish was a testament to the talent of yesteryear cooks in creating a lavish meal from very little.

Two Versions of Butter Chicken at Daryaganj with Amit Bagga

To hear the other side of the genesis story, I headed to Daryaganj, the brand launched by Kundan Lal Jaggi's grandson Raghav Jaggi and his business partner, Amit Bagga. The Aerocity outlet in south-west Delhi was busy and inviting. The claim to being 'the original' was evident right at the entrance. The copy beneath the logo boldly announced: 'By the inventors of Butter Chicken and Dal Makhani'.

The interior, with its exposed brick wall and palette of browns, had an earthy, polished elegance. Amit Bagga, the hurricane force behind the chain, welcomed me with a chipper greeting. An ebullient man with raven-black slicked-back hair, he exuded a raw, manic energy.

The restaurateur's passion for the brand was apparent as he ran me through a ninety-slide PowerPoint highlighting the origin of butter chicken and dal makhani through old photos, notes, and press clippings. As per the document, both dishes were invented by Kundan Lal Jaggi, and not Gujral, and the timeline was the late 1940s.

Though the former partners of Moti Mahal were like brothers, Amit said, the closeness did not carry through to the successive generations. The Jaggi family pulled out of the business for several decades until Raghav decided to honour his forebearer's legacy by setting up a new restaurant in 2019. Amit, who was Raghav's classmate at St. Columba's, joined him to conceptualize Daryaganj Restaurant.

Built around reviving 1940s nostalgia, the menu is full of retro classics. The first thing Amit set before me was tandoori chicken made according to the authentic recipe. A cavalcade of appetizers—mutton burrah, chicken pakora, mutton seekhs—followed, as the raconteur regaled me with stories from Moti Mahal's early days.

Tracing the roots of the legendary eatery, Amit shared that Jaggi and Gujral started off working for a gentleman named Mokha Singh, the owner of the first Moti Mahal in Peshawar. During Partition, the former employees came to Delhi as refugees, and had a joyful reunion standing in a long line to buy whisky. They found Mokha Singh too, in Kingsway Camp, and with his blessings, opened Moti Mahal in Daryaganj. 'Think about it. Whisky ne bichhadon ko mila diya (Whisky reunited the separated). If it hadn't been for the drink, there would be no Moti Mahal, or butter chicken!' he twinkled, evoking a Manmohan Desai-style potboiler with every word.

The two versions of butter chicken that made up my main course charted the changes the icon had undergone in the decades since its inception. 'Original Butter Chicken', with meat on the bone, was a joyful, robust iteration with a chunky tomato gravy. In contrast, 'Today's Butter Chicken', served boneless and with an ultra-smooth, velvety sauce, channelled a modern urbaneness. 'No prizes for your pick,' Amit teased, watching me happily crunch through the chewy parts of a bone.

The experience at the eatery was utterly relaxing and charming. Listening to Amit's stories, I lost track of time as well as the morsels consumed. Struggling with a giant gulab jamun that had landed on my plate, I glanced at my watch. I had been eating for three hours!

As I lurched out the door, Amit said our session was to continue. 'Come back for keema kaleji and dal meat soon,' he said. I couldn't wait.

Butter Chicken Trail in Gurugram

Gurugram, as I learnt from Ashish, has many other butter chicken eateries and chefs of repute. With Daryaganj checked off my list, I decided to stay for a few days with my Welham pal Juhi at her place in the Satellite City and try some more joints.

'Butter chicken Punjabiyan di shaan hai (Butter chicken is the pride of Punjabis),' said a beaming Sweety Singh in a tangerine polo T-shirt, as he ushered me into his takeaway outlet kitchen, Delhi 2 By Chef Sweety Singh, in Gurugram's Paras Trinity complex. Nailing the perfect bird, he believes, is all about drawing out flavour at every stage of the preparation, right from slowly simmering the tomatoes in butter, to finishing the dish with cream.

Bemoaning the lack of technique and short-cuts in cooking the classic, Sweety decried the 'lazy' versions of butter chicken rampant today. 'People these days have no idea about what butter chicken is. They've made it sweet by adding sugar and honey! They use purée instead of fresh tomatoes and stock instead of bones. Have they forgotten that purée and stock are for making soup?' Sweety fumed, indignant that the icon had paid a heavy price for its popularity.

The dish he served me won my heart with its rustic hominess. Created with the passion and the heart of a Punjabi home-cook, it had no unnecessary flourishes and was strictly eat-by-hand fare. Brimming with zingy acidity, the immediate flavours of tomatoes came through, imparting a sunny vibrancy to the plate. I polished off every last drop.

If Sweety's butter chicken was a love letter to tomatoes, Punjab Grill delivered an ode to butterfat. Over a glass of Chivas, Chef Sareen

Madhiyan served me an uber rich, royal recipe that was low on spices and heavy on cream and cashew-paste. Strained thrice for a super smooth texture, the sauce was geared toward a more refined palate. I also demolished a crusty butter chicken kulcha crammed with enough filling to make it truly decadent.

The primary appeal of butter chicken, Sareen believes, derives from fat, which explains why contemporary versions have been getting richer and more refined. 'Fat makes us happy. We get that dopamine high. And aren't we all trying to be happier and happier?' he said, grinning. The future of the dish, he opined, was all about mastering the art of refinement. 'It's all about processing the dish more and more. For the version we serve in our Washington DC outlet (now rebranded as Rania), we use a Thermomix to emulsify the gravy, so there's no butter visible,' he shared.

Butter chicken is also an obsession for Chef Gautam Chaudhry, who has been putting his own spins on the classic over the years, including a basil butter chicken served with rosemary garlic naan (for Tanzore, Beverly Hills), and a European take featuring a tandoori chicken served with his signature white makhani sauce made from parmesan, garlic, kasuri methi, and cream (for The Pink Poppadom at Hyatt Bengaluru).[5]

The ruggedly handsome Punjabi man with curly, slightly greying hair, told me that the addition of fenugreek and garlic to the butter chicken recipe has yielded massive flavour payoffs. Though not foundational ingredients, both add contrast and character to the original, thereby adding to the dish's appeal.

'It's important to remember that the original butter chicken was an accidental dish. Like all accidental preparations, it has matured over a period of time. Authenticity is nothing but a moment in a lifespan. It's relative,' Gautam said, even as he cautioned against turning the dish into some kind of haphazard parody.

'Butter chicken took over the world because it's a perfectly balanced flavour bomb of sweet, salty, bitter, spicy, and tangy. Regardless of the approach, the dish must remain carefully calibrated. No ingredient should outshine the other,' he emphasized. It made me realize that India's most indulgent dish, at its core, is not about unchecked abandon but judicious restraint.

Butter Chicken with Vaibhav Bajaj at Pandara Road

In a key passage from Marcel Proust's *Remembrance of Things Past*, the protagonist dips a madeleine in his lime-blossom tea, and suddenly finds himself back in Combray in north-central France, where his aunt would feed him madeleines as a child. The taste of the shell-shaped cookie triggers a deluge of involuntary memories, enabling him to relive the sensations and perceptions of his early years.

Havemore is my madeleine. It was at this historic Delhi eatery at Pandara Road that the butter chicken sprees of my childhood would take place. That livewire chatpata flavour has stayed with me all these years.

Returning to my pre-teen ideal after two decades made me nervous as hell. If I hated it, it would make me angry about being let down. If I loved it, I wouldn't know how to process my emotions. Either way, I would be a mess.

As I walked in after nearly twenty years, the smell of smoke and butter floated through the air. Except a few upgrades, the joint retained its old-world aura, with dim lighting and uniformed waiters scurrying about. Within seconds, my mind had wandered off, thinking about all the butter chickens I had eaten here and the memories that accompanied them. I had goosebumps and was close to tears.

I was so lost in my thoughts that I barely noticed the arrival of Vaibhav Bajaj, the third-generation owner of Havemore, and my lunchmate for the afternoon. 'Are you okay, ji?' he asked gently, noticing how tightly I was gripping my water glass. 'Oh, hi,' I mumbled, taking a moment to gather myself.

Vaibhav's boyish, goofy humour was exactly what I needed to bring me back to the ground. The ultimate Delhi salesman, he rattled off a list of signature meaty dishes for me to try. 'You have to try our mutton burra. Uff, when you tear into it—the bite, the juice—it's too good. And our brain masala—it's cooked in butter, it is actually amazing. And the butter fish is yummy. Completely fab. OH. MY. GOD.'

Moments later, he sheepishly confessed that he was vegan. 'What? Why?' I asked, bursting into laughter.

'Yes, ma'am,' Vaibhav said. 'I'm a Sadhguru follower, and haven't touched meat for several years. It's been difficult for me but I can't go back to it because it affects my practice. Meat makes me sluggish. I would rather be in a more vibrant mode,' he said.

The idea of a solitary carnivorous feast wasn't appetizing. I decided to stick to butter chicken with garlic naan, and a cool glass of chaas or buttermilk. As I tore a piece of the garlic naan to mop up the deep-orange gravy, a blizzard of flaky shreds flew out and fell on my plate. A briny jolt from the furiously pink sirke wale pyaz (vinegar-onions) completed the taste. That first bite was intensely gratifying. Bright, bracing, and compelling, it ran the danger of doing me in before I'd even begun.

It was hard to tell apart my enjoyment of the meal from the childhood significance it had for me. I found myself crazy in love all over again, surrendering all cynicism in the wake of the familiar, cherished taste.

As I sat there picking at the last of the buttery bits on my plate, Havemore seemed like exactly the right place on the planet to be.

But my journey was far from over. Sated on the classic orange butter chicken, I was now eager to try other versions of the dish, including its yellow and white avatars, and some modern iterations too.

YELLOW

Baba's Butter Chicken at Infinity Tower

The idea of butter chicken without tomatoes seems rather joyless (if not downright sacrilegious) to me. But many believe butter chicken has reached its apotheosis in Baba's butter chicken, a smooth, buttercup-yellow incarnation with nary a hint of the pulpy red staple.

When I stepped into the warmly furnished casual dining place, its Punjabi roots were evident. The paintings and pictures on the walls depicted vignettes of rural Punjab—paranda-braided beauties frolicking on swings, men doing the Bhangra, and village folks lounging on a charpai or manji.

The butter chicken at Baba's came with a naan slathered with fresh cream instead of butter. At first taste, I sorely missed the orange-red colour, and the sweet-tart punch of tomatoes. But after a few bites, I had to admit it *was* a nice dish—milder, smoother, and creamier than the tomato version. Though unashamedly rich, it was perfectly balanced. With no acidity from tomatoes to cut the creaminess, the richness of onion paste, cream, and butter blended in to yield a mellow, uninterrupted taste.

Over a phone call with Avneet Singh, the Ludhiana-based owner of the chain, I learned that the dish was over sixty years old, and was first cooked up by his grandfather Sardar Himmat Singh, lovingly known as Babaji. 'He developed his own style of making the sauce with onion paste, ginger, and spices grown on their own farms. Though a little cream goes into it, no cashew-paste is used. The yellow colour comes from a (secret) spice—no, it's not turmeric—and the dish is cooked entirely in white butter and milk from beginning to end,' he revealed.

When I broached the topic of tomatoes, Avneet pointed out that Punjab's idea of butter chicken was vastly different from Delhi's. 'As soon as you step out of Delhi and NCR, butter chicken is no longer red. Tell me, how can a gravy made mostly with tomatoes and cashew-paste be called butter chicken?' he argued, believing the Delhi version to be a misnomer.

I wasn't quite convinced. No doubt, Baba's silkily textured dish was impressively nuanced and quite delicious. And it had certainly got a leg up on the present-day 'extra creamy' craze. But was it butter chicken? The idea would take some getting used to.

WHITE

Butter Chicken with Anubhav Sapra at Aslam Chicken

'Until you've crossed the threshold of Aslam Chicken in Jama Masjid, you haven't eaten real butter chicken. That place has changed the way we eat the dish in the city,' raved Anubhav Sapra, making a strong case for visiting the Old Delhi restaurant. The founder of Delhi Food Walks knows his onions. I was intrigued by his recommendation.

We decided to visit the eponymous Delhi 6 eatery together. It was the month of Ramzan, and Matia Mahal was bustling with festivities. We arrived right in time for iftar to see the party spilling onto the street. The stalls offered infinite choice. Walking from one to the next, everything looked equally inviting. It took every ounce of self-control to resist a feast en route to our destination.

Wandering down the charming lane, we entered Aslam's through a haze of tandoor smoke. The no-frills interior featuring a black and white mosaic wall, a large vintage wooden clock, and a tiny washbasin, looked like it had not been touched for years.

The owner, Mohammad Aslam, a dynamic presence amid the crowd, was just sitting down to break his roza. His loosely cut chestnut-brown kurta was the same colour as his eyes. 'Anuman bhai, aaiye (Please come, Anuman bhai),' he greeted, inviting us to share in his faith and traditions with steaming hot bowls of haleem. 'Adab, Aslam bhai,' Anubhav said with a warm smile, not seeming to mind the distortion of his name.

Seated at a communal table, I was introduced to a family from Moradabad. Regulars at Aslam's during their visits to the capital, they had a distinct disdain for the version of the butter chicken served in New Delhi. 'I don't like it,' the man said bluntly. 'It's sweet.'

Pleased with the drift the conversation was taking, Aslam piped in, 'Sirf mera butter chicken asli hai. Baki sab farzi hain. Poochh lo aap kisi se bhi (Only I serve the real butter chicken. All others are fake. Ask anyone).'

Aslam shared that the eatery came into being in the 1980s when his father Nasiruddin set up a small cart outside the Jama Masjid. A master at coaxing the best out of spices, Nasiruddin created a secret blend with which he would marinate his tandoori chicken. More than a decade later, when Aslam combined this magic mix with butter, herbs, and fire-kissed chicken tikkas, he knew he had a winner on his hands and launched Aslam Chicken in 1998.

Rashid Bhai, his nephew and trusty lieutenant, detailed the making of the inimitable dish. Each morning, chicken tikkas, rubbed with a secret spice-mix, are left to marinate for hours before being half-browned on the tandoor. In the evening, with deft hands, the juicy chunks are tossed in a tangy sauce of spiced yoghurt, coriander, and green chillies before getting a final glug of melted Amul butter.

I snapped up a piece, savouring the smoky succulence of the

chicken. Tearing into the crisp-skinned segments, I lapped up the lemony, buttery flavour. Before I knew it, I had devoured my plateful with two rumalis.

I could see why Anubhav had been so eager to get me to Aslam's. This was not even a remote cousin of any butter chicken I had eaten. But its charred butteriness and lip-smacking flavour elevated it to greatness. I felt a pang of regret at not having discovered it earlier.

INNOVATIONS

As a new breed of chefs dish up the future of butter chicken, many are beginning their own traditions. They may not be classics yet, but some are already legacies in the making.

Delhi SOCIAL's Chef Glyston Gracias, who loves to play with flavours, contrasts, and combinations to evoke an emotional response from diners, infuses his butter chicken with Black Label Johnnie Walker Whisky. Flambéed right in front of me at the table, it made for a theatrical experience.

At SAGA, Atul Kochhar's (now-closed) luxe temple of fine dining in Gurugram, I tasted the 'Butter Chicken Ball', a frame-worthy stunner designed to wow the senses. To create a multidimensional plate, the chef filled classic makhani sauce inside a panko-ball of fried chicken. The dish, served over a bed of dal makhani, was heated at the table, causing the sauce to boil up and ooze out of the ball. It was spectacular.

But it wasn't all about entertainment. The London-based chef stressed that in the days to come, provenance would become even more crucial than the spicy flavours we crave in butter chicken. 'As different breeds of chicken become available, chefs will proudly state in menus where the bird has come from. Flavours will remain the pillar of the dish, but the taste of the chicken itself will be just as much of a big deal,' he predicted, making me equally curious what a faux-chicken version would be like.

Customization is top-of-mind for the husband–wife team of Chiquita and Sumit Gulati, who launched their brand Yours Truly Butter Chicken to cater to different kinds of lovers of the dish. Devoted solely to the creamy classic, they offer eight versions—choose from 'Breakup Wala Butter Chicken' (so hot it makes you cry), 'Meat Wala Butter Chicken' (featuring keema and eggs, and akin to a meat lover's pizza), 'Diet Wala Butter Chicken' (made with lighter alternatives like milk instead of butter, cream, and khoya), 'Lactose-free Butter Chicken' (made from almond milk, on special request), and even a pale yellow 'NRI Butter Chicken' (inspired by the creamy and non-spicy versions available abroad, crafted especially for the chilli-intolerant and those with a preference for mild flavours).

Back in Mumbai, I caught up with Saransh Goila, another evangelist for innovation. A welcome interloper in the butter chicken world, the chef earned a spot on the globe's culinary map with his uber smoky, complex take on butter chicken using the dhungar technique.[6]

Admittedly not a fan of butter chicken in his early years, an article entitled 'The Kitchen Conundrum'[7] opened the chef's eyes to the untapped global potential of the tomato-rich classic. 'Heinz developed a ketchup recipe which suits the palates of 70 per cent of people across the world without changing the taste,' he said. 'A big part of the credit goes to the taste of tomatoes. With its balance of acidity and sweetness, it gives an umami kick to the ketchup. You want to keep licking it. It's addictive. Butter chicken has the same universal appeal.'

The chef believed butter chicken gravy could do for Indian food what ketchup had done for the Western world. 'The sauce—that's where the journey of butter chicken is headed. It has the pull of ketchup and can work as a base for *anything*. I will not shy away from innovating around the product, whether it goes on top of a pizza or inside a pie,' he said.

The launch of the 'Goila Butter Chicken Burger' at his London outlet was a step in this direction. The description sounded drool-worthy—fried tandoori chicken inside a brioche bun along with sirke wale pyaz, chutney, generous dollops of makhani gravy, and a bed of garlicky mayo at the bottom. 'This is just the start,' Saransh said, all smiles.

My peregrinations ended on a high. Rediscovering the dish after long years, I was stunned to see so much incredible invention coming out of the simple, straightforward staple I grew up on. The idea that the vivid, luxurious makhani sauce could have a life beyond the classic was exciting. Given the limitless possibility of riffing with the magical ingredient, the butter chicken formula could be adapted brilliantly and endlessly.

Not bad for a dish created by accident.

◆

The good thing about not eating butter chicken all these years: an element of genuine surprise was stirred into rediscovering it. Eating my weight in the buttery stuff felt bloody good. I had missed my first love.

The conclusion I arrived at after my excursions was that, far from being overrated or clichéd, butter chicken is India's most misunderstood dish. Many are trying to topple the classic from its pedestal. But in undermining it, they forget that it does indeed bring something sensational to the table. The creamy mouthfeel of fat combined with the sweet-sour tang of tomatoes hits every flavour note and channels a deep sense of euphoria.

An icon that has been embraced joyfully across the globe needs to be celebrated. It would be a crying shame for India's most charismatic dish to fall by the wayside as a casualty of culinary snobbery or bad PR. Let us not undermine butter chicken in a bid to push other classics forward. On the contrary, its remarkable evolution can be a beacon of innovation for other Indian foods.

My odyssey left no doubt that the icon is here to stay and rule. It did, however, leave one tricky question unanswered: what exactly is butter chicken today?

Long before the staple assumed so many forms, it was a dish associated with happiness and indulgence. To me, that remains its true essence. Much as I relished the suave, debonair siblings of the dish, I ended up reverting to the simple, soul-satisfying taste I'd eaten and loved for years. The childhood favourite was still very much at the top of the pecking order.

If that makes me a boring traditionalist and a supporter of clichés, so be it. I'd rather be happy than cool. As the formidable Jay Rayner, renowned British journalist and restaurant critic, writing in the context of French food, once noted, 'Food cliches are cliches for a reason: because they are just so damn lovely.'[8]

MOTI MAHAL'S BUTTER CHICKEN

SERVES: 4 TIME TAKEN: 30 MINUTES PLUS MARINATION

INGREDIENTS

Boneless chicken	700 gms cut into 4-cm pieces
Lemon juice	1 tbsp
Chilli powder	1 tsp
Garam masala powder	1 tsp
Salt	1 ½ tsp
Plain full fat yoghurt	¼ cup
Ginger	1 tbsp, minced

For gravy,

Oil	2 tbsp
Onion	1, finely chopped
Tomatoes, Roma variety	1 kg, chopped
Salt	to taste
Kashmiri chilli powder	1 tbsp
Garam masala powder	1 tbsp
Cumin powder	1 tsp
Butter	2 tbsp
Cream	⅓ cup

METHOD

Marinate the boneless chicken pieces in lemon juice, chilli powder, garam masala, salt, yoghurt, and ginger.

Set aside for 30 minutes.

Grease a baking sheet with oil.

Spread the marinated chicken on the tray and bake in a preheated oven at 200°C for 15-18 minutes until the chicken is just cooked through.

For the sauce, heat oil in a pan over medium heat. Add the chopped onion and cook for 2–3 minutes until softened. Stir in the tomatoes, cover and cook for 10–12 minutes.

Use a spatula to press the sauce through a fine mesh strainer back into the pan.

Blend the strained sauce with a stick blender or in a mixer and put it back in the pan.

Switch on the flame and stir in the spices and salt until well-blended. Add the cooked chicken pieces and stir.

Cook for 3–5 minutes, until heated through.

Add butter just before serving, and once the butter has melted, add the cream. Stir well. Mix and serve hot.

Tip: Instead of cooking the chicken in the oven, you could cook it with 1 tbsp oil in a pan for 8–10 minutes. Once the chicken is cooked, remove it and set aside.

Use the same pan to cook the gravy to add flavour.

You could also add 1 tsp crushed kasuri methi in the end to enhance the flavour.

DARYAGANJ'S 'TODAY'S BUTTER CHICKEN'

SERVES: 4 TIME TAKEN: 30 MINUTES PLUS MARINATION

INGREDIENTS

For marination,

Boneless chicken thighs	500 gms, cut into tikka-size pieces
Hung curd	4 tbsp
Deggi mirch powder	½ tsp
Salt	1 tsp
Lemon juice	1 tbsp

For gravy,

Butter	4 tbsp
Green chillies	4, slit
Ginger paste	2 tbsp
Deggi mirch	1 tbsp
Fresh tomato purée	2 cups

Cumin powder	1 tsp
Cashew paste	2 tbsp
Garam masala powder	1 tsp
Kasuri methi	1 tsp
Salt	2 tsp or as per taste
Fresh cream	½ cup

For garnish,

Ginger juliennes	1 tbsp
Butter	2 tbsp
Fresh cream	2 tbsp

METHOD

For chicken tikka,

Marinate the cleaned and washed chicken in hung curd, deggi mirch powder, salt, and lemon juice.

Set aside for 20 minutes.

Cook the chicken in a tandoor until done. Baste it with 2 tbsp butter and set aside.

For gravy,

Melt butter in a pan, add green chillies, ginger paste, deggi mirch, and cook for a minute.

Add fresh tomato purée and cook for 5 minutes on a slow flame.

Add cumin powder and cook for 30 seconds. Then add cashew paste and cook for 1 minute.

Add the cooked chicken tikka pieces, garam masala, kasuri methi, and salt.

Let it cook for 5 minutes and check for seasoning and consistency.

Finish with fresh cream and butter.

Garnish with ginger juliennes, butter and serve.

ATUL KOCHHAR'S 'BUTTER CHICKEN BALLS'

SERVES: 4 TIME TAKEN: 1 HOUR PLUS FREEZING PLUS OVERNIGHT SOAKING

INGREDIENTS

Makhani sauce	4 tbsp
Dal makhani	2 cups
Boneless chicken thighs	500 gms
Refined oil	2 cups, for frying
Salt	to taste
Pepper	a pinch
Flour	1 cup
Eggs	2, beaten
Panko breadcrumbs	1 cup

For makhani sauce/tomato balls,

Tomato	1 kg, chopped
Garlic	1 tbsp, chopped
Red chilli powder	1 tbsp
Cashew nuts	2 tbsp
Butter	2 tbsp
Honey	1 tbsp
Sugar	1 tsp
Green cardamom	2–3

For dal makhani,

Whole black urad dal	1 cup
Red rajma	⅛ cup
Deggi mirch	2 tsp
Salt	to taste
Tomato purée	1 cup
Butter	¾ cup
Ginger-garlic paste	3 tbsp
Kasuri methi	1 tsp, crushed
Refined oil	¼ cup
Full cream milk	1 cup

METHOD

For tomato balls,

Put chopped tomatoes, garlic, chilli powder, cashew nuts, and green cardamom in a pan.

Cook on a slow flame for 20–25 minutes until the tomatoes are soft and sauce is reduced.

Purée the sauce and strain it.

Add butter and honey to the sauce and let it cool.

Make small balls of the sauce and chill for 2 hours.

For dal makhani,

Soak the black urad dal and rajma overnight.

Wash and rinse the dal and put in a pressure cooker with 1½ cup water, 1 tsp deggi mirch, and salt.

Cook the dal for 2–3 whistles, until tender.

When cooked, stir the dal with a ladle to mash it.

Take a lagan (broad-based metal pot) and heat refined oil in it.

Add ginger-garlic paste and cook for a minute.

Add tomato purée and cook well for 10 minutes.

Add the cooked dal and milk and let it simmer for half an hour on a slow flame until it becomes nice and thick.

Finish it with butter and hand-crushed kasuri methi.

Use as required.

To process the chicken,

Clean the chicken thighs, cut each thigh into two.

Place each chicken thigh in between two sheets of cling wrap. Gently pound the chicken thigh with a meat hammer or a heavy rolling pin until the thigh becomes thin and even.

Season them with salt and pepper.

Add the tomato sauce balls in the centre of each flattened chicken thigh.

Fold the edges of each chicken thigh over the sauce to form balls. Freeze them for 2–3 hours until firm.

Dust the chicken balls with flour, then dip in beaten egg, and coat with Panko breadcrumbs, retaining the shape of the balls.

Heat 2 cups of oil in a kadhai and fry the chicken balls on a slow flame so that the chicken cooks completely from inside. Fry them till nice and golden.

For assembly,

Reheat the dal makhani and put it at the base of a plate.

Arrange 2 fried chicken balls on top per portion.

Serve hot.

Tip: Wrap the chicken thighs after stuffing with makhani sauce tightly in cling film and then freeze; it will help retain the ball shape.

Vada Pav

ONE FOR THE ROAD

Why do I love vada pav? Let me count the ways: the spicy, batter-fried potato ball coddled in squishy-soft bread and enlivened with sinus-clearing chutneys is a flavour bomb. Its carb-on-carb foundation makes it a miracle for hunger pangs. It's inexpensive—the average price is ₹20. It's easy to carry around. And oh, it takes just a minute or two to wolf down.

But that's only half the story. The truly magical thing about a vada pav is eating it on the street—constructed right in front of you by a hawker, with a bit of theatre. As you're enveloped by the piercing perfume of fried green chillies, jostled by fellow street-food pilgrims, something almost alchemical occurs. The city's faultlines vanish. You're immersed in a real community.

In 1999, when I first moved to Maximum City,[1] the inexpensive eat fuelled me through many a graveyard shift as a lowly cub reporter working for a leading daily. Hunched over my office desk with a mouthful of the bready comfort, I would tackle monstrous deadlines and impossible bosses. As I got achy and fatigued, vada pav would put me right quick. It was like having a 'bantai' (Mumbai slang for buddy) by my side.

After work, I would flag the same kali-peeli taxi to Churchgate Station and vent my frustrations to Vinayak, my cabbie friend, philosopher, and guide. 'Khali peeli tension nahi lene ka, madam. Mast rehne ka (Don't stress, madam, just be happy),' he would console, infecting me with his joie de vivre.

During that first year in Mumbai, I went from vada pav novice to serious fancier in the space of a few months. Propelled by my fervour to find the best, I ate at a lot of carts. Wait times could be long. Moving through the serpentine lines, mingling with strangers, I got the best crash course in Mumbai life.

The men behind these carts had always intrigued me. During the pandemic, my curiosity peaked. As silence pervaded our streets, I found myself thinking more and more about the real-life drama of their lives. Who were they? What were their personal stories and philosophies?

When the city unlocked, I wanted nothing more than to meet these unsung heroes up close. I decided to revisit some of my favourite carts and also check out some new ones.

Narendra Vaidya's Stall outside Dadar Station

Outside Platform 1 at Dadar station, time has stood still around a weathered folding table, a large stainless-steel platter, and a fading signboard, for over fifty years.

It was here, in this nondescript corner of Mumbai, that a street vendor named Ashok Vaidya first spawned the city's favourite snack in 1966 by brilliantly crossbreeding batata vada, a Maharashtrian staple of batter-coated potato dumplings, with pillowy pav bread.

The impetus to start a snack for the proletariat was both functional as well as politically expedient: functional, because the punishing work schedules at Mumbai's textile mills meant that the factory workers needed something substantial to fuel them through the long hours. And expedient, because right-wing political party Shiv Sena's supremo Bal Thackeray preached a doctrine of Marathi enterprise and gave a boost to the vada pav business to counter the growing influence of south Indian Udupi eateries. In the early 1980s, many textile mill workers, who lost their livelihoods after the Great Bombay Textile Strike of 1982, supported themselves by starting vada pav carts.

Ashok's son Narendra, who continues his father's legacy from the same Lilliputian space, had agreed to meet me at his perch. There was a whirlwind of energy around him as I watched him grab and split open pavs, smear them with chutneys, ram vadas inside, and dole them out to a horde of hungry customers, all at warp speed. He could barely stop to catch his breath, let alone talk to me.

Signalling for me to wait, the slim-built vendor stretched his arm over the crowd to hand me a vada pav. The blend of crisp, soft, and chewy textures combined with a parade of flavours from the chutneys—sweet, salty, spicy—made it irresistible.

Just moments later, I watched stupefied as the whole set-up was disassembled with astonishing efficiency. As his helper neatly folded everything and tucked it away in a corner, Narendra hurriedly explained that he had to go under the radar for a bit each day when the authorities were on their rounds.

Dismantling done, he nodded to his partner and whisked me to the nearby Shagun Café, an Irani joint, for a proper chinwag. 'We can talk peacefully now,' he said cheerfully, as he ordered tea.

'Your father invented the vada pav, and you still don't have a licence?' I asked, mystified. 'Yes,' he admitted sheepishly, revealing that their licence was revoked in 2001 after the Supreme Court declared the station a no-hawking zone due to the fire risks involved.

The Brihanmumbai Municipal Corporation (BMC) had given him a place at the Hawker's Plaza near Flower Market in Dadar, which he didn't consider a viable option. Who would climb to the first floor of a building to buy vada pav? Besides, there were too many emotions attached to Dadar station, a hub of Mumbai culture and a major transit point. So he came back. 'My father spent his whole life at this place. It's something I want to protect,' he said with steely calm.

Wrangling with authorities aside, Narendra's love for the trade was palpable. The long hours, the scorching heat, the endless pressures of hawking—all paled before the intimacy of the personal bond he shared with each of his customers. 'Nothing beats the energy of being on the street. Attending to so many people all at once at rush hour gives me a high. I love the satisfaction on their faces when they eat my vada pav. My day is made,' he said, flashing a wide grin.

Narendra, who started helping at the stall while still in school, has vivid memories of his pioneer father. 'Baba was a rebel and loved to try new things in the kitchen. He would feed us Irani omelettes spiced with chutney and dosais stuffed with chicken. Before inventing the vada pav, he used to sell poha, which he renamed as Indian biryani. That's how creative he was,' he said.

The idea of making vada pav took root when one of Ashok's customers asked for a bun to eat along with poha. 'That's when Baba got the idea to serve batata vada with pav, a meal by itself, which he served with chutneys. It took many tries before he found the perfect recipe,' Narendra revealed.

After Ashok succumbed to a sudden heart attack, the torch was truly passed on. A trusted guardian of the authentic vada pav traditions his father started, Narendra has kept the taste scrupulously unchanged through the years.

Narendra chafes at the very idea of calling vada pav 'Bombay burger' (à la Anthony Bourdain).[2] 'Vada pav should never try to be a burger. It's a 100 per cent Maharashtrian snack with the besan-coated batata vada and pav bread. The whole fun of vada pav is with Indian chutneys, whereas a burger plays with cheese and sauce,' he said.

Back at the cart, he requested me to finish the interview at his home in Matunga a couple days later. On a sunny Sunday morning, welcoming me into his cosy home, Narendra introduced me to his mother, his older brother Vinayak, and his sister-in-law Ameeta. Over cups of tea and homemade chaklis (crunchy besan spirals) he showed me old pictures of his father with his mentor Bal Thackeray.

Vinayak, an MBA degree-holder, with past stints at JWT and Hindustan Thompson, has some lofty ambitions, including setting up more shops and having a presence at the airport. His dream, though, is for the Maharashtra government to grant heritage status to vada pav. Carts like theirs, he argued, ought to be landmarked as heritage symbols, being integral to the city's cultural fabric. 'Heritage doesn't mean just buildings. Street food is culture, too,' he argued passionately.

Narendra remains more modest in his expectations. 'If the government gives me a licence to sell from my spot at the station, I will be happy. The cart is my dream world. It's my whole life,' he said emotionally, sharing that though he had no plans to marry, he hoped to eventually pass on the baton to his nephew.

After an obligatory round of selfies and group photos, the family waved me a cheery goodbye. Vinayak promised to invite me for dinner soon. 'Next time, we'll call you over for fish curry and rice,' he said.

'And some wine,' Narendra chimed in.

Ashok Vada Pav Near Kirti College

The blue-and-yellow canopied kiosk outside Kirti College is hailed as legendary among Mumbaikars. Everything you crave in a vada pav, you'll find here: vadas fried to golden perfection; sweet-sharp chutneys that taste electric; and fried bits of besan batter, or chura, that underpin the snack's crunchy appeal.

Its owner Ashok Thakur has something mythical about him, too. Like the Holy Grail, he is notoriously elusive. After a month of follow-ups and a barrage of calls, the doyen finally agreed to grant me an audience.

As always, there was a snaking queue outside the minuscule shop. I spotted a construction worker squabbling with his wife in Bhojpuri, a teen telling her friend about her first date in detail, a cigarette-puffing corporate barking orders over the phone, and a bratty five-year-old having a meltdown.

An assistant of Ashok's took me to a small room behind the front counter, where a Tintin-esque wavy-haired man held out his hand for me to shake. A large platter of mashed potato balls was at the ready, waiting to be deep-fried into vadas. Leaving the task to an assistant, Ashok ushered me outside to a quiet corner of the road.

'Madam, recorder chalu kiyela (Did you turn on the recorder)?' he asked in a teasing tone before launching into the story of his travails. Ashok's father was a mill-worker at Jalan Mill in Lower Parel and his mother washed utensils for households. Ashok was the fourth in line of five brothers, two of whom were disabled. The family lived in a 10 x 10 kholi (small room) and struggled to make ends meet.

When trade unionist Datta Samant called for the textile workers' strike in 1982, Ashok was struggling to find a job. His elder brother, a union leader in the Kamgar Union (a workers' union) asked him not to join corporate companies as it would betray the workers' cause. 'Uss din main bahut roya, madam. Maine socha, main mere bhaiyon ko kaise zinda rakhunga (That day I cried a lot, madam. I wondered how I would keep my brothers alive),' he whispered, eyes welling up.

To make ends meet, Ashok started assisting a vada pav seller. Standing at the cart all day, he developed not just an understanding of the trade, but also a deep appreciation for the dish. 'Vada pav Mumbai ki pehchan hai. Ameer garib dono khata hai. Yeh dukh sukh mein kaam ata hai (Vada pav is Mumbai's identity. It's eaten by the rich and the poor alike. It comforts in good and bad times),' he said.

Determined to shine, he started his own cart. Today, he is acknowledged as the undisputed master of the vada pav in Mumbai, emulated by his peers and revered by fans.

'How did you get this far?' I asked.

'Anubhav se. Thokar kha ke. Maine apna tann mann laga diya vada pav par (With experience—and learning from each failure. I devoted my entire life to perfecting this food. I put my heart and soul into it),' he replied.

The golden-fried bits of chickpea batter Ashok stuffs into his vada pav have contributed greatly to his lore. He credited the idea to a bunch of famished students from Kirti College who would hang around his stall. They couldn't afford a vada pav, so they would ask him to add chura to the pav. Now, regular customers say that their favourite snack simply does not taste right without a layer of the crisp crumbs.

Though Ashok wanted to leverage his fame to build a larger commercial enterprise, funding was an issue. 'My plan is ready. I'm just waiting for someone to come to me and say, "Ashok bhai, take my millions and do what you want with it." But you need a big heart to part with money,' he joked.

For now, he lives by a simple and age-old business philosophy: keep the customer satisfied. As I was leaving, Ashok spotted a cab-driver struggling with his stuffed-to-bursting vada pav. The chura was about to slip out of the bun, so Ashok promptly gave him a piece of newspaper to place under it. The cabbie flashed him a bright smile and thanked him.

'Dekha, madam, customer kya hai? Woh bhagwan hai (See, madam, what the customer means? He is God),' Ashok said.

Ashok Satam's Cart outside CTO in Fort

If street food is all about setting, there are few better places to snarf a vada pav than the diminutive stall outside the Central Telegraph Office

(CTO). Ringed by Art Deco buildings and a stone's throw from the nymphs of Flora Fountain, this beloved landmark stands out as much for its mise en scène as for its gustatory pleasures.

'You don't need a history book to know about Mumbai. Just come to my stall. My stall is Mumbai's diary,' said Ashok Satam, the amiable, medium-built co-owner[3] of the cart, as we caught up for a rendezvous on a muggy afternoon.

It wasn't an empty claim. From his corner, Ashok had seen the real-world effects of booms and crashes of the stock market, the city's worst upheavals, its shootouts, gangster wars, and legal trials. Blessed with a photographic memory, Ashok shared a few gems with me in a sun-dappled corner of the street.

The cart, set up by his father Manohar Mangesh Satam, dates back to 1971. Ashok, who was eleven then, recalled the tense days of the India–Pakistan war when the government had passed strict orders for Mumbaikars to keep their windows closed and covered with black paper and their lights off, as part of a city-wide blackout to minimize visibility in case of an aerial attack. 'Think about it, madam,' he said. 'I've been here since that time.'

Some of his most vivid memories were from the early 1990s, when stockbrokers, hot from trading, would flock to his stall until late night. It was the era when scamster Harshad Mehta, the then-Big Bull of the Indian stock market, ruled Dalal Street. There was no internet and people would come to trade in person. 'Traders would call for parcels of my vada pav in the evening and eat them late in the night,' he recalled. When the market had a high, so did Ashok. 'Even today, I follow the stock market closely. Its rise and fall impacts me directly,' said the veteran.

Later in the same decade, he had a tryst with the underworld when sellers of unauthorized liquor tried to extort money from him. 'With folded hands, pita ji and I pleaded with them: "We are poor people. We sell vada pav to feed our family and educate our children. How can we give you money?" They understood and let us go.'

On 26 November 2008, when Pakistani militant Ajmal Kasab and his fellow assassins attacked, Ashok had just wrapped up for the day and left for Chhatrapati Shivaji Terminus. As the train left the station, he heard a huge explosion. Only after reaching home did he realize he could have died that day. 'The sound of the firing still echoes in my ears,' he said, shuddering at the thought.

Unlike Narendra, Ashok had a vendor's licence as his cart stood outside the non-hawking zone. Money was good, and he had even managed to get an education loan to send his elder son to Auckland for an MBA (the younger is working in IT). Though he took great pride in selling vada pav on the street, he had discouraged his children from joining the trade. 'Why?' I asked. 'Too much struggle and uncertainty, madam,' he said.

The pandemic had wreaked havoc on him—he lost two of his brothers and suffered great financial losses due to the work-from-home arrangement—but Ashok believed the future of street food was bright. 'A hawker must be strong and have faith in himself. There is no space for self-doubt in this business.' Fortunately, his nephew, who was laid off during the pandemic, has been learning the ropes.

Watching history unfold before his eyes, Ashok had become somewhat stoic. It was his father's credo that kept him going through thick and thin: 'Hawking business mein sar par baraf rakho aur zabaan par shakkar (In the hawking business, you have to keep your head ice-cool and your tongue sugary sweet),' Ashok quipped.

Our chat had spanned the entire afternoon. As Ashok returned to work, I grabbed a vada pav to go. The taste brought on a rush of memories. I would snack here during my stint at Cox & Kings in 2018. The fiery, toasty vada, with just detectable coriander and curry leaves, was exactly the same, as was the drizzle of bright-red dry garlic chutney sprinkled on it.

The simple snack was as no-frills as they come, yet layered with so much history. I felt like I was carrying a piece of Mumbai in my palm.

Aram Vada Pav at Capitol Cinema Building at Fort

Propitiously located in front of the Chhatrapati Shivaji Terminus and surrounded by landmarks like the *Times of India* office, the Press Club, and the BMC building, Aram serves as the snack hub of the historic Fort area in south Mumbai. The popular Maharashtrian eatery, which serves a variety of inexpensive local dishes, is thronged by commuters and office-goers all day.

It was noon when I arrived. As always, I paused to admire the pale-blue Victorian façade of the eatery, housed in one of Mumbai's oldest (and now closed) theatres. A relic from the past, Capitol Cinema was in full swing in the 1920s. I could almost see the trams standing at the very spot where I now stood.

The joint was crammed elbow-to-elbow as usual. Ochre-and-red-jacketed waiters scurried about, a digital monitor flashed the menu options, and patrons hungrily devoured everything from kothimbir vadi (steamed cakes made of besan and coriander) and misal pav (sprouts curry with fluffy bread) to thalipith (multi-grain savoury flatbread).

Kaustubh Tambe, the calm and smiling third-generation owner of Aram, was tending to the cash counter and joined me a few minutes later. As he revisited the eatery's chequered past, I learnt it was once a British bar. Kaustubh's grandfather Shrirang Shankar Tambe leased it from Globe Theatres in 1939 and started selling dairy products like ice cream, mawa, curd, lassi, and sweets under the name Aram Milk Bar. 'He called it "Aram" because he wanted people to come and relax here,' Kaustubh said.

The menu was altered when Kaustubh's father Madhavrao Tambe took over the business. A BCom graduate, Kaustubh started coming to the shop in 1992, at twenty-two. When he introduced vada pav to the menu in the mid-1990s, he thought everyone would be happy with the classic version. It didn't take him long to change his mind. People would constantly ask, 'Azun kai ahe (What else do you have today)?'

Sensing a niche, he pioneered an anything-goes approach to vada pav fillings and chutneys. Starting with a fiery Kolhapuri vada pav brushed with thecha (chilli and garlic chutney), Kaustubh introduced a panoply of variants—butter, cheese mayo, grilled cheese. Vada pav and Schezwan sauce might seem like an odd pairing but it's one of the bestsellers at Aram.

So much fusion from such an old shop might seem incongruous, but it seemed like a perfectly viable idea to Kaustubh. Inherent in the sandwich genre, he argued, is the tendency to innovate and improvise. Besides, though unmistakably Maharashtrian in flavour, the foundational elements of vada pav aren't native to India. Its core ingredients—potatoes,[4] chillies, even pav[5]—came to India via the Europeans (mainly the Portuguese) during the sixteenth century.

Kaustubh wasn't against commercialization either. Standardizing the taste of vada pav, he believed, was important to scale up the business. 'We need to be consistent with the quality of the bread, the frying, and the masala. That can only happen if we invest in better machinery and hygiene. One can learn so much from chains like McDonald's.'

Interestingly, there is a McDonald's right next to Aram. But Kaustubh didn't fear any competition from the McAloo Tikki Burger sold by the American giant as part of its Indian menu. The besan-coated vada, he pointed out, had a distinctly different taste and texture from the crumb-fried McDonald's potato patty. Vada pav also scored better on account of its nutrition value. 'Though the vada is deep fried, besan or chickpea flour is a source of good protein, and potatoes give carbs. Provided it's fried in good oil, vada pav is a fantastic snack. It's not junk food. Even nutritionists approve of it,' he opined.

His plans for the future include setting up 250-square-foot outlets selling vada pav and other Maharashtrian items in Mumbai and other cities. So far, his children haven't shown interest in carrying on his legacy. One wants to be a lawyer, while the other two are pursuing business administration. But Kaustubh didn't seem too troubled by the future of his business. 'I want my kids to study and carve their own paths. Recently, my son made me watch *The Wolf of Wall Street*. I loved it as it taught me so much about the ways of money and business. My kids constantly open my eyes to new worlds,' he said.

Khidki Vada in Kalyan

'Certain things in life you want to stay the same. Like the taste of your vada pav. If you lose that, it's all over,' Nilesh Vaze said passionately when we met up at his shop, the famous Khidki Vada in Kalyan.

With his shining pate, towering frame, and a traditional pearl bhikbali (earring) dangling from one ear, the scion of one of

Maharashtra's oldest vada pav families[6] could pass off as a seasoned Marathi actor.

Smiling bashfully, he even admitted to completing a diploma in acting. But the pull of family ties proved to be stronger. At eighteen, Nilesh and his younger brother Shailesh joined their father Yeshwant Vaze, who started the famous Khidki Vada in 1968.

A former clerk at Mumbai's Kohinoor Mill, Vaze senior started the shop as a side gig from their home in Kalyan. He would hand out vada pav from a window, which opened directly onto the street. Only his hands were visible, but people remembered the taste of that robustly spiced potato. The people of Kalyan were soon saying, 'Jo khidki mein milta hai woh vada leke aao (Get the vada that is sold from the window).' That is how the shop got its name, Khidki Vada.

Nilesh, who assisted his father for several years, wanted to push his parents' legacy forward, but in the right direction. Ready to up his game in his early forties, he wondered how to retain a strong regional identity for vada pav in an increasingly homogenizing world.

Inspiration struck when he realized that most of his competitors were focussing their attention on chutneys, playing with tweaks on the tamarind-date and dry-garlic versions. In the process, the main star of the show, the vada itself, was being ignored.

Nilesh knew the key to a delicious vada pav lay in the spice mix that flavours the potato ball. Growing up, he would watch his mother Uma Yeshwant Vaze grind fresh spices in a khalbatta (iron mortar and pestle) in a steady circular motion. Daily, she would grind green chillies, ginger, garlic, onion, coriander, and cumin paste to make the masala for the vadas. 'The chillies would sting her eyes and hands, and she would cry,' he recalled.

Dead against the rampant burgerization of vada pav and the monocultures of large chains, Nilesh decided to bottle the taste of his mother's hands. Putting innovation at the heart of his model, he shifted bag and baggage to the seaside town of Dapoli to set up a masala factory.

After much trial and error, he and his wife—who also holds a diploma in vegetable preservation—got the proportions spot-on. The duo developed a wet paste for the vada that can last without preservatives for a whole year. 'The balance of the masala is superb, and you can really get the local taste. You just need to add the masala to boiled potatoes, make balls, coat in besan batter, and deep-fry,' Nilesh said.

The masala is the quickest way for people to make an authentic and hygienic vada pav. 'And since you are making it at home, you can be assured of enjoying our classic taste in your kitchen,' he vouched.

Over the years, the masala business has proven to be as successful as their traditional vada pav fare. Partnering with a big international distributor overseas, Nilesh has been able to sell the paste in markets like London, the US, and Germany. 'We are supplying the masala to several vada pav sellers, Indian expats, and students located abroad, who use it on a regular basis,' he shared.

The Vazes have applied for a patent for the recipe and guard it like the formula of Coca Cola. When I asked him the secret to making the paste last so long, he gave the entire credit to his 'elder brother', the vada pav. 'I consider Khidki Vada Pav, invented two years before my birth, my elder brother. He gives me whatever I ask for.'

Nilesh believes that with the masala, he has uncovered a whole new way to take vada pav into the future without compromising its regional flavour. His Cornell-educated son has no intention of joining him, but he doesn't see that as a problem.

'Hum rahen ya na rahen, Khidki Vada ka naam hamesha rahega (Whether I'm there or not, Khidki Vada will live on forever),' he declared with a theatrical flourish.

Vada Pav Bao with Glyston Gracias at Khar SOCIAL

Glyston Gracias, city chef, SOCIAL, turned into a wide-eyed fanboy when talking about his childhood snack. 'I mean, who doesn't love vada pav, right? He's my hero!' he exclaimed.

The vada pav of his childhood was an impossibly delicious snack that Aunt Ivy, a Catholic nun who worked at his school canteen in Malad, would smear with her signature coconut chutney. 'She would use these very sweet coconuts and jaggery along with coriander and green chillies, which made the chutney extra sweet. I was crazy about it,' he said.

Admittedly a bit bored of seeing his idol wear the same threads, the chef decided to give 'him' a cool makeover for SOCIAL's hip Gen-Z audience. 'I wanted my vada pav to wear a funky new jacket. I also wanted him to trend on social media, so I made him very Instagram-friendly,' he said.

Captivated by Asian flavours, he whipped up a panko-fried potato patty which went inside pita bread, nestled alongside a blistering fried green chilli, and a luxe side of garlicky mayo. Voila, the vada pav bao was born.

The trendy riff was a smash hit and won raves for its double whammy of sweet-and-spicy flavours. Pitched at a younger, uptown audience, it was a funky reminder of the versatility of the snack. Different, yes, but also juicy, snappy, and undeniably fun.

Gorging on the starchy treat with a glass of chilled beer, I found it robust, naughty, and completely irresistible. The bright flavours popped in my mouth. The reinterpreted street-treat fit in seamlessly with the swanky setting too.

Riyaaz Amlani, the CEO of Impresario Entertainment & Hospitality, who joined us, thinks of the clubby version as natural evolution. 'Humans are attracted to novelty. Our neurons start firing when we see something unique. It's just psychology 101,' he said. Newness doesn't mean a lack of seriousness, though. 'If you're messing with a classic, it better be good. We need to do it responsibly and sustainably,' he insisted.

For Glyston, modernizing street food is a way of showcasing it to new audiences and taking it forward. Sixty years after its invention, we have only nibbled at vada pav's full potential, he believes. The bao wasn't his first riff—he had experimented with vada pav gnocchi earlier—and it certainly wouldn't be his last. 'Watch this space,' he said confidently.

'Toast to that?' asked Riyaaz. I nodded, holding up my empty beer glass for another round.

Shree Krishna Vada Pav with Sujay Sohani in London

As it blazes a fresh trail, the art of vada pav is getting its share of international attention, courtesy of the creativity of NRIs. To get a sense of its global march, I got on a call with the owner of Shree Krishna Vada Pav (SKVP), the eatery that reportedly introduced the snack to London in the early 2010s.

Like most success stories, the saga of its co-founder Sujay Sohani began with a setback. A native of Mumbai, Sujay graduated in Hotel Management from Rizvi College and moved to London to work. However, he was laid off during the recession of 2008.

As he and his friend (and business partner) Subodh Joshi explored new ventures, they gravitated towards the idea of setting up a vada pav outfit. 'We had no capital to open a proper restaurant, but vada pav seemed doable. It's the cheapest way to open something of your own and the best thing to make with easily available ingredients. Also, it's something we missed eating in London,' Sujay said.

To test the waters, they started operations from the pantry of a rundown Polish ice cream parlour. Subodh's wife gave them the recipe for a typically homemade batata vada and chutneys that they would eat in Mumbai—coconut, garlic, coriander, and sweet tamarind. The pav posed a bit of a problem, as it was difficult to get the sourish taste associated with Mumbai's laadi pav (rows of pav, merged). But they got a dedicated pav-maker to approximate the taste.

Much trial and error, a few misadventures, and punishing hours followed. Sujay recalled how he and Subodh would carry tea for the shops at the high street in a thermos just like in India. 'The business operated on a typical Indian credit model too. "Account mein likh dena (Put it on the account)," our clients would say,' he said, laughing.

The slog paid off. From a small mom-and-pop storefront, SKVP has now branched into thirteen outlets across the UK. Though they sell a range of street food, vada pav remains their top seller. The crowd they draw is fairly cosmopolitan including not just Asian, but a mix of British, Romanians, Polish, and Germans.

'We can proudly say that we were the first to bring vada pav to the UK and make it commercially viable. Following our success, other

Indian high-street brands started selling vada pav and other Indian street food too,' Sujay said.[7]

He believes that vada pav could be the next food to capture global imagination. Though not a huge fan of batata vada by itself, he considers its pairing with pav and chutneys a sure-fire hit. 'Vada pav's appeal revolves around simplicity and convenience. You can eat it on the go. It's veg *and* vegan. Everyone loves it.'

The entrepreneur sees this as a chance to build global reputation for Indian street food. It's all about promoting it the right way and encouraging people to try it, he believes. 'South India has proved it with dosai and idli. Could you ever have imagined that there would be a Saravana Bhavan in Amsterdam and that the Dutch would eat dosai?'

Globally, Indian food is equated with butter chicken and naan, but Sujay is determined to shake up the cliché. 'The main philosophy behind starting SKVP was to show that there are many other kinds of Indian food—vada pav, chaat, and other items which we ought to be proud of,' he said.

According to Sujay, being true to its Mumbai origins is what would make vada pav a global hit. 'If pizza, a very basic food of Italy, can be known as pizza everywhere, then why not vada pav? Our dream is to make vada pav as famous as pizza. One day, people across the globe will ask for it by name.'

His words echoed in my ears as I put the phone down. It was an exciting thought. Vada pav's greatest achievement may be yet to come.

◆

The world of vada pav is ruled by some riveting personalities.

They invent patent-worthy pastes. They educate their sons at Cornell. They watch *The Wolf of Wall Street*. They call you home for wine. Call me stereotypical (not to mention elitist, presumptuous, and downright ignorant), but I never associated them with these things. Getting to know these dynamos and entering their worlds allowed me to see them in a new light. It also enabled me to appreciate the interesting crossroads at which vada pav sits.

With more eateries around the country and the world featuring the snack,[8] and innumerable upscale variants being dished out, there has never been a more exciting time to be a vada pav lover.

Yet the future of the handheld treat seems uncertain.

Shorn of its street context and diversity of tastes, vada pav risks losing its identity and distinctness. The quirky charms of new variants cannot be denied. But the fact remains that the iconic snack has achieved its exalted position thanks to the hundreds of hawker stalls that weave through the city. Each is renowned for a specific taste brought to life by a secret recipe, ingredient, or technique. These beloved local institutions aren't merely places to carbo-load. They make our streets deliciously vibrant.

Today, one cannot drive very far without having a vada pav cart come into view. But that may not be the case in the future.

Running unauthorized businesses, braving the elements, our hawkers lead precarious lives. Many still don't have licences. Post-pandemic, the existential hustle is even harder. As hygiene-related concerns surround street food, many have been abandoning their businesses. Others continue to hold strong, but don't have successors to carry on their legacy.[9]

Each time a hawker closes shop or retires in the absence of a successor, we lose beloved tastes along with untold skills, wisdom, stories, and heritage.

Mumbai without my favourite street carts is unimaginable to me. To lose them would be to lose a small part of myself.

Recognizing the imperative of protecting this precious legacy, countries across the world have been taking active steps to safeguard hawkers and elevate their status. Hawker Culture in Singapore features on the UNESCO Representative List of the Intangible Cultural Heritage of Humanity.[10] The country also devised a Hawker's Succession Scheme[11] in which veteran hawkers are paired with aspiring vendors to pass on their skills.

In Thailand, researchers at the National Science and Technology Development Agency (NTSDA) have developed a smart food-vending cart with modern features such as a mini wastewater treatment system, a water sink, a kitchen hood, a refrigerator, and two stoves. Even Michelin Guides have been honouring hawkers.

India too must upgrade the quality and reputation of its street food through dedicated societal and government support.[12] If we wish to preserve our street eats, we must protect the ecosystem that surrounds them. This begins by recognizing our hawkers as rich cultural assets and significant contributors to the economy.

We love our street food. It's time we nurtured it too.

Recipes from My Travels

NARENDRA VAIDYA'S VADA PAV

SERVES: 4 TIME TAKEN: 30 MINUTES

INGREDIENTS

Boiled potatoes	500 gms, peeled and mashed
Oil	2 tbsp
Green chillies	3–4, chopped
Garlic	6–7 cloves
Ginger	1-inch piece, chopped
Curry leaves	10–12
Mustard seeds	1 tbsp
Cumin seeds	1 tbsp
Asafoetida	a pinch
Turmeric powder	1 tsp
Fresh coriander	a handful, chopped
Salt	to taste

For coating,

Besan	150 gms
Turmeric powder	1 tsp
Baking soda	½ tsp
Water	200 ml
Oil	2 cups, for frying

For green chutney,

Fresh green coriander	1 cup
Spinach	½ cup, boiled

Green chillies	3–4
Garlic	4–5, cloves
Ginger	½-inch piece, chopped
Lemon juice	1 tbsp
Cumin powder	1 tsp
Salt	to taste

For dry chutney,

Red chilli powder	2 tbsp
Garlic	10–15 cloves, fried
Fried chura of besan	½ cup, crispy
Salt	to taste
Pav	8

METHOD

Heat oil in a kadhai.

Add cumin seeds, mustard seeds, and asafoetida and let them crackle.

Add chopped green chillies, garlic, and ginger, and cook for 30 seconds.

Add curry leaves, mashed potatoes, turmeric powder, salt, and fresh coriander. Mix well and set aside to cool.

For the coating, mix besan, water, turmeric, salt, and baking soda. Whisk well to a smooth coating consistency.

Make small balls of the potato mixture.

Heat 2 cups of oil in a kadhai, dip the potato balls in the besan batter, and deep-fry on medium heat until golden brown.

For the green chutney, grind together all the ingredients until smooth.

For dry red chutney, grind together red chilli powder, fried garlic, fried chura of besan, and salt.

Stuff the batata vada inside the pav smeared with the two chutneys.

Tip: Instead of fried chura of besan, you could use readymade khaari boondi (fried besan batter drops) to make the dry red chutney. Do not blend hot besan chura for the chutney, or it might make it greasy.

For more flavour, you could add ½ cup toasted shredded coconut or ¼ cup roasted peanuts while blending the chutney.

SOCIAL'S VADA PAV BAO

SERVES: 4 TIME TAKEN: 30 MINUTES PLUS REFRIGERATION

INGREDIENTS

Boiled potatoes	500 gms, peeled and mashed

For tempering,

Soyabean oil	2 tbsp
Mustard seeds	1 tbsp
Cumin	1 tbsp
Curry leaves	10–12
Ginger	1 tbsp, chopped
Garlic	2 tbsp, chopped
Green chillies	1 tbsp, chopped
Asafoetida	a pinch
Turmeric powder	1 tsp
Kitchen king masala	1 tbsp
Fresh coriander	a handful, chopped
Salt	to taste

For batter,

Besan	1 cup
Salt	to taste
Chilli powder	1 tsp
Water	1½ cup

To coat,

Panko breadcrumbs	100 gms
Soyabean oil	2 cups, for deep-frying

To serve,

Pita bao (available at SOCIAL, or use pita bread)	8 pieces

Garlic mayonnaise	100 gms
Chilli pickle	20 gms

METHOD

Heat 2 tbsp oil in a pan. Add all the tempering ingredients and sauté well for 2 minutes.

Add the mashed potatoes to the pan and mix well.

Season with salt and add chopped coriander.

Take out the mixture from the pan, let it cool a bit, and then make patties of approximately 60 gms each out of the mixture.

Whisk the batter ingredients until thick and smooth.

Coat each patty with this batter and then coat it with panko breadcrumbs. Refrigerate for an hour.

Heat oil in a kadhai and deep-fry the crumbed patties until golden and crisp.

Spread some garlic mayo and chilli pickle inside each pita bao. Stuff the bao with the fried vada.

Serve with fries and garlic mayo.

Tip: Garlic mayo can be made by whisking together 40 gms readymade dry garlic chutney with 60 gms mayonnaise.

Dhansak

AN INVITATION TO GLUTTONY

I got my first taste of dhansak during the mid-1990s on a visit to Mumbai with my childhood friend Anupama.

Jeroo Nariman, the matriarch of Parsi Dairy Farm, knew Anupama's family well, and had invited us to join her weekly Sunday dhansak ritual with the brood at her 100-year-old home on Princess Street.

Jeroo's family—her nieces Meheru and Shernaz along with their respective husbands and kids—was big-hearted and zestful, and welcomed us to the table without a shred of formality. The mutton dhansak arrived along with its cavalcade of caramelized white rice, golden prawn kavabs,[1] and crunchy kachumber or salad of finely diced onions, cucumbers, and tomatoes. The spicy dal, with large chunks of meat, had so many parts that it felt more like a production than a dish to me.

As the achingly tender meat fell apart in our mouths, we oohed and aahed over its luscious texture. Platters were passed, conversations sparked, banter exchanged, and frustrations vented. The meal ended on a high note with Jeroo's spectacular caramel custard, and Rambo the dalmatian scoring a regal dollop of white butter.

All too soon it was late afternoon. Replete with Duke's Raspberry Soda and buoyed by the boisterous bonhomie of our hosts, we headed back.

It was a good Sunday, and a fine lunch.

◆

The deep love for good food and hospitality that made Jeroo's dhansak so memorable has long been a hallmark of Parsi culture, traceable to the community's Persian ancestry.

The Zoroastrian descendants of Parsis sailed across the Arabian Sea to escape religious persecution in Persia and landed in Gujarat, sometime during the eighth century CE.[2] Before the Arab conquest of their homeland in the seventh century, they were a part of the great Sassanid or Sasanian Empire, one of the most developed and prosperous empires of the ancient world.

Many elements of dhansak, including the love of meat, would have existed in Sasanian Persia. According to food historian K. T. Achaya, 'pulses would have taken the place of rajmah beans and spinach used in Iran.' He notes that 'at least three dals, and even up to nine' went into making dhansak, which also included 'pieces of fatty meat, tripe and vegetables'.[3]

One can only imagine the early journey of the dish. Stew-loving Zoroastrians, with their rich tradition of meat-and-vegetable blends from Iran, would have arrived in Gujarat. The unique taste of Indian spices and produce would have piqued their interest. Before long they would have succumbed to the Gujarati passion for sweet, tangy, spicy flavours, leading to the creation of dhansak.

Over the centuries, the dish would have evolved, replacing the mellow preparations of Persia with a spicier concoction through the liberal use of Indian spices and condiments. Filtered through the hands of countless cooks and melded with the local ingredients and Gujarati culture, dhansak would become, well before the twentieth century, the flagship food of the Parsis.

The version of yore was cooked on wood fire and made with masalas prepared at home. Though the essential recipe hasn't changed, it has become less elaborate, calling for fewer ingredients and steps. The nine dals Achaya talks about got reduced to one or two, the use of tripe got omitted, and everything went into blenders and pressure cookers.

DHANSAK LESSONS WITH HOME-COOKS

The basic recipe for making dhansak calls for vegetables—pumpkin, onions, eggplants, methi (fenugreek) leaves, and mint—to be cooked along with lentils, before straining the mixture to a smooth, velvety blend. A vaghar or slow tempering of tomatoes with masalas is then prepared, to which the lentil and veggie mush and boiled mutton (or chicken) are added and left to meld.

Each ingredient plays its part in producing the astounding range of flavours—sweetness derives from pumpkin and onions, bitterness from methi, citrusy notes like coriander and mint, tartness from tomatoes, heat from red chillies, and complexity from spices.

With as many dhansak variations as there are cooks, the devil is often in the details. Some home-cooks like to use only toor (tuvar) dal, others prefer a combination of two or three lentils (mostly masoor, toor, and moong). Some swear by the tried-and-tested red pumpkin and eggplants, others add carrots or even pineapples. Some like their dhansak smooth, others like it a bit grainy. Some like to add jaggery and tamarind, others shun them. Some dump all of its ingredients into a pressure cooker, others believe in more thoughtful assembly.

Mahrukh Mogrelia, a food entrepreneur who owns a brand called Mahrukh's Kitchen, holds that the flavour of dhansak should derive from the natural sweetness of vegetables like pumpkin, and not from sugar or jaggery. 'Dhansak shouldn't be obviously sweet; it should have that spiciness. And the dal must be strained to a smooth consistency. God forbid if a pumpkin piece gets into a Parsi's mouth; he will know it has veggies, and never eat dhansak again!' she said, laughing.

Homogenizing the ingredients made it easy for Mahrukh to sneak some nutrition into her unsuspecting children's diet. 'Mum would grind all kinds of veggies into the dhansak without letting us know. Once she added beetroot, and I asked her, "Why is the dhansak red today?" But she just said, "It's so tasty. Chaakhi le, dikra (Taste it, son)!" And I lapped it up!' her son Khurshed recounted with mock horror.

Jeroo Shroff, a gourmet chef and culinary teacher of forty years' standing, strongly disapproves of the current practice of using masoor dal instead of the traditional toor. 'Nowadays, people use masoor because it's cheaper, but it alters the taste,' she said. She also emphasized on the technique of giving the vaghar the love it needs. 'You have to put the vaghar on a very slow flame and for a very long time, and cook the tomatoes till all the water dries up. Only then add in all the masalas.'

Food photographer Yasmin Khambatta's preferred way of making dhansak, following her mother's recipe, is to use a combination of four dals—toor, chana, masoor, and moong. 'Mum did not use eggplants as they made the dal very dark. Instead, she added carrots along with pumpkin to make the dish a bit sweeter. And she always served dhansak with murabba made from small mango pieces cooked in sugar syrup,' she said.

The choice of meat elicited sharp reactions, dividing the cooks I met into the mutton and the chicken camps. The former stressed that mutton dhansak cooked with the meat bones adds flavour to the dal, whereas the latter, like Khurshed, preferred the soupy texture of chicken dhansak. 'Trust me, chicken dhansak tastes better. Always,' he declared.

The strikingly different ways home-cooks worked with the dish is a testament to its adaptability. The ultimate validation of this flexibility comes from that most revered of Parsi cookery bibles, *Vividh Vani*. Authored by Meherbai Jamshedji Wadia, the late nineteenth-century tome mentions not one but three recipes of dhansak, each with slightly different ingredients and techniques. And it clearly says that either chicken or mutton could be used.

Interestingly, my own practical lesson in dhansak-making was replete with rule-flouting. Magan, my lawyer friend Pervez Rustomkhan's cook, was a reluctant teacher. The veteran brought a devil-may-care impunity to his cooking. He omitted the vegetables and methi leaves, sneaked in some curry powder, and threw in a handful of curry leaves.

It was a killer dhansak.

Dhansak Masala with Keki Umrigar and Family

Dhansak is a jigsaw puzzle of spices.

Three key spice blends go into the preparation—dhansak masala, Parsi sambhar masala, and dhana jeera (ground coriander and cumin mix). Each stands apart with its distinct ingredients, which vary depending on the recipe of the spice-maker. The finished dhansak dal usually includes a mix of milder, aromatic spices like cinnamon, star anise, nutmeg, and mace; and sharper, more robust accents from mustard oil, fenugreek, garlic, and red chilli powder.

Trying to decode these blends, I ended up at the home of Keki Umrigar, the proprietor of Umrigar Stores at Bora Bazar in Fort. Umrigar, a reputed Parsi spice-maker, supplies masalas to a loyal clientele, including leading Parsi and Irani restaurants of Mumbai.

Keki's daughter-in-law Farida greeted me with a cup of phudna ni chai (mint tea) at their three-storeyed home Keki House, which has a water-well within its precinct. Wells play an important role in Parsi purification rituals, and all fire temples—places of worship for Zoroastrians—have one. Keki's son Parvez told me that theirs was frequented by Parsi visitors who wished to have a moment of peace to themselves and light a divo (prayer lamp) or an agarbatti (incense stick). 'Keeping the well open to people of faith is a part of my father's religious service. Till he turned eighty, he would go around cleaning all the fire temple wells in Mumbai himself,' Parvez said.

The Umrigar repertoire of spices includes both raw masalas as well as blends like curry powder, tandoori masala, garam masala, sambhar masala, vindaloo masala (spice blend for making Parsi-style vindaloo), and dhana jeera. Dhansak masala is among their bestsellers, a recipe passed on from their native village in Gujarat's Valsad district and refined over time. Parvez took me to a small room in their house, where the masalas were stored in large mason jars. He made me sniff a few. The smell was so overpowering that I had to hold the jars away from my nose. 'Now you know how pure our quality is,' he said.

Given the potency of the blends, the amount used can make or break a dish. 'To foolproof things, we make packages with exact proportions required to make the day's quantity of dhansak for our restaurant clients,' Farida told me.

Later, Parvez took me up the wooden stairs of the house and introduced me to Umrigar senior.[4] Frail yet alert, the elderly Keki strained to listen to my questions, which Farida translated into Gujarati. After some persuasion, he revealed that his dhansak masala is a concoction of twenty-two roasted items such as coriander seeds, cumin seeds, black pepper, sesame seeds, poppy seeds, nutmeg, cloves, cinnamon, star anise, and mace, all used in fixed proportions with Parsi sambhar already present in this mix. 'This masala is all you need,' Farida said.

A stickler for quality, Keki said that malpractices were common among Parsi spice-makers. 'Nowadays people often sell fake masalas. But we get the best quality of raw spices from Masjid Bandar and do our own mixing, oiling, roasting, and packaging,' he said. In fact, their association with their wholesale suppliers spans decades.

As I said my goodbyes, Farida presented me with a packet of dhansak masala to take home. It was no ordinary gift. Zealously guarded for generations, its contents revealed an absolute mastery of spice proportions.

On my way out, I jokingly asked Keki if he would share his dhansak formula with me. He smiled faintly and looked straight ahead. I think he pretended not to hear me.

Mutton Dhansak at Ripon Club

When I entered the Parsi-only (non-Parsis can visit with a member) Ripon Club at 8 a.m. along with my friend Pervez on a Wednesday, the kitchen staff was working at blinding speed. One was frantically chopping onions, another was painstakingly dicing pumpkins, a third was tearing apart bunches of methi, and a fourth was busy cleaning mutton. It was dhansak day, a beloved tradition at the club since its inception in 1884.

A couple hours later, their boss and then-caterer Nargis Mistry arrived.[5] As she prepared the dhansak masala, tables were set. The buffet wouldn't start for a while, but the club's dining room, with its whirring fans, ornate chandeliers, and retro swing doors, was already coming to life.

Chatting with Nargis, I learnt that Ripon Club's Wednesday dhansak ritual started as a mid-week treat for its members, mostly lawyers, businessmen, chartered accountants, and other professionals who would drop in from work. 'They came, and continue to come, for the best dhansak in town. It's a parampara (tradition),' she said proudly.

Headwaiter Nicholas aka Necklace, who has been working at Ripon Club since 1987, joined us for a bit. He painted a vivid picture of the Parsi bastion during its heydays in the '80s. 'There were so many parties at the club those days. We had a pop show every Saturday, with both Hindi and English songs. There was a bar upstairs, and people would play cards and snooker,' he reminisced.

On Wednesdays, the club would throb with frenetic activity, keeping the staff on its toes. 'Boley toh daud ke jana padta tha guest log ke paas. Itna rush hota tha (We had to run to the guests to take orders, such was the rush),' Necklace recalled, adding that people would make reservations for dhansak days in advance.

The crowds thinned considerably after regular service of liquor and playing cards were stopped, the former due to the prohibitive cost of getting an alcohol permit. The number of dishes dwindled, too. 'Earlier, at least four to five items were served along with dhansak. Now, it's just a couple of dishes like bheja (goat brain) cutlets or farcha (Parsi-style fried chicken),' rued Necklace.

Nargis blamed it on the steep hike in the prices of ingredients. 'In the good old days, ingredients were cheaper. Now, there is GST on everything. Middle-class folks have to pay taxes as well as GST.' Despite facing rough weather, the club has retained its old-world chops. It's perhaps the only place in Mumbai where you will find bawas (Parsis) eating bhonu (food) outside their homes and spot an elderly man catching a post-lunch catnap on a long-armed easy chair.

As the buffet was laid out, I breathed in the earthy aromas and filled my plate. Giant portraits of Parsi bigwigs stared down at me, a reminder that the meal I was savouring was once the weekly highlight of the club's legendary co-founders and members Pherozeshah Mehta (president of the Indian National Congress held in 1890 and planner of the municipal charter for Mumbai), Jamsetji Tata (founder of the Tata Group), and Sir Dinshaw Maneckji Petit (one of the entrepreneurs who set up the first cotton textile mills in India), and other illustrious members.

It didn't seem too big a leap to suggest that some of the sharpest Parsi minds were fuelled by dhansak. I could imagine these giants of politics, trade, industry, and science sitting here, chatting, debating, planning over platefuls of the puréed goodness.

It would have been one hell of a power lunch.

Dhansak Nostalgia with Jimmy and Mehroo Kadkhodai

Another dhansak shrine, the fabled Paradise Restaurant in Mumbai's Colaba, was my weekly bright spot when I was working at *Verve,* the culture and fashion magazine of the Mahindras, in the late 2000s. The eatery closed for good a while ago, but I decided to pay its owners Jimmy and Mehroo Kadkhodai[6] a visit at their home in Tardeo.

Jimmy, sporting a velvet Parsi topi, and Mehroo, clad in a mid-length floral dress, welcomed me cheerfully. Their tiny apartment had an air of cosy intimacy, with its ivory lace curtains, carefully preserved teakwood furniture, sepia-tinted photographs, and a votive prayer lamp burning on an antique sideboard.

Chatting with the charming elderly couple over tea and batasas (crumbly savoury biscuits), I learned that Jimmy is Irani. Unlike Parsis, Iranian Zoroastrians came to India as part of a different diaspora some 150 years ago. Jimmy's family, originally from Yazd in Iran, was part of this migration. 'Like many others, my ancestors braved the stormy sea to escape persecution by the Arabs. They left all their possessions behind. Many rolled off into the sea and never made it to India,' he said, regret shadowing his deep brown eyes.

Among those who did were enterprising Iranis who started Mumbai's beloved Irani café tradition. Jimmy began by selling soup, chicken rolls, and sandwiches along with his uncle at Excelsior Cinema, and launched Paradise in 1957. It was Mehroo, a self-taught cook, who introduced typical Parsi dishes like sali boti (mutton curry with potato straws), dhansak, curry rice, patra ni machhi (fish coated with chutney and steamed in banana leaf), khichri saas (fish in white gravy served with khichri), and atheli margi (marinated chicken cooked with onions and tomatoes) to the menu.

Dhansak, their crowd-puller, was on offer twice a week—mutton on Wednesdays, chicken on Saturdays. Both were boneless versions. 'Guests would mostly come in from office. They would want to eat with a fork and knife and finish the meal fast, so we left the bones out,' Mehroo said.

Getting her own masalas ground allowed the former restaurateur to channel her inner control freak. 'I would go to Saat Rasta to buy the masalas and get them pounded myself. It was the best, most amazing blend, and would stay fresh for over a month,' she recounted.

To guard her precious 'masalo' (masala mix) from her staff, she would carry exact pre-marked quantities of the blend required for the day in her special green dabbas along with her round spoons to the restaurant every morning. 'My men were very cunning and forever looking to steal my masalas. But I never let them,' she said, snickering.

It is, however, this 'evil' squad that Mehroo credited for the success of Paradise. 'I loved working with my men. They worked hard and never fought. I was forever after them to improve their hygiene. "Haath dho, plate dho, mooh dho (Wash your hands, wash your plate, wash your face)," I would tell them constantly. So, they named me Madam Dho Dho Dho.'

Listening to her stories made me appreciate the role hired cooks had played in shaping Parsi cuisine. Workers from Gujarat, known as laliyas in vernacular Gujarati, would prepare the food at most Parsi restaurants. But the best cooks, as per Mehroo, were the Goan Catholics. 'We had one Charlie, who was very naughty. If I shouted at him, he would throw the entire dish down the drain. I would tell him, "Charlie, tum bau kharab hai (Charlie, you are very bad)." But no one could cook like him,' she said, eyes twinkling.

The conversation was laced with wistfulness. The couple clearly missed being at the restaurant, which they had to close after Jimmy suffered a stroke. 'I forgot everything when I was at the restaurant. No bad thought ever entered my mind. Only my food and my guests mattered,' Mehroo said, her voice laden with emotion.

'We provided sixty-one years of service to the human stomach,' Jimmy said. 'Paradise was a very personal experience. It was like people's own dining room. Guests never realized they were sitting in a restaurant. Everyone knew the waiters by name. "Arey Francis, idhar aao (Francis, come here)," they would say....'

The legacy of a lifetime was lost. But for a few moments, the couple's nostalgia-soaked stories conjured a lost culinary paradise, a world in which Madam Dho Dho Dho reigned supreme and turned out knockout dhansaks.

Dhansak with Shezad and Hilla Marolia at Café Farohar

Was the dhansak of Gujarat any different from that of Mumbai? To find out, I journeyed to Udvada in Gujarat's Valsad district.

The holiest town of the Parsis is steeped in prayer. It is also a place for eating copiously. This became evident to me as Shezad and Hilla, the owners of Café Farohar at Sodawaterwala Dharamshala, sat me down to a king-sized Parsi breakfast at eight in the morning. Having arrived early, I was hoping to save my appetite for dhansak and hang around the kitchen with the mother-son duo. But Shezad had other plans.

He rattled off a slew of specialties for me to try: khurchan or spiced lamb offal, leela lasan nu edu or scrambled eggs seasoned with tender-green garlic shoots, bhakras or Parsi fried doughnuts with toddy, sev or sweet vermicelli garnished with rose petals and served with a hint of sweet curd, and poro, that most decadent deep-fried Parsi omelette.

I squirmed. All this in the morning? Does that mean our dhansak plan was off? 'Not at all,' Shezad said cheerfully. 'We shall eat dhansak at noon.'

As we polished off the hearty repast, the diminutive chef shared that the desire to recreate authentic specialties inspired him to move from Mumbai to Udvada and start Café Farohar. 'I introduced an à la carte menu to offer a larger selection of Parsi dishes to my diners. At Farohar you can eat dhansak any day of the week, and also try specialties like papri ma gosht (mutton cooked with broad beans), Bhatia chicken (chicken with potatoes), and atheli margi.'

After breakfast I ambled into the backstreets of Udvada. Admiring the glorious winged-bull façade of the fire temple from a distance, I spotted white-robed priests and elderly women spinning the sacred thread called kusti, on traditional looms. Many of the once-spectacular Parsi houses lining the narrow lanes had been abandoned, giving the town an almost ghostly feel. Clicking photos of the cottages with their double otlas or porches, swings, and wells, I managed to cover every street within a couple of hours.

Back at Farohar for lunch, the dhansak, made using homemade masalas, and brown rice arrived in earthen matkas. The taste was not significantly different from other versions I had eaten earlier, though the addition of fried onions into the dal at the time of boiling gave this version additional depth and complexity.

Breaking into her impish smile, Hilla recalled the days when her father Cawasji, a quartermaster of a ship, would cook dhansak for the family on Sundays. 'The oldies would take a pack of rum and ask for kavabs even before the meal was ready. "Thoda chakhna mangta hai (We need some snacks)," they would say. Post drinks, there would be a call for lunch. "Jamva chalo ji (Come, let's eat)," dad would say, and we would pounce on the food. Afterwards, everyone would sleep till five in the evening. The idea was khavanu, peevanu, ane majja karvanu (eat, drink, and make merry). That's our Parsi philosophy.'

Glancing toward the neighbouring table, I noticed an elderly man with a shock of grey hair enjoying a plate of whole fried boi (white mullet). I made a mental note to try it on my next visit. We finished off the meal with doodh na puff, or sweet clouds of milk froth that arrived in cutting-chai glasses.

Unable to conquer my greed, I bought scoops of mango ice cream (handchurned using a traditional wooden device called sancha) which was being peddled from a rickshaw, as I walked down the street from the restaurant to my hotel.

In the room, the day's gluttony finally took its toll. I collapsed on the four-poster bed and passed out.

Dhansak with Sarka ni Kachumber, with Firdose and Zenobia Tavadia

The following day, I made my way from Udvada to the nearby town of Sanjan. It was at this historic port, located on the banks of the Varoli river, that the Zoroastrians received sanctuary when the first band of migrants landed in Gujarat.

I was visiting to keep my rendezvous with Firdose Tavadia, who manages the the Bai Maneckbai P. B. Jeejeebhoy-WZO Sanatorium. The sprawling bungalow, which serves as a retreat for visiting Parsis, boasts an excellent café and catering services. Though only Parsis are permitted to stay, walk-ins for lunch are allowed.

Just in time to watch dhansak being made in the spacious kitchen,

I cottoned on to Firdose's tips for making a standout dish—the dal should be cooked with mutton stock, and small methi greens should be used. 'In the olden days, we would add local greens called dal patta to give a distinctive flavour. But they're not to be seen these days,' he said.

The secret ingredient in Firdose's dhansak is his special mutton masala, so named because he and his wife Zenobia make a dish called black pepper mutton with it. Later, as we sat down to eat, Firdose told me that he actually got the masala recipe from a television show: 'We tried it and were hooked.'

The dhansak was perfectly made, but the show-stealer was the sarka ni kachumber, made with finely sliced onions, tomatoes, cucumbers, and green chillies mixed with salt, black vinegar, and a sprinkling of red chilli powder. Crunchy and tangy, it cut through the richness and fat and met the dhansak's sweetness straight on. 'This is the original kachumber. Today many people don't like vinegar, so they use lemons instead,' Zenobia told me.

As we forked up the dhansak and brown rice between bitefuls of malty kachumber, Firdose attempted to piece together the early incarnations of dhansak. 'The word dhansak comes from "dhan", which means rice; and "shak", which refers to vegetables blended with lentils, and meat added for flavour. I think first, we would have concocted masala ni dar. Then someone would have added meat. Veggies would have been the logical next step given that our Persian ancestors loved stews. You can write in your book that Parsis are the best chefs. We blend things beautifully,' he said.

It seemed apposite that this conversation was happening in the town where, according to a legend chronicled in the 1599 epic poem 'Qissa-i Sanjan', Jadi Rana, the raja of Sanjan offered the Zoroastrians a filled-to-the-brim glass of milk when they first came to his kingdom seeking asylum.[7] The royal's gesture was to signify that his kingdom was full and could not accommodate the refugees. The tenacious Zoroastrians responded by blending some sugar into the milk to reassure the king they would not crowd his kingdom but enhance its sweetness. Jadi Rana was impressed by the immigrants' ingenuity. Not only were they granted sanctuary, they were also permitted to retain and follow their faith.

This seamless blending in, the couple believe, typifies every aspect of Parsi life. 'Like a well-made dhansak, our ancestors melded into their new home. We speak Gujarati and many of our customs have Hindu elements. Even the saris we wear during weddings are in the Gujarati seedha-palla style,' Zenobia said.

We chatted late into the afternoon, discussing food, history, and culture. I had eaten dhansak many times before, but savouring it in this history-laden town gave it a newfound poignance. It helped me mine the dish for its deeper significance.

Reimagined Dhansak with Viraf Patel

Back in Mumbai, I got a taste of Chef Viraf Patel's limited-edition menu titled The Modern Parsi, for SodaBottleOpenerWala restaurant. In Viraf's maverick hands, dhansak transformed into a grainy lentil stew with strong Iranian echoes. The dish, which came with fall-off-the-bone tender lamb shanks, was still pungent and spicy, but with more texture as the grains were left whole.

'When we talk about dhansak, it's all about nostalgia and comfort, but that doesn't mean it can't be updated or tweaked. We Parsis are very adaptive,' Viraf said, sharing that the inspiration for his creation came from the stew's Persian roots. 'I've done a bit of research on this. Given the hilly, mountainous terrain our ancestors lived in, cooking one-pot meals would have been common. Persians cooked stews like this with the meat and pulses left whole. There was no straining, puréeing, or blending. And the lentils would have been there too. So, this "modern" version is probably closer to the ancient prototype. It's actually very, very old,' the chef explained, sharing that his idea was to celebrate old Parsi food and culture while simultaneously pushing them forward.

However, not everyone takes well to messing with classics. My photo of the tweaked dish on Facebook the following day elicited a strong backlash from a Parsi PR professional. 'For a thousand years dhansak has been made in a certain way, and this is not that. Why are people trying to screw up Parsi culture?' he complained.

To me, the new incarnation was refreshing. Viraf had embraced the spirit of the dish, playfully blending it with his own creativity. If anything, it left me yearning for a taste of other such true-to-the-classic experiments. May there be more.

◆

The many dhansaks I had are proof that the dish can reveal strikingly different faces.

Evidently, the maximalist dish is the ultimate reward for working hard. 'After slogging through the week, we want a rich treat. We want to enjoy the whole day with drinks and kavabs and heavy food,' Nargis, my host at Ripon Club, told me.

Its spicy exuberance does more than just soothe aching bones. It embodies the Parsi penchant for extravagance and richness. Dhansak is pure gratification, a dish eaten with the *intent* of no-holds-barred feasting.

Arduous and time-consuming, it is also testament to a cook's dedication. Consider that it took someone the better half of the day to prepare, and suddenly consuming the opulent dish doesn't seem like a voracious indulgence. It's only fair.

The association of the food with mourning—dhansak is eaten on the fourth day after a near one's death—gives it an unexpectedly sombre dimension. 'Parsis abstain from eating meat for three days after a person dies as a sign of respect and grieving for the deceased. On the fourth day, dhansak is cooked and first offered in prayers offered for the departed soul. Thereafter, the whole family partakes of it,' Mahrukh (owner of Mahrukh's Kitchen) said. It is for this reason, she revealed, that the dish isn't served at a Parsi wedding, a Navjote (Parsi religious induction ceremony), or Navroz (the Parsi new year).

Author Murzban F. Shroff, a proud Parsi and an ardent lover of his community's cuisine, ascribed the popularity of the stew to something a lot more mundane. 'The whole object of a good dhansak is to lead you to overindulge and flatten you out for a few hours,' he said. The soporific effect of the dish spells disaster for the libido, though. 'We Parsis like to rib each other about something called a baporiyu. If a Parsi couple is not contactable in the afternoon, they are teased about indulging, probably, in a baporiyu, an afternoon romp. But dhansak negates any chances of that. You have no option but to give yourself a delicious snooze, no scope for other appetites,' he added, with a twinkle in his eye.

In the end, the stew's layered identity makes it difficult to pick out any one reason for its legendary status. Celebratory feast. Mourning food. Metaphor for Parsi adaptiveness. Best sleeping pill ever. It is all of these.

But perhaps the most persuasive argument for partaking in the darkly sumptuous mess is simply this:

Dead or alive, it's a good thing to be happy.

Recipes from My Travels

NARGIS MISTRY'S MUTTON DHANSAK WITH BROWN RICE, KAVABS, AND KACHUMBER

DHANSAK

SERVES: 4

TIME TAKEN: 1 HOUR PLUS SOAKING

INGREDIENTS

Mutton	500 gms, curry-cut
Ginger-garlic paste	1 tbsp
Toor dal	250 gms, soaked for 30 minutes
Orange masoor dal	50 gms, soaked for 30 minutes
Pumpkin	50 gms, cut into cubes
Eggplant	50 gms, cut into cubes
Methi (small variety)	1 bundle, cleaned, and leaves picked
Onion	1, chopped
Tomato	1, chopped
Ghee	50 gms
Coriander	a handful, chopped
Green chilli, garlic, cumin seed paste	1 tbsp
Dhansak masala	2 tbsp (try Mangal brand)

Dhana jeera powder	1 tsp, roasted
Parsi sambhar powder	1 tsp
Turmeric powder	½ tsp
Mint leaves	a handful, chopped
Salt	to taste

METHOD

Boil the mutton with ginger-garlic paste, salt, and 1 cup water in a pressure cooker for 3–4 whistles.

Boil the dals in a pressure cooker along with pumpkin, eggplants, methi leaves, and salt until cooked, till around 1 whistle.

Heat ghee in a pan, add the chopped onion, and fry until golden-brown.

Add the chopped tomatoes, chilli-garlic-cumin-seed paste, dhansak masala, dhana jeera powder, sambhar powder, turmeric powder, chopped coriander, and mint.

Let it cook for 5 minutes and then add the boiled dal to it. Cook for another 10 minutes.

Add the mutton with its water to the dal and let it cook for 5 minutes.

Mutton dhansak is ready.

BROWN RICE

SERVES: 4 TIME TAKEN: 30 MINUTES PLUS SOAKING

INGREDIENTS

Basmati rice	250 gms, washed and soaked for 1 hour
Sugar	2 tsp
Water	500 ml
Cloves	2–3
Black peppercorns	5–6
Cardamom	2
Bay leaf	1
Salt	1 tbsp

METHOD

Take a big vessel and put 2 tsp sugar in it along with 2 tsp water.

Let the sugar caramelize, then add 500 ml water to it and bring to a boil.

Add the whole garam masala and salt to the water.

Add rice and cook for 10 minutes on a high flame.

Cover and simmer for 5 minutes and switch off the flame.

Let the rice rest for 10 minutes. Fluff the rice with a fork and serve hot.

MUTTON KAVABS

MAKES: 12–15 KAVABS TIME TAKEN: 20 MINUTES

INGREDIENTS

Mutton	300 gms, minced
Boiled potatoes	2, peeled and mashed
Ginger-garlic paste	1 tsp
Red chilli powder	1 tsp
Dhana jeera powder	1 tsp
Turmeric powder	½ tsp
Oil	2 cups, to deep fry
Eggs	2
Green coriander	a handful, chopped
Mint	a handful, chopped
Suji	1 cup
Salt	to taste

METHOD

Mix the mutton mince with potatoes, ginger-garlic paste, chilli powder, dhana jeera powder, turmeric powder, salt, chopped coriander, and mint.

Make small balls of desired size and set aside.

Beat 2 eggs in a bowl. Dip the meat kavabs in the beaten egg and then coat them with suji on all sides.

Heat 2 cups of oil in a kadhai and fry the meat kavabs until golden on medium heat.

Serve hot.

KACHUMBER

SERVES: 4 TIME TAKEN: 5 MINUTES

INGREDIENTS

Onions	2, diced
Cucumbers	2, peeled, deseeded, and diced
Tomatoes	2, diced
Lemon juice	1 tbsp
Green chillies	1–2, chopped
Salt	to taste

METHOD

Mix everything together and serve.

Tip: Dhansak masala and dhana jeera masalas are readily available online

VIRAF PATEL'S NINE-BEAN-AND-LENTIL STEW WITH LAMB SHANKS

SERVES: 4 TIME TAKEN: 2 HOURS PLUS OVERNIGHT SOAKING

INGREDIENTS

Lamb shanks	4, trimmed
Mixed beans (kidney beans, black beans, black-eyed peas, chickpeas, navy beans, whole red lentils, yellow lentils, Bengal gram, whole green gram)	1 cup, soaked overnight
Ghee	4 tbsp

Onion	1, large, chopped
Garlic	3 cloves, chopped
Ginger	1-inch piece, grated
Cinnamon sticks	2
Cloves	4–5
Green cardamom	2
Bay leaves	2
Cumin powder	1 tsp, freshly ground
Coriander powder	2 tsp, freshly ground
Turmeric powder	1 tsp
Red chilli powder	1 tsp
Tomatoes	4, chopped
Tomato paste	¼ cup or 1 cup tomato purée
Water or lamb stock	6 cups
Green coriander	½ cup, chopped
Mint leaves	¼ cup, chopped
Salt	to taste

METHOD

Heat ghee in a large pot.

Season and sear the lamb shanks on all sides until browned. Remove and set aside.

In the same pot, add chopped onions and sauté until golden brown.

Add chopped garlic and grated ginger, and sauté for another 2 minutes.

Add cinnamon sticks, cloves, cardamom pods, bay leaves, cumin powder, coriander powder, turmeric powder, and red chilli powder. Stir well to coat the aromatics with the spices.

Add the chopped tomatoes and tomato paste. Cook until the tomatoes are softened and the mixture becomes thick.

Drain the soaked nine beans and add them to the pot along with the rinsed lentils. Stir to combine.

Place the lamb shanks back into the pot.

Add 6 cups of stock and bring the stew to a boil.

Reduce the heat to low, cover the pot, and let it simmer for 1.5 to 2 hours until the lamb and beans are tender.

Add salt to taste.

Add freshly chopped coriander and mint to the stew. Stir well and let it simmer for an additional 10 to 15 minutes.

Discard the cinnamon sticks, cloves, cardamom pods, and bay leaves.

Serve the nine beans and lentil stew with lamb shank and a side of brown rice or bread.

Layered with spicy mutton mince and eggs, Junior Kuppanna's kari dosa is a meat-lover's delight.

Photo: Junior Kuppanna

Dosa tacos at ITC Grand Chola's Avartana, comprising mini dosas wrapped around fillings like slow-roasted aubergine (shown in the photo) and Chettinad chicken.

Photo: ITC Grand Chola

Narendra Vaidya's vada pav comes with a trio of palate-rousing chutneys—dry garlic, coriander, and tamarind.

Photo: Yasmin Khambatta

Simple yet indulgent, Moti Mahal's legendary butter chicken has withstood the test of time.

Photo: Monish Gujral

Mutton dhansak served along with brown rice, kavabs, and black vinegar kachumber, at the Bai Maneckbhai P. B. Jeejeebhoy WZO Sanatorium in Sanjan.

Photo: Yasmin Khambatta

Chef Avinash Martins gives Goan prawn hooman a spiffy makeover with his tapas-style presentation and bite-size accompaniments.

Photo: Avinash Martins

Low on oil, Shatbhi Basu's undhiyu is seasoned with a special masala made from fresh coriander, green garlic, green chillies, coconut, and ginger.

Photo: Yasmin Khambatta

Tabinda Khwaja's turai ke shami is a standout family recipe that substitutes ridge gourd peels for mutton mince.

Photo: Syed Ahmad Bilal

Ranjit's SVAASA'S amchur wale sukhe chane make for a great fibre-packed breakfast or early-evening snack.

Photo: Sona Bahadur

Loaded with crunchy mustard greens, smoked pork with lai haak is a beloved winter staple in Assam.

Photo: Yasmin Khambatta

Indian Accent's smoked duck shami with crispy sevia and barberry chutney pairs fabulously with a robust malbec.

Photo: Indian Accent

The subtly spiced Ambur mutton biryani cooked with long-grain Basmati rice, a specialty of Chennai's The Ambur Canteen.

Photo: Yasmin Khambatta

With its striking yellow colour and lively citrus accents, Oiendrila Ray Kapur's kamala bhog is perfect for entertaining.

Photo: Oiendrila Ray Kapur

Baked rosogollas are hot-sellers at Kolkata's iconic mishti chain Balaram Mullick & Radharaman Mullick.

Photo: Balaram Mullick & Radharaman Mullick

Manzilat Fatima takes a break after cooking up a feast of royal Awadhi dishes at a restaurant pop-up.

Photo: Manzilat Fatima

Junior Kuppanna's business head, S. M. Bablu, showcases a freshly made kari dosa at the restaurant's Nungambakkam outlet in Chennai.

Photo: Yasmin Khambatta

The author (extreme right) with Mohammad Aslam, the owner of Aslam Chicken (second from left), at the famed Jama Masjid eatery in Delhi.

Photo: Sona Bahadur

Narendra Vaidya, the son of vada pav inventor Ashok Vaidya, continues his father's legacy from his tiny cart outside Mumbai's Dadar station.

Photo: Yasmin Khambatta

Shezad and Hilla Marolia at Udvada's Sodawaterwala Dharamshala, which houses their popular Parsi eatery Café Farohar.

Photo: Yasmin Khambatta

The Kar brothers of Odisha's Bikalananda Kar family display giant brown rasagolas, known as khirmohan, at their sweet shop in Salepur.

Photo: Sona Bahadur

Chef Avinash Martins lucks out with a prize catch at a local fish market in Goa.
Photo: Avinash Martins

An earthen pot being stuffed with beans, tubers, and greens to make umbadiyu at Magan Bhai's stall in Valsad.

Photo: Yasmin Khambatta

Sufia Kidwai holds up a plate of freshly made shami kebabs in her sun-soaked garden.

Photo: Sona Bahadur

Bahadur, the eponymous owner of Amritsar's Bahadur Kulcha Corner, poses with his famous chhole-kulche.

Photo: Sona Bahadur

Home-cook Nayana Swargiary Phangsho prepares oma narzi, a Bodo delicacy made with smoked pork and dried jute leaves, in her Guwahati kitchen.

Photo: Sona Bahadur

Goan Fish Curry

BEING HOOMAN

All along Goa's coastline, a deep love of fish curry prevails. While vindalho (or vindaloo as it's more commonly known) hogs a lot of glory, it is this humble staple that forms the backbone of Goan cuisine.

Over countless visits to the susegad state, I've found Goa's simplest dish the hardest to pin down. I've often marvelled at its variations in texture, colour, and taste, and tried to look for clues hiding in each plate.

The classic, distilling as it does the essence of everyday Goan cooking, thus became the focus of a ten-day culinary exploration. The idea was to undertake a curry-consuming marathon to gauge the state's obsession with this staple and to acquaint myself with its various guises.

Done with over-visited purveyors of the dish, I wanted the real deal—the curries made in homes, hole-in-the-wall 'rice-plate' joints, and obscure village tavernas. I knew this quest would be best navigated with locals, and that as long as I stayed away from tourist haunts, I was in for a treat, and a real adventure.

HOOMAN

Mackerel and Teflam Curry with Vidya Naik

My curry expedition began on a languorous Sunday afternoon with clear blue skies and a briny sea breeze. I was seeking out Peep Kitchen and Bar in Taleigao, known for its authentic Hindu Goan cooking (distinct from the Christian community's style).

Vidya Naik, a homemaker-turned-restaurateur who runs the popular eatery along with her sons Gaurish and Amey, had offered to give me a Hindu Goan curry 101 over lunch. It seemed fitting to start with mackerel curry, that most quintessential of Hindu Goan curries, along with some fresh urrak (first distillation of cashew fruit) from their spiffy bar.

'Goan fish curry is the magic of five ingredients,' Vidya said. 'Coconut, tamarind, coriander seeds, and turmeric were available in Goa before the sixteenth century. Then the Portuguese arrived and gave us chillies. All our curries are basically a blend of these ingredients. Only the proportions and consistency vary.'

Understanding the divergent Hindu and Christian styles of making the dish begins with some basic nomenclature. Goan Hindus use the term 'hooman' for a curry, whereas Christians say 'codi' or 'koddi'. 'When Hindus say kadi, we refer to the tart digestive drink made with kokum[1] and coconut juice that accompanies a hooman,' Vidya clarified.

The ingredients vary as well. Catholics often use cumin seeds and garlic to season their curry; Hindus typically don't, sometimes using asafoetida instead. Christians like Kashmiri chillies; Hindus prefer the stubby Goan ones from Mapusa or Canacona for heat and a specific flavour.

Regardless of these differences, both communities eat the dish for lunch almost daily, accompanied by fried fish or prawns, kokum kadi, and a seasonal vegetable like tambdi bhaji (red amaranth), pumpkin, or okra. 'Hooman completes our day. You could have a table overflowing with the best food, but if fish or prawn curry isn't on the table, it isn't a meal,' Vidya said, as my hooman arrived with a slew of accompaniments.

Mackerel's classic pairing with teflam (variously known as tefla, tephal, tephlam, tirphal, chiphal, and teppal),[2] a local spice related to the Szechuan pepper family, provides a delicious balance between the oily texture of the fish and the sharp, astringent tang of the pepper. One bite and all my taste buds were awake.

The key to unleashing this deliciousness, Vidya pointed out, lies in the masterful blending of the vatap or finely ground paste of grated coconut, tamarind, red chillies, and spices. The restaurateur recalled how, growing up in a large family of fifty to sixty people, she and her cousins would take turns grinding the masala for the hooman on a rogddo, or traditional Goan grinding stone. It was a gruelling task, made worse by the stiff competition to turn out the finest paste.

'Our fingers would burn with the sting of chillies. But it was that curry, made in pure coconut oil, using hand-pounded masalas and slow-cooked on coals, that was the *real* hooman,' she said, making it clear that there are no shortcuts to curry nirvana.

Curry Basics with Sangita Gaunecar

The bold, beautiful flavours of my inaugural meal had piqued my curiosity. To delve deeper, I sought the help of Sangita Gaunecar, another ace home cook who continued my education over tall, chilled glasses of rose falooda at Panaji's Fidalgo restaurant.

While conceding that the hooman defies easy categorization, Sangita offered an ingeniously simple explanation. 'Just remember, curry is always about the fish,' she said, adding that the type of seasoning used depends first and foremost on the choice of seafood.

Teflam works like magic in curries with oily, fatty fish like mackerel and sardines as they impart punch and pucker, neutralize the strong smell, and aid in digestion. However, it's too strong a taste for prawns and delicate white-fleshed fish like pomfret and ladyfish, which are typically seasoned with onions and sharpened with green chillies.

These two basic formulations, teflamche hooman (curry made with teflam) and kandyanche hooman (curry made with onions), constitute the most popular hooman styles. Partial to the former, Sangeeta recounted how after a recent visit to Europe, she missed the staple so much that she drove straight to her cousin's restaurant from the airport to quell her cravings. 'I felt like I was home before I actually reached,' she said, smiling.

As we chatted, I learnt that caste and class, along with geography, season, choice of souring agent (tamarind, kokum, bimbli or star fruit, raw mangoes, hog plums, and the like) and the type of chillies used, all play a part in influencing the taste of the dish. Variations abound among

Goan Hindus. 'The hooman made by our Goud Saraswat Brahmin community, for example, is made without garlic and is a lot milder than the spicy version made by the Kshatriya community. And my Gouda domestic workers make theirs sizzling hot,' Sangeeta explained.

My befuddlement amused her. 'Too many curries, too little time. You'd better cancel your flight back to Mumbai,' she said, ending my tutorial with a peal of laughter.

Mackerel Hooman with Sapna Sardessai

Mackerel hooman headlined the menu again the next day at lunch with Sapna Sardessai, a book publisher-turned restaurateur with several cookery books to her credit (including a translation of Padma Mahalé's iconic *Ishtann*), along with twin restaurants called Kokum Curry in Candolim and Panaji. Her husband Girish and some friends joined us.

Beautifully laid out on banana leaves, the meal comprised a stunning array of Saraswat delights: foddi, or shallow-fried raw slices of breadfruit; shelle, a tangy chutney starring raw jackfruit; chicken xacuti, a spicy chicken curry; eggplant bharta, or roasted eggplant, skinned and mashed with onion and chillies; sweet-sour saasav made with sucking mangoes, coconut chutney, and jaggery; kismur, a salad made from roasted dried mackerel; prawn pickles; Goan papadum, and three types of sol kadi made from fresh kokum and dried kokum shells.

The hooman arrived in a traditional Goan earthen pot known as kuinnem. The simple recipe calls for coconut ground with local Goan chillies, turmeric powder, and tamarind. The blend is simmered before mackerel and teflam are added. The last layer of flavour is added with a generous pour of coconut oil.

What might have been a mundane dish in lesser hands burst with flavour, thanks to Sapna's inspired cooking and love for hyper-local ingredients. The kokum was from her own garden, the Goan button chillies from Mapusa market, and the fresh-pressed coconut oil from a nearby oil mill. Even the sea salt, sourced from local saltpans, was redolent of Goa.

Girish, in charge of the daily fish-buying, expounded on Goa's piscine treasures—muddoshi or ladyfish, tamso or red snapper, and small river fish called karbat. 'The traditional Goan male will not do a scrap of work in the house, but he'll gladly go out and buy fish every day,' he said.

'Look who's talking,' Sapna said.

As I polished my plate clean, she prodded me to eat my second helping of rice with sol kadi instead of fish curry. 'Kadi should be eaten with rice, not drunk from a glass. Only tourists do that,' she said. Not expecting a rap on the knuckles halfway through the meal, I tentatively poured a tiny bit of the bright pink liquid on my rice. 'Go on,' Girish encouraged, 'We eat a third of our rice with fish curry, and the rest with sol kadi. It's lighter, easier on the tummy, and plays up the taste of the accompaniments through contrast.'

He was right. The combination of rice with the bracing taste of sol kadi instantly lightened things up and made the meal a lot brighter. It hit so many different notes—sweet and sour, tangy and zesty, refreshing and soothing.

It made me happy and giddy—almost like a child.

Prawn Hooman with Yatin Kakodkar

Not too long ago, a Panaji-based businessman, who happened to be my co-passenger on a flight from Goa to Mumbai, described in mouthwatering detail his idea of the perfect Goan prawn curry.

'A great Goan prawn curry will have the perfect balance of flavours. A spoonful should bring out the sweetness of coconut, the earthiness of coriander, the pungency of red chillies, and the sourness of raw mango or tamarind, all at the same time,' he said.

'And where would I find such a masterpiece?' I asked. 'My home, of course,' he said, extending an open invitation to drop in for a bite.

A year later, I found myself ringing Yatin Kakodkar's doorbell to find out whether his fabled prawn curry was really that good.

Renovated with a sleek modern design, his Porvorim home stood out with its massive kitchen. 'It shows how important food is in our household,' Yatin said, welcoming me with his signature gin gimlet and a platter of rice flour-coated Goan prawn cutlets called dangar, seldom found in restaurants.

Chatting with his friends, I was delighted to find myself in a room full of fellow prawn curry lovers. Each had a different take on the classic. Some liked making it with grated coconut, others preferred using coconut juice. Some stuck to using tamarind as a souring agent, others experimented with hog plums and raw mangoes. All agreed, though, that the simple tweak of adding a seasonal vegetable—most commonly, radish, drumsticks (moringa pods), or okra—elevates the dish manifold.

The silken curry Yatin served us that night was devoid of vegetables, though no less delicious. The sharp, tart notes of raw mango were mellowed by the sweetness of the coconut. The prawns, sourced fresh from Mandovi jetty, were perfectly cooked. 'I kept it simple with just red chilli and turmeric powder, and raw mango for sourness,' he said.

Yatin remembered vividly the taste of the prawn curry made at his ancestral home, where his maternal grandmother would work with great prowess in the kitchen. 'I loved how she would add a twist to her prawn hooman by adding bimbli or okra for a vegetable. Somehow, the addition of okra did wonders to that dish.'

The use of ingredients like Kashmiri chillies, garlic, and cumin seeds was a strict no-no for his conservative Hindu grandmother. It was only years later that Yatin started making the Catholic-style fish and prawn curries in his own kitchen. 'That's the great thing about a Goan curry. It unites. Hindus and Christians are constantly adapting each other's recipes, leading to countless variations over time,' he said.

'Which one do you like more?' I asked.

'Why choose when you can have both? The more the curri-er!' he replied.

Sungtachem Hooman with Shubhra Shankhwalker

Sensing my eagerness to try south Goa's acclaimed prawn hooman, my friend Shubhra drove me to an unassuming eatery called Mom's Recipe in Verna village. An avid cook who promotes her native cuisine through pop-ups at various cool venues, Shubhra swore by the place's spot-on local flavours. 'Even my fussy ex-hubby approves of it,' she said.

The scene at the bare-bones eatery was crowded and convivial as waiters ferried hot thalis from the kitchen to the tables. Starring drumsticks and freshwater prawns, the hooman here was a sunny, happy yellow, the luminosity of the turmeric shining through. I loved its bright, slightly tart flavour.

As we ate, Shubhra narrated her culinary journey. Growing up, she rarely cooked. It was only after she married and moved to her then-husband Raya's home that she developed a newfound curiosity about her native cuisine. 'My former mother-in-law taught me to cook, gently guiding me on how to buy fish at the local market and differentiate between the taste of sea prawns and those from the backwaters,' she said.

Breaking into a chuckle, the curly-haired cook recounted the first time she made hooman at home. To her horror, she found that the prawns Raya had bought were still alive. 'They were moving. I had no idea what to do with them!' she said. A few hours later, her mother-in-law called to check whether she was done cooking. 'No. I'm still waiting for them to die,' she muttered. The MIL, unfazed, offered a less time-intensive strategy to solve the dilemma. 'Just put them in the freezer, silly girl,' she had said.

KODDI

Soi-mirem, Rossachi Koddi, and Toca Boca with Margarida Tavora

The following afternoon found me at Nostalgia,[3] a quaint eatery in the historically resonant village of Raia. It is here, in this culinary bastion of Goa, that I discovered a legion of vintage Goan and Indo-Portuguese dishes, from apa de camarao (prawn pie) to sans rival (a retro-style almond cake). This visit was all about grasping the intricacies of the Catholic-style fish curry.

The restaurant was vibrating with music when I entered. It was Easter Sunday and a massive feast was being lined up for the evening. Owner Margarida Tavora, a dear friend, had thoughtfully offered to host me for a curry lunch, despite her frenetic schedule.

Kicking off my lesson, Margarida underlined that the Christian koddi reflects geographical variation and regional diversity as much as its Hindu counterpart. 'Traditionally, the Catholics of north Goa make a grated coconut curry known as soi-mirem, whereas those from the south like to make rossachi koddi using coconut juice,' she pointed out.

Margarida, who grew up eating mackerel and prawn soi-mirem at her parental home in Panaji, discovered the pleasures of the coconut-juice version only after she married and moved to south Goa. It was her in-laws who taught her how to make a creamy curry using a blend of both thick and thin coconut milk. 'Now I prefer it to soi-mirem. It tastes richer and better,' she said.

Her late husband, Chef Fernando Costa, the founder of Nostalgia, was a juice curry fan too. 'I wish my Ferdy were here today. He would have loved to meet you,' she said with a sigh. Famed for his deep knowledge of Goan cuisine, the passionate chef had traced the evolution of koddi in an essay entitled 'United We Eat'. Margarida read out the passage for me. 'The locals, poor as they were, generally used grated coconut in their preparations of soi-mirem, but the Goan upper classes, who had the advantage of closeness with the Portuguese, taught them how to use the extract, thus upgrading the product quality.'

Both types of Catholic curries showed up at lunch—deep-red mackerel soi-mirem, and vivacious-orange juice curry featuring pomfret. There was piquant mori (shark) ambot tik (a hot-and-sour Goan curry) too, that other beloved of Goan Catholics, paired with pillowy steamed rice cakes called sannas.

A seemingly endless lineup of accompaniments crowded the table. Boiled Goan sausages, clams sukhem (a dry, coconut-based clam dish), salted mackerel salad, lime and mango pickle, small green mangoes in brine, bimbli pickle, sweet and spicy mango chutney, and papadums. 'We call them toca boca. It's a class of side dishes that accompany a Catholic-style fish curry,' Margarida said, as I filled my plate with sampling portions.

Fragrant with coconut, the juice curry was mild and luxuriously velvety, the delicate pomfret falling apart at the touch of my fork. The soi-mirem, in sharp contrast, delivered a gut-punch of tang and pungency. Choosing between them was like comparing Ray and Tarantino. I liked each for very different reasons.

Toca boca, Margarida explained, literally means 'touch of the mouth' in Portuguese. Though it's usually something simple like fried fish, pickles, or papadum, its repertoire gets more elaborate during the monsoon when fresh fish goes off the tables (owing to the fishing ban imposed in Goa during the rains). That's when the Catholics make another type of fish curry called samarachem koddi, with dried prawns and dried mango seeds, especially stockpiled for the wet season.

Margarida's gentle eyes gleamed with delight as she recalled how her stash of toca boca came to her rescue during her boarding school days in Bengaluru: 'My siblings and I took time to get used to the canteen food. The first time we were served rasam, we couldn't fathom how we could mix our rice with something so thin. Fortunately, we had our pickles and papadum to see us through,' she said with a giggle.

Leppo Koddi with Ralph de Sousa and Chef Francisco

Fish curry is also Goa's cucina povera or peasant food, a way of using small cheap fish to make affordable yet nourishing meals.

I got a taste at the home of Ralph de Sousa, a Saligao-based Catholic hotelier. As I entered, a portly man named Francisco aka Francis[4] was prepping for a soi-mirem. Into the blender went two marble-size balls of tamarind, one coconut, six dried Kashmiri chillies, a few peppercorns, a tablespoon of coriander seeds, an inch-long piece of ginger, and four cloves of garlic.

Francis was a traditional mesta (head cook in old Goan homes), whom Ralph had specially called to make a rustic tongue-sole (a kind of fish known as leppo in Goa) curry. Having worked as an assistant to renowned cooks, he had gathered the secrets of cooking traditional Goan food as well as Portuguese-Goan cuisine. 'That's why I call him *Chef* Francis,' Ralph said, making Francis blush.

While the curry bubbled in the pan, Ralph showed me around his beautiful Lusitanian-style heritage home. Dating back to 1790, the mansion originally belonged to the Abreus, a prominent family from Saligao's landed gentry. The kitchen, overlooking a well, still retains much of the original layout. There is a window for drawing well-water and several types of grinding stones used for Goan cooking, including the flat fator and the heavy, round rogddo. 'We still use them,' Ralph said, visibly proud of his kitchen heirlooms.

Ralph's wife Calusha and son Carlos joined us for lunch in the dining area overlooking the living room furnished with vintage Goan furniture dating back to the 1600s. Francisco's vibrantly hued curry sat in the middle of the ornate ten-seater table along with an array of Catholic specialties whipped up by Calusha—breadfruit foddi, prawn chilli fry, mullet recheado (mullet stuffed with Goan red paste), sautéed red amaranth, and a salted mackerel salad.

Though bony, the leppo was delectable, its mild, clean taste coming through the warm sauce. 'Now you know there's life beyond pomfret and mackerel curry. Bigger fish doesn't always mean a better dish,' Ralph said, urging me to try other local Goan catch.

Ralph, sharing anecdotes about his home and family dishes, admitted that traditions were difficult to maintain in changing times. 'Our mothers were brilliant, painstaking cooks. People of my generation still crave those tastes. That's why mestas, like Francis, are so precious. Sadly, they're a dying breed too,' he said with a heavy sigh.

Afterwards, as we clicked photos in the beautiful garden, Ralph urged me to revisit during the monsoon to try Francis's dried prawn curry known as samarachem koddi. 'It's special,' Francis said, flashing me a smile.

Marine conservation scientist Aaron Savio Lobo, whom I met later over a coffee, also rooted strongly for local fish such as tarle and pedve (sardine), and verleo (silver sides) as more sustainable options for a fish curry. 'It is advisable to focus on eating the smaller seafood species that are lower on the food web, which include shellfish such as tisreyo (clams) and kalvam (oysters) and small fish such as sardine, while avoiding the larger predatory fish such as chonak (Asian sea bass), gobro (grouper), and mori (shark),' he said, even as he confessed his own weakness for the sour-spicy kick of ambot tik made using leppo.

Tarle Koddi with Marise de Lima

Marise de Lima, the former president of Alliance Française, Panaji, fed me another peasant-style meal at her Dona Paula home, pairing tarle or sardine curry with streaked assgo rice native to Chorao Island. There was beetroot soup too, along with a plate of fried anchovies known as patoshim (or potasi), all made by the cook, Filu.

The combination of sardines with raw mangoes gave the curry an unusual depth of flavour. But what brought oomph to the meal was the patoshim. The size of about two fingers, the freshwater fish has a delicate texture and a unique aroma.

I lost count of how many I ate as Marise held forth on Goa's no-waste 'poor cooking' traditions, evolved over thousands of years by humble farmers and fishermen. 'Like all staples, curry-rice is the diet of scarcity. We have centuries of rural heritage to thank for the dish we all love,' she said. As nothing edible was ever discarded, rustic versions of the curry involved making use of bits of the fish—like the head and tail—that might not otherwise be eaten. 'The poor use the head of the fish to flavour a curry and slice the body to fry and enjoy with the meal.'

Kalchi koddi, the practice of thickening leftover curry and eating it the following day for breakfast, was another way of making a pot of curry last longer. 'Back in the day, the curry would sit on wood fire or a sand pit oven all night, slowly gathering layers of flavours. Can you imagine how good that tasted?' she exclaimed.

Tavern-style Prawn Koddi with Hansel Vaz

The meal at Marise's whetted my appetite for typical village-style fare. While I didn't quite have the stomach for a head curry, I was keen to try a meal at a real taverna. I had often driven past these watering holes with the words 'rice plate' written outside, but never stopped to eat there.

Hansel Vaz, the affable founder of Cazulo Premium Feni, raved about the food at these tavernas. 'The curry is kosher, the masalas homemade, and the fish always fresh. You'll never get those flavours at a shack,' he said.

A twisting drive amid lush paddy fields got us to his favourite rice-plate joint in his native Seraulim. The heady aromas drifting though the doorway told me we were at the right place. 'What's this joint called?' I asked, not seeing a board at the entrance.

'It doesn't have a name. It's simply known to the locals as Uncle's hut,' Hansel said.

'Uncle' is the mild-mannered, elderly Fernando, the owner of the place, who promptly arrived to take our order. 'What curry do you have today?' Hansel asked him. 'Sungtachem koddi,' he replied, referring to the plat du jour of prawn curry. We ordered it, along with a side of fried leppo and lemon sodas.

The tiny taverna was teeming with patrons, drawn by the promise of honest, tasty food. 'Fernando's wife Reny does all the cooking herself. She makes the masala fresh in small batches and sources the ingredients personally. Her food reminds me of home,' Hansel told me.

Despite being a regular visitor himself, Hansel said he wouldn't bring his wife Wenona here. 'Nah. She's too propah. My in-laws would only put a good piece of fish in a curry—never the head—and use only the first extract of coconut milk.'

Eating her curry-rice without a piece of fried fish was a no-go for Wenona. 'When we got married, she was secretly miserable when she found out that we don't make fried fish every day in our home. She recently told me that my mum-in-law would keep a piece for her every day, just so she could sneak in on her way back from work to get her daily fix!' Hansel recounted with a chuckle.

'Is fried fish that important?' I asked.

'Oh yes. At a restaurant, if you're eating curry and ask for extra rice, it will come with a piece of fried fish. They'll just assume you want both!'

The fried leppo arrived on cue, accompanied by prawn curry and white rice, a side of dried mackerel, sautéed ridge gourd, and some sweet mango chutney. It was served family-style, in communal bowls and not in pre-plated thalis.

'That's the norm in these parts,' Hansel told me. 'Even the tiniest Catholic place in south Goa will bring the curry and rice separately. The Hindus will serve in thalis.'

Primal and potent, the dishes bore a strong rural influence. The golden fried leppo was crispy and tender by turns, and the small white prawns in the curry had a richer, deeper taste than the farmed red ones usually served at restaurants. My favourite was the accompanying pickled mackerel, known as parra. The natural mineral flavour of the mackerel, intensified by drying, packed the fish with a briny punch.

Silence fell over the table as we ate. Hansel didn't seem to mind. He knew I was busy discovering real food.

A Whiff of the Past with Raphael Viegas

As Goa's indigenous fish and rice are replaced by industrial produce from outside the state, the taste of Goan fish curry has been changing profoundly.

The elderly Raphael Viegas, whom I met at his 1910 Indo-Portuguese home in the predominantly Catholic village of Curtorim in Salcete, had witnessed first-hand the erosion of Goa's rich agrarian heritage and its impact on the local cuisine.

Hailing from a family of gaonkars (clansmen who laid the foundation of the village) he is from an era when comunidades, the system of collective ownership of land, still prevailed in Goa before the end of Portuguese rule in 1961.

The former chemist, who worked in a soil-testing laboratory for the Goa government before he retired, spoke dreamily of the xit-codi (rice curry) he grew up eating. Strongly rooted in a sense of place, it derived its magic from native species of fish and rice that went into it. 'Our generation ate the best fish. The mundkars, who looked after our property, would bring us the freshest catch from Curtorim's rivers—shevte, tamso, muddoshi, tigur,' the nonagenarian reminisced.

The bucolic world he painted was a far cry from the current times when overfishing has destroyed much of Goa's marine reserves, and most of its fish comes from Maharashtra, Andhra Pradesh, and Tamil Nadu. 'Today, people are making fish curry with sea bass. Can you imagine?' he asked, visibly recoiling.

Goa's characterful rice cultivars, so intimately associated with its distinctive terrains—kolyo from morod or uplands; kendal and kochri from kherlands or midlands; and khorgut, assgo and xit'to from the saline khazan lands—are likewise disappearing, destroyed by the aggressive pushing of high-yielding varieties like Jaya and Jyothi.

The challenges faced by Curtorim's rice cultivators, so poignantly captured in filmmaker Vince Costa's documentary, *Saxtticho Koddo* (*The Granary of Salcete)*, saddened Raphael greatly. 'With education and urbanization, our youth is moving away from agriculture. Goan rice is no more. Our paddy fields are being abandoned,' he rued.

As monocultures of agriculture and aquaculture wipe out native rice and fish, Goan curry is losing its authenticity and charm, lamented the locavore. The cherished tastes of his youth, so deeply rooted in the terroir of Curtorim, were gone forever.

To relive precious memories of yore, Raphael ferreted out a tattered 1924 cookery book entitled *Preparados Praticos da Cosinha*. Written in Portuguese, the tiny heirloom remained his only link to his mother's cooking. He flipped to the page for carile de peixe (fish curry). With just four ingredients and minimal instruction, the recipe was barely a few lines. Raphael read it out loud to me, dwelling lovingly on each word.

'I dream of this curry,' he said longingly.

The Curry in Modern Times

Goa is awash in change and taking its culinary cues from the rest of the world. Chef Vasquito Alvares detailed this transformation during our meeting at the atmospheric Clube Nacional in Fontainhas. 'When the average Goan goes to a restaurant today, he or she is likely to get chicken lollipops and French fries for starters, butter chicken with naan, and maybe some fried rice for mains. It's the standard order. Even my family and friends get that,' said the chef, who currently helms a restaurant called Casa Lusitana.

Admitting that the very notion of Goan food is changing, Vasquito recalled an 'authentic' Goan menu advertised by an old-school club for its fiftieth anniversary celebration, which listed French fries, Russian salad, and Hakka noodles as its first three items. 'I made fun of it at the time but if you think about it, it *is* an authentic Goan menu because that's what Goans are eating today,' he said.

Change is simmering at the haute end as well. Attracting much hipster buzz, Goa has grown attuned to the trendiest food movements afoot across the world. 'Farm to table, vegan, pop-ups, food trucks, and keto are all an accepted part of the city's food fabric today,' he noted.

Curry-rice, happily, is holding up supremely well amid this avalanche of change. Though some may trade it for the occasional salad, the quotidian staple continues to tether Goans to a place of familiarity, comfort, and tradition. Vasquito has refrained from tinkering with the icon thus far. 'The problem with Goan fish curry is that very few people want any new takes. They just prefer a dish made well.'

Ruta Kahate, who used to serve hip, San Francisco-style fare at her now-closed café, Ruta's Roadhouse, in Assagao, echoed Vasquito's view and dished out the perfect little gem to reinforce the curry's staying power. 'Once, we had a large family over at the café. One of the diners, pleased with his order, said, "This is so good. How am I going to go home and eat lunch?" I asked him, "Didn't you just eat lunch?" He said, "Oh that? That was a…sandwich. Lunch is fish curry-rice."'

I did manage to hunt out an out-of-the-box version of the classic at Chef Avinash Martins's restaurant Cavatina in Benaulim. The creative perfectionist is known for his 'local-heart, global-soul' renditions of Goan cuisine, and his updated seafood thali didn't disappoint.

Reimagined tapas-style, the common prawn hooman sparkled anew with its bevy of accompaniments and marine-themed plating. Beautifully creamy and subtly accented with turmeric and teflam, Avinash's poem of a curry was eclectically paired with crab xec xec goujon (deep fried strip of crab cooked in aromatic coconut sauce), kismur fritter (dry fish salad croquette), seeded recheado chonak (seed-crusted Asian sea bass spiked with a fiery red paste), cloud-light mini sannas, and sol kadi foam. The bite-sized morsels, stunningly presented on sea shells, were elegant, innovative, and above all, respectful of produce.

Like others I met during my visit, Avinash believes that the future of Goan fish curry is inextricably entwined with the preservation of its ingredients. Strongly opposed to bull trawling, a method of commercial high-speed fishing with trawl boats, he mourned the disappearance of precious Goan marine life. 'I don't like this mega business of harvesting and harnessing anything from the sea at any given point of time,' he said. It is the distinctive taste of local fish, the chef emphasized, which gives a defining edge to a Goan curry. For the dish to retain its magic, it is important to bring back disappearing species like shevto, or the striped gray mullet, which have been impacted severely by industrial fishing and the growing influence of foreign fish like tilapia.

'The sea is like our mother. It should be allowed to rest during the rains. It must be allowed to recover,' he said fervently.

◆

My currython convinced me of Goan fish curry's exceptionality. It might appear to be the most unassuming of dishes, but greatness lurks beneath. Woven into the very warp and weft of Goa's fabric, it epitomizes inclusivity.

In a state sharply cleaved along religious and geographical lines, it's a minor miracle that *all* of Goa's major communities—Hindus, Christians, Muslims, and aboriginals—eat this dish for lunch almost every single day.

The genius of the staple lies in its minimalism. It rocks the plate with a few inexpensive ingredients. Just two elements—the kick of kokum or tamarind and the heat of red chillies—are enough to add pizzazz to the humblest meal.

Cheap, nourishing, and easy to cook, the egalitarian staple honours the tables of all classes. The wealthiest with state-of-the-art kitchens make it, as do the less financially affluent, often on wood fire. It is daily fuel, a beloved culinary tradition, a rich cultural artifact, and above all, a simple pleasure to be enjoyed with loved ones.

Yet, for all its simplicity, the story of Goan fish curry is nuanced and complex, and has a sprawling sweep. It is striking how the same basic, rustic recipe is infinitely interpreted and adapted across the state—as teflamche hooman and kandyanche hooman, as soi-mirem and juice curry, as fish-head curry and kalchi koddi, and so many others.

At the end of my visit, Goa's most loved dish still brimmed with mystery. I would have to tease out its nuances slowly, over successive visits. Bit by bit, bite by bite, it would unravel its secrets to me.

But even then, I would never know it all.

Recipes from My Travels

SAPNA SARDESSAI'S MACKEREL CURRY WITH TEFLAM

SERVES: 4 TIME TAKEN: 30 MINUTES

INGREDIENTS

Fresh mackerels	3
Coconut oil	4 tsp
Green chillies	2, slit
Ginger	½ tsp, finely chopped
Turmeric powder	1 tsp
Goan Szechuan peppers (teflam)	10–12, lightly pounded
Coconut	1½ cup, grated
Chilli powder	1 tsp
Goan dry red chillies	4–5
Tamarind	marble-sized ball
Kokum shells	3
Salt	to taste
Water	2½ cups

METHOD

Wash and clean the mackerels, cut into curry pieces, discard the heads, apply salt, and set aside for 15 minutes.

Heat coconut oil in an earthen pot, add sliced green chillies and ginger.

Lightly wash the mackerel pieces again and add to the pot.

Add ½ tsp turmeric powder and Szechuan peppers. Add 1 cup water and allow cooking, covered.

Finely grind together grated coconut, chilli powder, the remaining turmeric powder, dry red chillies, and tamarind along with 1 cup water. The paste has to be nice and fine, not grainy.

Add this ground coconut paste to the pot and mix gently.

Add ½ cup water to the mixer and remove all residue paste. Add to the pot.

Add salt and check for seasoning. Add kokum shells.

Put off the flame and drizzle some coconut oil over the curry.

Cover immediately to keep the flavours intact.

Serve hot with steamed rice.

Tip: In case you don't find teflam, you can use black peppercorns, though the flavour will be a bit different. Instead of mackerels, you could use any firm-fleshed fish like rawas, basa, or singhara.

AVINASH MARTINS'S PRAWN-AND-BIMBLI HOOMAN

SERVES: 4 TIME TAKEN: 30 MINUTES PLUS MARINATION

INGREDIENTS

Prawns	15–20
Bimbli	5–6, sliced
Turmeric powder (for marination)	1 tbsp
Chilli powder	1 tsp
Coconut	½ cup, grated
Turmeric powder	½ tsp
Tamarind	marble-sized ball
Black peppercorns	5
Coriander seeds	½ tsp
Byadagi chillies	2–3
Oil	1 tsp
Onion	½, chopped
Water	1¼ cup
Salt	1 tsp

METHOD

For marination,

Shell the prawns; devein them by removing the thick black thread from the middle of each prawn's back.

Apply turmeric powder, chilli powder, and salt.
Leave it for 15–20 minutes.

For gravy,

Grind together the grated coconut, turmeric powder, tamarind, black peppercorns, coriander seeds, and red byadagi chillies with ½ cup water to make a thin smooth paste.

Add ¼ cup water and marinated prawns in a pan, add 2 tbsp of the ground paste, and let it cook for 2–3 minutes.

Add in the rest of the gravy and ½ cup water along with the sliced bimbli and cook on a medium flame for 5–8 minutes.

Switch off the gas.

Heat oil in a tempering pan, add the chopped onions, and fry until they are slightly burnt. Add the onions to the gravy and close the lid.

Add salt to taste and check seasoning.

Tip: Instead of bimbli, you could use 1 tbsp tamarind paste or 1 tbsp vinegar as a souring agent in the gravy.

Undhiyu

ROOTING FOR CHANGE

The appeal of undhiyu, Gujarat's favourite winter dish, made from mixed seasonal root vegetables, legumes, and greens, was lost on me the first time I ate it. Its exotic ingredients were unfamiliar. I had never eaten ratalu (purple yam); or tuvar lilva (green pigeon peas); or the elusive Surti papdi bean, which rarely ever makes it to north India.

The taste confounded me. Far from being simplistic, it was a thing of labyrinthine complexity. Eaten in one bite, it was a thousand flavours—earthy, pungent, salty, sweet, savoury, bitter, bland, starchy, and grassy—all at once.

The dish grew on me over time. Once I had broken down the multitude of sensations, it became apparent that the combination was actually delicious. The medley of oddball vegetables intrigued me. I had to know more about it.

I intended to begin my investigations with south Mumbai's cult undhiyu haunt, Hiralal Kashidas Bhajiawala, but its owner Gaurang Shah insisted there was no tastier way to get acquainted with undhiyu than eating it in the city of its birth.

'Head to Surat first,' he urged. And so I did.

SURAT

Undhiyu Shopping at Bhagal Market with Gaurang Sukhadia

An outstanding undhiyu begins in the mandi. Ingredients are king in this parade of winter ingredients, some of which are associated exclusively with Surat.

The region's deep black soil and tropical climate have long made it Gujarat's cornucopia. Unlike the rest of the semi-arid state, here vegetables virtually leap off the ground.

Gaurang Sukhadia, who helms S. Motiram, a leading sweet shop in Surat, had offered to take me to Bhagal market. One of the city's top produce spots, it's the best place to get familiar with the array of tubers, greens, and beans that go into making undhiyu.

The city's trademark scent of paunk (tender sorghum grains) enveloped us the moment we stepped out of the car. Seasonal produce, fresh and happy, was everywhere. Blazing-red tomatoes, neon green limes, festoons of marigolds.

Gaurang's pride in the plenitude of his land was palpable. 'We're pretty spoilt in Surat. Having fertile soil means we have it all here,' he said, as we strolled past just-picked bounty to halt at his favourite stall. 'Say hello to Surat's super bean,' he said, gently splitting open a flat, tender green pod of Surti papdi, locally known as Katargam papdi, to show me three soft, tiny beans inside.

The legume, which plays a starring role in undhiyu, is dependent on Surat's topography, and is hard to grow elsewhere, Gaurang explained. Though the nearby village of Katargam, where the bean was originally grown, no longer harvests the legume, the name has stuck.

Like all Surtis, Gaurang is a sucker for its subtle sweet flavour and tender bite. 'There is no bean like it. It's in a class by itself,' he said. I bit into one. It had a mild, tender, mellow flavour.

As I took in the incredible variety on display, Gaurang pointed out undhiyu's other salient ingredients—purple yams with violet-brown skins known as kand or ratalu; oblong, blocky sweet potatoes known as sakaria; small potatoes; ripe bananas; serpentine coils of green chillies; local cucumbers known as ariya kaakdi; fragrant stalks of garlic greens known as leela lasan; and ringan, or round, smooth eggplants the size of golf balls.

Each ingredient plays a role in creating the beloved taste. The tubers form the backbone of the dish, giving it heft; the beans give a nutty crunch and aroma; the eggplants give it a melting tenderness; and the ripe bananas impart a sweet creaminess set off by the slightly bitter flavours of the crisp muthiya, a Gujarati snack made of mixed flours and fenugreek leaves. 'Bring them all together and it's a feast in a dish,' said Gaurang, beaming.

The final dish, of course, is not just about the ingredients. At the heart of undhiyu is the special green Surti masala used to season the classic. Made with green chillies, fresh coriander leaves, green garlic, grated coconut, peanuts, sesame seeds, and spices such as nutmeg, cumin, cinnamon, black stone flower, salt, and star anise, the judicious use of this mix breathes new life into the vegetables.[1]

The undhiyu I ate at Gaurang's shop was redolent of this verdant blend. Blanketed with chopped green garlic, and sweetened with sugar, it came with a brazen amount of groundnut oil.

'An undhiyu that isn't swimming in oil isn't undhiyu,' Gaurang said, laying out the more-is-more culinary philosophy of the Surtis, who view food as a symbolic expression of supremacy and wealth.

Ghari, a Surti specialty he fed me before I left, was just as staggeringly decadent. Made with dry fruits, mawa or thickened milk, sugar, and ghee, the sweet came swaddled in an additional outer layer of solid ghee.

I jokingly asked whether he made low-cal versions of these dishes. 'Na, majja nahi aave chhe (No, that's no fun at all),' he said dismissively.

Undhiyu Tutorial with Mina Patel

A wander through the tatty, winding laneways of Gundi Sheri in the old city offers a sense of Surat's historic past. There's no ignoring the imposing old buildings, which keep alive a bygone charm and reflect centuries of Surti history.

Walking through a warren of nooks, crannies, and corridors, I arrived at the ancestral home of Mina Ben, a local home caterer of repute, who had offered to teach me her time-tested method of making Surti undhiyu from scratch.

A soft-spoken woman with smiling eyes, Mina Ben was clad in a floral salwar kameez, her hair swept back in a tight bun. Welcoming me to her home, she introduced me to her family—her husband Deepak, son Anand, and daughter-in-law Hemali—before sitting me down on a well-worn sofa, the only piece of furniture in the room not cluttered with her grandson's schoolbooks.

Mina Ben, who traced the origin of the dish to the Leuva Patels of Surat, made it clear that the classic can't be rushed. You need to persevere to be richly rewarded with a dish of delicious complexity.

Her tutorial, delivered in breathy, emphatic tones, was full of tips. Undhiyu can't be cooked in a pressure cooker. Only Surti green vegetables must be used. No oil other than groundnut oil will do. And there should be no bitterness in the methi leaves used for making muthiya.

As she began frying the vegetables on a slow flame in her trusty iron kadhai, the care she put into each batch was evident. 'Go low and slow. Ahista ahista. That's what is going to make it tasty.'

Hemali, meanwhile, boiled the papdi beans, stuffed the bananas with Surti green masala, and fried the muthiyas with a pre-prepared dough of atta, besan, green chillies, methi, and sugar.

Next, Mina Ben made a vaghar or tempering by frying up crushed peanuts, sesame seeds, hing, dhana jeera powder, ginger-garlic paste, green chillies, salt, dried coconut or khaman, sugar, and shop-bought undhiyu masala.

The assembly of the undhiyu allowed me to see how much detailing goes into creating the balance of tastes and textures. The vegetables were layered artfully. First, the papdi and tuvar lilva; then a layer of eggplants followed by the yams, tubers, stuffed ripe bananas, and vaghar mix. The muthiyas went in last so as not to disintegrate and melt away.

The dish was finished with a flurry of coriander leaves and green garlic, and a generous glug of groundnut oil. 'The more the better,' Mina Ben said, blaming the excess on the hot weather. 'Food spoils easily in Gujarat. That's why we use so much oil.'

The undhiyu gently simmered on the stove, filling the kitchen with a celebratory fragrance. Twenty minutes later, Mina Ben beamed triumphantly, 'Undhiyu bani gayu (Undhiyu is ready)!'

Not one to do things by half measures, Hemali had cooked up a storm of Surti dishes as well—bhagat muthiya, a lively tomato-and-onion curry with lentil and dumplings, purple yam, corn, peas, and potatoes bobbing in it; moraiya khichdi made from barnyard millet; a sauté of sweet potatoes, purple yam, and potatoes; cucumber; green garlic raita; and green garlic papad. There were kesar (saffron) jalebis too, the only shop-bought item.

When Hemali finished plating, my thali was a rainbow of colours. Fresh, lively flavours bounced off the plate as I tucked into the food with discs of puffed pooris. It left no doubt in my mind that Gujarat has some of the best vegetarian food in the world.

From start to finish, the most important element in Mina Ben's undhiyu was the taste of indulgence. Drenched in oil, the dish made for some serious carbo-loading. By the time I finished, I was full to bursting. 'No more,' I groaned.

But Mina Ben wasn't having any of it. 'Eat some more. The season won't last forever,' she said, placing another ladleful of the rich, comforting mess on my thali.

VALSAD

Umbadiyu at Magan Bhai's Stall

Come winter, the tiny village of Dungri in Gujarat's Valsad turns into one giant culinary festival. Campfires and makeshift roadside eateries are everywhere. Their primary offering—a rotund clay pot of mixed vegetables known as umbadiyu,[2] draws crowds from as far as Mumbai, Surat, and Ahmedabad.

Regarded as undhiyu's rustic counterpart, the smoky treat comprises peak-winter vegetables fired up in an upturned earthen pot known as a matla. It is from this ancient cooking method that undhiyu derives its name. 'Undhu' in Gujarati translates to 'upside down', so there's definitely a connection between the two delicacies.

A toasty smell hung in the air as I drove into the sleepy hamlet on a crisp December morning. With no time to scour the various stands, I headed straight to Magan Bhai's stall, famed for its honest-to-goodness umbadiyu.

The tiny kiosk was wreathed in smoke as I entered. Magan Bhai, a gregarious man with gleaming eyes, welcomed me inside. 'Come, come, come. Magan Bhai na umbadiyu best in Valsad! No, best in Gujarat. No, best in India! No, best in world!' he cried excitedly.

Speaking in a mix of Gujarati, Hindi, and English, Magan Bhai explained that umbadiyu started as the diet of adivasis or local tribals, who would roast veggies in a clay pot to eat during the winter. The dish became popular when the Dhodia Patels of Valsad started pairing it with their toddy before the days of Prohibition. An adivasi himself, Magan Bhai learnt to make the dish from his father, who would light up the matlas in the fields of rich landlords like the Desais.

Showing me around, his wife Dhanu Ben pointed out the key components of ubadiyu: sacks of potatoes, heaps of purple yam, eggplants, and field beans. While tubers are common to both dishes, she explained, umbadiyu uses the local papdi in place of Surti papdi, and replaces the tuvar lilva with green peas and corn kernels.

I watched her layer the vegetables in clay pots with a familiar hand—first the beans, then the tubers, peas, and corn kernels. Kalhar, the wild aromatic greens used to stuff and seal the pot, play a pivotal role in the dish. Dhanu Ben bruised a couple for me to smell. Velvety to touch, they had a clean, menthol-like perfume.

Unlike its maximalist cousin, the key to a great umbadiyu is its sparse use of spice. I was curious about the blackish masala that went into the mix, but Magan Bhai refused to spill the beans. 'No, no, no! I not tell recipe. Top, top, top secret,' he declared. (Dhanu Ben, though, let it slip that it was carom seeds mixed with salt, green chillies, and a few dry spices.)

The pots were inverted, covered with firewood, and fired for an hour. In the meanwhile, I snuck out for a bit to explore a lively Sunday fair replete with stalls selling ber (jujubes), sugarcane, peanut-and-sesame brittle, paunk, and much more.

When I returned, Magan Bhai was busy flipping the contents of the piping hot umbadiyu onto a piece of butter paper on the table. A bracing glass of cool buttermilk accompanied the treat.

As I dug into the slow-cooked feast, I understood why umbadiyu had such a cult following. An hour of roasting under the embers had slow-cooked the veggies, playing up their sweetness. The skin of the purple yam was lacquered to a golden crisp, the sweet potatoes had caramelized and acquired a gorgeous creaminess, and the beans, cooked to a crisp tender, retained their colour and snap.

The scorched, sharply pungent taste was enhanced by the delightfully rustic setting. I couldn't imagine this dish as takeaway. It was made to be relished in situ.

Basking in the happy haze of the mild winter sun, I knew I had consumed more than a pot of roasted veggies. I had partaken in an earthy pleasure rooted in village life.

As I bade Magan Bhai farewell, he cried, 'Madam, make Magan Bhai famous. Write in paper. Magan Bhai's umbadiyu eat. Come Mumbai. Come New York. Come Dubai. Come all!'

AHMEDABAD

Undhiyu with Kotha ni Chutney, and Other Versions

Although undhiyu was birthed in Surat, the classic Surti version represents only half the culinary story—the rest emerges in innumerable regional adaptations across the state, each with a different cadence.[3]

Ahmedabad, with its blended population, is the perfect place to taste this diversity. The variety of undhiyus served here reflects the varying culinary approaches to the dish.

The undhiyu I ate at The House of MG, the city's premiere boutique hotel helmed by heritage entrepreneur and educationist Abhay Mangaldas, was typical of the Amdavadi version. Drizzled with sesame oil, and with the consistency of a medium-thick gravy, it was flavourful yet not as rich or spicy as the one I ate in Surat. Though made using classic Surti green masala, the vegetables were steamed and not fried.

The show-stealer was the accompanying kotha ni chutney, a tangy relish made with wood apple pulp, red chilli powder, cumin seeds, and jaggery. Not to be confused with the north Indian bel or bael (also known as wood apple in English), kotha or *Limonia acidissima* grows in (but isn't endemic to) to Gujarat. Like Katargam papdi, it makes a brief, much-awaited cameo in the winter.

The side made an essential contribution to the undhiyu. Sweet, tart, and intense, it cut the richness of the vegetables, giving them a zip of flavour. The sour notes from the wood apples were a brilliant counterpoint to the sweetness of the yams. Elevated by its supporting cast, the familiar dish suddenly acquired a new edge. The simple addition of acidity took it to a new height.

Abhay, who joined me for a bite at HMG's Green Café, is a fan of undhiyu's wintry flavours. He recalled how growing up at his ancestral home in Mangalbaug, undhiyu was always special. 'Nobody ever got tired of undhiyu. One, it's only made in the cold season, limited to a couple months in a state with a scorching climate. Two, from tubers to greens to herbs, there's something for everyone. And three, it was accompanied by pooris and kesar jalebis,' he said.

On regular days, the less expansive panchkutyu shak, made with five veggies, stood in for the traditional dish. Sometimes, a lentil undhiyu made of moong and moth bean sprouts, soaked chickpeas, potatoes, purple yam, bananas, sweet potatoes, and green eggplants would be made.

Shaan Zaveri, the soft-spoken owner of the iconic Swati Snacks, treated me to sambhariyu, another undhiyu variant. More of a home dish, it is made with stuffed vegetables or bharelu shak—stuffed eggplants, tendli (ivy gourd), and potatoes—along with sweet potatoes along with onions, peas, tuvar lilva, and chutney.

I got a taste of their classic version too, featuring steamed veggies, and no visible oil. The green, low-fat dish was served with bajra no rotlo or pearl millet flatbread, chilli-garlic chutney, jaggery, and white butter.

Unlike Abhay, Shaan believes that undhiyu is highly contentious and evokes strong opinions, as not all the vegetables find favour with everyone. As someone who falls in that camp, he happens to like his without eggplants and bananas. 'That's why I like sambhariyu,' he said. 'For me, it's undhiyu without the offensive veggies.'

To make the dish more democratic, he shared, Amdavadis have invented the tawa undhiyu. A rage at weddings, it allows one to build one's own undhiyu. 'We call it "live" undhiyu because it's assembled on a tawa right in front of you. You can indicate your preference of vegetables and adjust the spice levels to your liking. Plus, it looks so much nicer.'

Although I didn't get to attend a Gujarati wedding, I did try another unique creation—the chicken undhiyu concocted by Tanjim Makda, who belongs to the Jhalawar Gujarati Muslim community from Surendranagar. Made like a home-style chicken curry with root vegetables and legumes, it is cooked till the meat falls off the bone. Tanjim used eggplants of two or three varieties, potatoes, papdi, green peas, pigeon peas, val beans, white peas, methi muthiya, and green chillies.

The dish became an immediate hit when she concocted the recipe in 2019 for the festival of Uttarayan or Makar Sankranti (a period that marks the transition of the sun into the zodiac sign of Capricorn, known as Makara in Sanskrit), by adapting the original for a non-veg clientele. 'The idea was to leave out the yams and sweet potatoes, as people don't like the sweet taste, and make it extra spicy,' she said.

Featuring dry whole masalas—cumin, cinnamon, bay leaves, black pepper—it was deliciously warming. But save for the vegetables, it bore little resemblance to the classic.

Sushila Subodh's Matla nu Undhiyu

The highlight of my Ahmedabad visit was my meeting with Gujarati gourmet and cookbook writer Sushila Subodh[4] at her Shahibaug residence. Regarded as a doyenne of Gujarati cooking, the spry nonagenarian was a font of undhiyu lore, willing and able to talk about the dish's intricacies with great nuance.

Some of her earliest and happiest memories had to do with growing up on her family farm outside Vadodara and eating matla nu undhiyu.[5] 'My father and uncles were landlords. Each winter we would visit the farm with all the cousins. It was a time when all we wanted to do was spend more time outdoors with the people we loved,' she said.

The undhiyu would be made in matlas. All the ingredients—papdi, lilva, small potatoes, sakariya, ringan, and ratalu—would be harvested from the fields. The bountiful pot would be stuffed with kalar leaves, and sealed with wheat flour. No oil or water would be added, allowing the vegetables to cook in their own juices. Seasoned with just salt and carom seeds, the vegetables would release their flavours and aromas inside the matlas.

An array of accompaniments would complement the fire-roasted veggies—raw sesame oil, kotha or wood apple chutney, leela lasan chutney, and khatiyu or tamarind water seasoned with jaggery, chillies, ginger, and garam masala. There would be boiled sweet potatoes, thin slices of ratalu, fried and served with a squeeze of lime, and the ultimate treat—fresh paunk ground into coarse green barfis.

A large table would be set up outdoors where the mellow, sun-kissed breeze provided the perfect accent to the field-inspired lunch. The veggie-loaded feast was a true winter bonanza, as delicious as it was convivial.

After she married into a prestigious textile family in Ahmedabad, where she found herself surrounded by luminaries like painter M. F. Husain, she would dazzle her food-loving family and guests with her undhiyu. But for Sushila, the stove version paled in comparison to the alfresco dish of her childhood.

A woman of strong opinions, she firmly believed that the undhiyu was not meant to be cooked indoors but in the open, using fresh produce from the fields. It's no surprise, she observed, that the dish is synonymous with Uttarayan. Celebrated mid-January to signal the end of harvest, it's a time when seasonal produce is at its best.

'Close your eyes and imagine the scene. Harvest is over, and everyone is celebrating in the fields. A bunch of farmers have gathered for a feast. One has brought ringan, another papdi, a third ratalu, and sakaria. They toss them all into a common pot in a gesture of thanksgiving. Yes, that's how it probably started,' she whispered, lost in her own imagining of the ancient ritual.

MUMBAI

Surti Undhiyu with Gaurang Shah at Hiralal Kashidas Bhajiawala

It made sense to conclude my undhiyu journey in Mumbai. Gujarat was, after all, a part of Bombay State before the latter was reorganized along linguistic lines in 1960.

Hiralal Kashidas Bhajiawala (HKB) in Girgaon remains a cornerstone of the city's undhiyu scene. Dating back to 1936, the shop was started by the eponymous Hiralal K. Bhajiawala, a renowned cook from Surat who moved to Mumbai after a difference of opinion with his family.

Recognizing an unexploited market niche in Bhuleshwar, a hub for Gujarati settlements, Hiralal opened his own ideal restaurant—a neighbourhood takeaway where he would cook authentic Surti food and recapture some of the magic of the dishes he had grown up eating.

The sweet, slightly pungent whiff of bananas was in the air as I entered the shop. Ever the generous host, Gaurang, Heeralal's son, greeted me with his trademark warmth. Before I knew it, he had deluged the table with an array of Surti delicacies—paunk vada (paunk dumplings), paunk sprinkled with lemon juice and sev, mini batata vadas (batter-coated potato dumplings), kand bhajiya (purple yam fritters), sev khamni (crushed, spiced chana dal topped with sev). 'You won't find these anywhere else in Mumbai,' he said proudly.

HKB has honed its undhiyu to a precise formula. When Gaurang and his brother inherited the shop from their father, they figured two ways to keep the beloved dish tasting the same, sourcing authentic ingredients from Surat and standardizing the recipe. 'We formulated each and every item including kachori, batata vada, dhokla, and undhiyu. Everything is cooked by weight to ensure there is not much variation in taste,' he said.

In true-blue Surti style, the undhiyu here was made in pure groundnut oil and without a drop of water, and stood out for its deep, luxurious taste. The sweet-spicy play of flavours came together nicely. Accented with herbs, the dish was as comforting as it was indulgent.

My favourite bit was the muthiyas. Crunchy and golden, the delicious balls of crispy carbs were very moreish. When I complimented Gaurang on the texture, he chuckled. 'Try telling that to my meat-crazy Parsi customers. They buy my undhiyu and replace the muthiyas with mutton kebabs. One even puts a fried egg on top!' he quipped good-naturedly.

Eager to try a contemporary take, I treated myself to Chef Pinky Chandan Dixit's low-cal undhiyu at her restaurant Soam in Babulnath.

Baked in the oven, her modern approach left the veggies perfectly tender yet preserving their colour and crispness. Seasoned beautifully with spices and greens and served with golden pooris (unleavened wheat bread deep-fried in oil) and creamy shrikhand (a Gujarati dessert made from strained yoghurt), the ensemble was finger-licking good.

Varun Inamdar surprised me with his rebooted undhiyu version. The chef made a rice pulao using leftover undhiyu and plated the dish in two ways—an uber fine-dine style, and a large family platter sprinkled with garlic-flavoured sev. 'We need to experiment more with undhiyu,' he said. 'I guess we are just scared to tinker with it, or busy digging up and recreating lost recipes. Or maybe, we are just too boring.'

Home-style Undhiyu with Neha Shah

Home caterer Neha Shah, who hails from the KVO (Kutchi Veesa Oswal) community in Kutch, invited me for an afternoon of lunch and stories at her home in Azad Lane, a Gujarati neighbourhood in Mumbai's Andheri West.

Although she served me a classic Surti udhiyu, the bajra no rotlo that accompanied it was native to Kutch. Her dish was remarkable for its yellow-orange colour and earthy, spicy kick. The striking hue, I discovered, came from a rhizome called amba-haldi or mango-ginger. 'Very few people add it in undhiyu, but it works like magic,' Neha said.

She recalled how, growing up, undhiyu was more ritual than dish in her Lalbaug home, where she lived with her parents and many uncles, aunts, and cousins. 'We would wait all year long to eat undhiyu,' she said, recounting how a day before Makar Sankranti, the women of the house would collectively roll up their sleeves to make the labour-intensive dish. 'The idea was to finish cooking, so they could enjoy the festival the following day,' she said.

Prepping all those fiddly vegetables—washing, peeling, stringing, removing the leaves—took up all day. Yet, the women's all-hands-on-deck camaraderie would imbue even these most ordinary tasks with richness.

The day-long festival of kite-flying would culminate in a mammoth feast for Makar Sankranti, where young and old would come together to partake of undhiyu along with pooris and shrikhand. 'Now when I make undhiyu, it's a way of reliving those days,' she said with a nostalgic smile.

Though loaded with winter flavours, Neha's homemade undhiyu was considerably less oily than the ones I had eaten. It made me realize that underneath its calorie overload, the dish has an abundantly nutritious core.

My hostess was happy to list the benefits for me. 'Green garlic boosts the immune system, amba-haldi aids in digestion, and papdi beans are an excellent source of plant-based protein.

'Eat up. You'll get super powers,' she said.

Shatbhi Basu's Big Fat Undhiyu Party

Undhiyu is not meant to be eaten alone. Conviviality is a big part of its raison d'etre. I longed to experience a real-deal undhiyu shindig, touted as the epitome of wintry good times.

When Shatbhi Basu, Mumbai's reigning queen of cocktails and founder of STIR Academy of Bartending, agreed to host a get-together at her Mahim home, my prayers were answered. It's not every day that a mixologist offers to make undhiyu for you. I knew her cooking would be one of a kind.

The guest list comprised some of her closest friends—chefs Amit Puri and Varun Inamdar, alcobev professional Sweta Mohanty, culinary experience creator Suprio Bose, and oenophile Sujata Patil. Shatbhi kept the menu limited to undhiyu, which she believes is worth celebrating by itself. 'It'll be a no-frills, all-thrills party,' she promised.

Unlike Gujarat's Mina Ben, Shatbhi had no predilection for doing things the old-fashioned way. A proponent of hassle-free cooking, she broke down the labour to a three-day process and bought the muthiyas from a store.

I was invited for a sneak peek into her green masala-making ritual. A soundtrack of classic rock accompanied the afternoon prep work as she worked happily in her blue-and-yellow-tiled kitchen.

Though her own family was originally from Kathiawar, Shatbhi's undhiyu was adapted from a Surti friend's recipe, and largely stuck to the classic. However, she hacked the original by skipping the dry masalas, sugar, and bananas.

I was stumped when she showed me her secret undhiyu tool—a four-inch-deep dish pizza pan. 'It works like a charm. I don't have to layer the vegetables. I just divide the pan into four quarters, and put the purple yam along with the muthiya, the sweet potatoes, and the potatoes. People can pick what they like. Everyone's happy,' she said.

As I was leaving, Shatbhi whetted my curiosity by claiming there was a 'mystery' ingredient in her undhiyu. 'I'll tell you about it tomorrow,' she said, ending our meeting on a cliffhanger.

At the party, Shatbhi's big-hearted 'pizza' pan of undhiyu arrived, crusted with a glistening garnish of green garlic and coriander. One taste and we couldn't stop sticking our spoons into the moreish treat. Each bite was packed with rich, intense flavours.

To everyone's delight, she had replaced the traditional chaas with white wine sangrias. 'Undhiyu makes you thirsty. Hell, yes. So, why not pair it with some vino?' trilled our genial hostess.

It was a genius idea. The fresh, fruit-forward taste of the sangrias balanced the undhiyu's spiciness, while also notching up the fun quotient. The next three hours just melted away. Foodie stories and tips were shared, as were good-natured quips about the culinary quirks of Gujaratis.

The sangrias kept coming, making it hard to keep track of how much undhiyu was consumed. Later, a warm batch of gooey brownies stretched the revelry.

At the end of the bash, the big question still remained. 'So, what's that secret ingredient?' I asked.

'Oh that. *You* are the magic ingredient, my dear. Undhiyu is all about great company,' said Shatbhi, bursting into her big infectious laugh.

◆

American slow food legend Alice Waters, known for her love of fava beans and green garlic, once summed up her farm-to-table philosophy simply: 'If you eat seasonally, locally, and sustainably, it can bring you back to ripeness, beauty, and community.'

Undhiyu is delicious proof of this.

Made with great regional produce, , it is an expression of terroir. I know the term is overused and abused, but ingredients like Surti papdi, lilva, and ratalu bring out the dish's local character. Shining a light on the beauty of seasons, they teach us to use things when they are at their peak.

Ostensibly, undhiyu might appear to be nothing more than a hearty winter feast. But dig a bit deeper and it is a reflection of a more expansive worldview—one that's about eating more diversely. As we face some of environment's biggest challenges, a dish like undhiyu can help us think about food from a perspective of sustainability.

Separated by hundreds of kilometres, my undhiyu experiences shared one quality: local vegetables treated with respect. Researching the mushy-crisp mess of winter staples enabled me to appreciate that we have a lot of brilliant indigenous produce that we overlook.

The UN Food and Agriculture Organization estimates that 75 per cent of crop diversity was lost between 1900 and 2000, and that as much as 22 per cent of the wild relatives of food crops will disappear by 2055 because of the changing climate.[6] It further observes, 'Just 15 crop plants provide 90 percent of the world's food energy intake, with three rice, maize and wheat—making up two-thirds of this [sic].'[7]

In an era devoted to agricultural monocultures, undhiyu reminds us to reclaim our underappreciated vegetables. No less than eight combine to create this unique and dazzlingly varied dish, which, quite literally, roots for the underdog by utilizing underused local produce. For once, humble spuds and yams, usually seen as unsexy, have a moment outside of the street cart.

The best part about the classic, though, is that it doesn't make any overtly 'woke' statement. It just calls for some celebration, and shows that planet-friendly eating can be indulgent and joyful.

ANJALI MANGALDAS'S UNDHIYU

SERVES: 12 TIME TAKEN: 2 HOURS

INGREDIENTS

Purple yam	250 gms
Sweet potato	750 gms
Potatoes	750 gms
Coarse wheat flour	50 gms
Besan	200 gms
Fenugreek leaves	250 gms
Green eggplants	250 gms
Surti papdi	750 gms
Papdi (flat beans)	250 gms
Green tuvar	500 gms
Fresh coconut	½, grated
Ginger	50 gms, crushed
Green chillies	50 gms, crushed
Garlic (or chopped green garlic)	150 gms, crushed
Salt	to taste
Red chilli powder	2 tsp
Sugar	1 tbsp
Turmeric powder	1 tsp
Asafoetida	½ tsp
Whole red chillies	2
Ajwain (carom seeds)	2 tsp
Cooking soda	1 tsp
Garam masala	2 tsp
Sesame seeds	1 tbsp
Cumin-coriander powder	4 tbsp
Green coriander leaves	1 bunch, chopped
Oil	12 tbsp

METHOD

Wash, peel, and chop the potatoes, sweet potatoes, and purple yam into large pieces. Fry them all in oil.

To prepare the muthiya, mix coarse wheat flour, besan, salt, 1 tsp chilli powder, a little sugar, 1 tbsp cumin-coriander powder, and oil.

Chop and wash the fenugreek leaves. Rub salt in them and squeeze out water to get rid of bitterness. Mix these leaves in the flour, knead into a firm dough, and prepare small rolls (muthiya). Deep-fry the rolls.

Slit the green eggplants on two sides. Mix 2 tsp ginger, half of the green chillies, coriander leaves, sesame seeds and 1.5 tbsp cumin-coriander powder along with a little sugar, salt, a pinch of cooking soda, and garam masala. Fill the slit eggplants with some of this mixture.

Heat oil, add asafoetida, and cook the eggplants.

Heat oil in a large pan. Add whole red chillies, ajwain seeds, 1 tsp red chilli powder,turmeric, and asafoetida. Add the Surti papdi beans, flat papdi beans, and green tuvar. Add salt and cooking soda dissolved in a little water. Cover it and let it cook.

Chop the coriander leaves and place in a large flat plate. Add the remaining crushed ginger, crushed green chillies, sesame seeds, cumin-coriander powder along with grated coconut, crushed garlic or chopped green garlic, some sugar and salt. Mix them well.

Add the fried potatoes, sweet potatoes and purple yam in the mixture. Add the muthiya and cooked eggplants too. When the peas and beans are cooked, add all of the vegetables and the masala mix as well. Mix well.

Cook on a low flame till all the spices are cooked.

Garnish with fresh coriander leaves and grated coconut while serving.

Note: This recipe has been adapted from Anjali Mangaldas's book *Bhojan No Anand*. She was Abhay Mangaldas's mother.

THE HOUSE OF MG'S KOTHA NI CHUTNEY

MAKES: 200 GMS　　　　TIME TAKEN: 10 MINUTES

INGREDIENTS

Kotha (wood apple)	200 gms (2–3), peeled
Cumin	½ tsp

Chilli powder	½ tsp
Jaggery	100 gms, powdered
Salt	½ tsp
Water	3–4 tbsp

METHOD

Put all the ingredients in a blender and grind until smooth.

Use the chutney as required.

PINKY CHANDAN DIXIT'S LOW-CAL UNDHIYU

SERVES: 8

TIME TAKEN: 1 HOUR

INGREDIENTS

Surti papdi	½ kg
Green tuvar	1 cup, shelled
Purple yam	½ kg, cut into 1-inch cubes
Yam	½ kg, cut into 1-inch cubes
Baby potatoes	250 gms, peeled
Sweet potatoes	250 gms, cut into 1-inch pieces or cubes
Baby eggplants	6–8
Semi-ripe bananas	3

METHI MUTHIYA

For muthiya,

Besan	¾ cup
Rava	1 tbsp
Methi leaves	1 cup
Turmeric powder	½ tsp
Chilli powder	½ tsp
Dhana jeera powder	1 tsp
Ginger-green chilli paste	1 tsp
Salt	To taste
Sugar	1–2 tsp

Lemon	½, juiced
Oil	1 tbsp
Oil	to deep-fry

UNDHIYU

For undhiyu masala,

Fresh coconut	1 cup
Green coriander	1½ cup, chopped
Green garlic	½ cup, chopped
Dhana jeera powder	4 tsp
Sesame seeds	1 tbsp
Turmeric powder	½ tsp
Green chilli-ginger paste	2 tbsp
Cooking soda	¼ tsp
Sugar	1–2 tbsp
Lemon juice	2 tbsp
Salt	to taste

For undhiyu tempering,

Oil	¼ cup
Asafoetida	½ tsp
Ajwain	1tsp

METHOD

For the methi muthiya,

Combine all the ingredients in a bowl and mix well.

Add some water to knead into a firm dough and divide the mixture into 10–12 round balls.

Loosely bind them so that they are not hard.

Deep-fry them in hot oil over a medium flame till they are golden-brown.

Drain and keep aside to use in the undhiyu.

For the undhiyu,

String the Surti papdi, taking care not to split the two sides.

Wash the papdi, put it in a big bowl and add ajwain, green tuvar, cooking soda, salt. Mix well.

Make a criss-cross slit in the potatoes and eggplants, taking care not to separate the segments.

Cut the bananas into big pieces and cut a vertical slit in the centre of each piece.

Mix all the masala ingredients together and put half of the mixture in the slits of potatoes, eggplants, and bananas. Reserve some of this masala for the end of cooking.

Heat oil in a heavy-bottomed pan or an earthern pot.

Add asafoetida and layer the potatoes, yam, purple yam, stuffed bananas, Surti papdi, eggplants, and lastly, the methi muthiya.

Add ⅓rd cup of water and cover and bake in a preheated oven at 180°C for 40–50 minutes.

Remove from the oven and let it rest for 10–15 minutes.

Add the remaining masala mixture on top and gently stir.

Allow it to settle for a few minutes and serve hot.

Shami Kebabs

THE KEBAB WHISPERERS

I miss shami kebabs.

Growing up in Delhi, the discs of minced meat and Bengal gram lentils were the kebabs of choice at my home. Parties at our house always meant shamis, festooned with onion rings and scatterings of lemon wedges. We ordered them at family lunches at Kwality and Embassy, and even packed them for alfresco picnics at India Gate.

Over the last couple of decades, the meaty treat has lost its influence and lustre—incredible, when you consider that it was once the gold standard for kebabs. It's hard to find a shami in restaurants these days. People don't seem to care for it anymore.

The few versions available today are rubbery, bland, and suffer from too much dal. 'Who wants to eat dal for the price of kebab?' said a fellow shami-lover after being served a sub-par version at a popular eatery.

On the other hand, galawati kebabs (patties of ultra-fine mince with nary a trace of dal) enjoy a cult following. Gaining exotic status among gourmands, they hog all the press, feature on every 'refined' menu, and get a glut of fans on social media.

I have no beef with galawatis. They are meatier and make an impact with their melt-in-the-mouth softness. But that very same texture is a real downer for those of us who prefer something that holds its shape and is not forever in a state of disintegration. Galawati tastes cloyingly rich and disappears too quickly in the mouth. Shami, by contrast, is light yet full-bodied. Biting into one feels really good.

Part of my affection for shami is informed by childhood memories. But it's not all romantic throwback. The charming croquette combines satiety with sophistication. Crusty, earthy, and with a juicy bite—if this isn't a perfect kebab, I don't know what is.

Thankfully, not everyone has abandoned the munchie. Though the kebab's fan base has dwindled drastically, there are places where it is still embraced as enthusiastically as it was earlier.

Shami's imprint on culture can still be felt in the old havelis of Lucknow, where this retro kebab continues to be tethered to nawabi traditions. I decided to visit some of these bastions to see whether there is still hope for the beleaguered kebab, and whether or not it is primed for a comeback.

◆

'Kebab matlab shami kebab (Kebab means shami kebab),' my aunt would often say. And it's true. For my parents' generation, and several before them, this was almost axiomatic.

So how did such a beloved food disappear into near-darkness?

'Convenience is what it comes down to,' said Chef Ranveer Brar, a leading authority on Awadhi cuisine, as we caught up over a foamy cappuccino in Mumbai on the eve of my Lucknow visit. The Lucknow-born culinarian pointed out that kebabs broadly fall into two categories—pake gosht ke kebab and kacche gosht ka kebab. 'For a pake gosht ka kebab like shami, mince needs to be boiled before frying the kebabs. Galawati and seekh kebabs, on the other hand, are made with raw mince. Just one marination and you're done,' he explained.

Being a twice-cooked kebab, shami requires a few hours of dedicated time. Back in the day when help was abundant, the lady of the house had the means to get the mutton boiled along with the dal and then ground. 'Today, no one has that kind of time—not even chefs,' Ranveer said.

In the olden days, he said, the meat for shamis would be cooked along with the bone, so the flavours of the bony matter and marrow would be sucked up by the dal. The pulled meat and lentils would then be ground together to make the mince patties. But as people started using boneless meat, there was nothing left for the dal to absorb. 'Umami went missing from the shami and it became a blander concoction,' he added. This did not go down well with a changing, increasingly Punjabi-fying palate. 'People wanted their kebab to have that bite and robustness. The understated appeal of a pake gosht ka kebab was no longer appreciated.'

Shamis also lost out in the clash between Lucknow's two reigning kebab titans, Sakhawat and Tunday Kababi. Sakhawat was famed for his shamis while Tunday championed galawatis. Though Sakhawat's quality was peerless, he limited his enterprise to a single shop in Qaisar Bagh. Tunday, a far shrewder businessman, opened outlets across the city. As more people started packing galawatis and carrying them on flights back to their cities, word of mouth spread and restaurants outside Lucknow started capitalizing on the demand for galawatis.

The formidable marketing chops of Tunday dealt deadly blows to the shami. 'In the end, shami became a victim of its own subtlety. I suppose we are all to blame for the decline of this forgotten classic,' said Ranveer in a low, apologetic tone.

◆

In Lucknow, culinary legends teeter between myth and fact. An amusing and apocryphal piece of the city's lore credits the invention of shami kebab to the ingenious cook employed by a toothless nawab.

We know this is likely not true. As food historian Colleen Taylor Sen tells us in her book *Feasts and Fasts: A History of Food in India*, shami more probably originated in Bilad al-Sham or Syria[1] and may have been introduced to India during the Delhi Sultanate. By the time the kebab came to Awadh (the historic name given to Lucknow and surrounding areas) via the Mughals, it was already well-entrenched in Indian cuisine.

The late Jafar Mir Abdullah, an icon of old Awadhi traditions, held that the classic had its heydays during the reign of the nawabs, who ruled Awadh from the eighteenth century until the collapse of Lucknow's monarchy in 1856.

Sporting a bushy moustache, Jafar claimed a direct bloodline to royalty, spoke flawless Urdu, and oozed portly charm in his brocade silk achkan. His home, the historic Sheesh Mahal, used to be the residence of Nawab Asaf-ud-Daula who ruled Lucknow during the late eighteenth century. The antiquities at the haveli evoked a mood of elegiac elegance.

Listening to Jafar's rich, majestic baritone, it was easy to slip back into Lucknow's nawabi era, a time when eating was an obsession and food given the status of fine art. The nawabs of Awadh didn't fight many major wars after the Battle of Buxar in 1764, Jafar said. Ruling in an era of uninterrupted peace, the epicures loved to host elaborate banquets that showed off their wealth and brought in top culinary talent from Delhi and other cities to work in their bawarchikhanas (kitchens). 'Waqt tha, log the, daulat thi (There was time, manpower, wealth),' he drawled.

Refined in the bawarchikhanas of the nawabs, shami became a more finely nuanced kebab. Earthy yet refined, its success came to rely on impeccable ingredients. 'The meat had to be faultless, without string or fibre or any remnants of bone. The spices had to be meticulously ground or pounded, strained and clarified many times. And unlike the high-fire cooking of the Mughals, shamis had to be cooked on a slow flame,' the stalwart said.

Along with exotic spices, sourness became one of shami's great enhancers, giving it a bracing jolt and a touch of seasonality. Depending on the time of year, a touch of turshi or tartness would be added to the kebab through the use of raw mango, starfruit, or lemon juice.

All these refinements made the kebab sing. 'Badi nafasat aur nazakat wale kebab hain hamare (Our kebabs are the ultimate in sophistication),' Jafar said, gently pushing a platter of freshly made shamis my way. 'Nosh farmaiye (Help yourself).' I popped one in my mouth. It was delicately spiced, herby, and soft.

I gobbled quite a few before asking him whether there was any truth to the yarn about the toothless nawab. 'It's difficult to say for sure. But we love a good story in Lucknow,' he answered with a merry laugh.[2]

◆

We know from *Lucknow: The Last Phase of an Oriental Culture*, Abdul Halim Sharar's seminal account of Lucknow during the late eighteenth and nineteenth centuries, that shami kebabs enjoyed great prestige during the reign of the nawabs. Besides being part of lavish nawabi repasts known as dastarkhwans, they were part of the tora—the grand feasts and huge parcels of food sent to people's homes—and included alongside delicacies like pulao, muzafar (a sweet dish made with vermicelli or rice), shir baranj (milk-and-rice dessert), and korma.[3]

Today, they have fallen from grace. Only a handful of old joints in Lucknow, like Dastarkhwan, Naushijaan, and Sakhawat sell them. And even though shamis continue to inspire passionate partisanship among home-cooks, there are just as many who consider them too plain.

Theatre actor-director and doctor Rishad Rizvi, a devout galawati fan, regards the shami as a decidedly plebeian creation. 'Shami is not on restaurant menus because it's not a delicacy. Usse dawati nahi samjha jata (It's not fancy enough for serving outside homes),' he said.

The old-timer regards the galawati as the superior kebab as making it requires more technique and elbow grease. 'Shamis can be made in an ordinary frying pan, but you need a mahi tawa and a special khurpi (tool with a flat blade) to turn galawatis. In galawatis, there is a lot of room to play with fragrance—meetha attar, kewra (screwpine) water, rose essence, saffron, and sandalwood powder are all added to make them. But these khushbu ke masale are not added to shamis.'

Another indicator of excellence is that Lucknow's old khansamas, held in high esteem for their time-honoured culinary skills, patronize galawatis and kakoris. 'Shamis are not even in the picture,' he pooh-poohed. Even in homes, Rishad claimed, shami is a breakfast or a pre-dinner bite, whereas galawati is served at special dinners. 'That's because galawati enhances the taste and spiciness of a korma, when combined in a niwala (morsel).'

Though Rishad made no bones about his preferences, he did point out that there is more to Lucknow's kebabs than the two under discussion. 'There are seventy-nine different varieties of kebabs being prepared in the city right now,' he said. 'Many of these—such as ghutwan kebab (with a runny, paste-like texture), boti kebab (cooked with keema, small bits of meat, and organ meat), majlisi (similar to ghutwan but with slightly different spices) labirein (very fine-textured kebab made with meat beaten with a hammer, mallet, or stone), patili kebab (simple koftas or meat balls cooked in salan), and pasande (heavily tenderized strips of meat cooked in thick salan)—are vanishing from tables. We need to save them too,' he underlined.

The Rampur Connection with Noor Khan

Although Lucknow is shami country par excellence, Ranveer had traced the kebab's beginnings in Uttar Pradesh to Rampur. To investigate its provenance, I met Noor Khan, a renowned Lucknow home-cook and founding member of the Mahindra Sanatkada's Awadhi Home Cooked Food Festival. The former principal of Karamat Husain College, known to serve some of the best kebabs in town, has family roots in Rampur—the maternal side of her family and her in-laws were from there.

The food curator concurred that shamis enjoy greater prominence on the table in Rampur. 'Galawatis didn't exist there. It was either shamis served with peeli mirch ki chutney (yellow chilli chutney), or kacchi tikia or seekh kebabs, made with raw mince. There was no concept of adding raw papaya to tenderize meat, like they do for making galawatis in Lucknow,' she said.

The kebabs of western Uttar Pradesh, Noor pointed out, have a different flavour profile from those of Lucknow. With the spirit of the countryside, Rampuri kebabs are chunkier and more robust, a characteristic she traced to the predominance of Pathans in the region. 'Owing to their tribal Pashtun roots, Pathans like their meat with a little texture, so all kebabs from that side of the state are chewier, bigger, and coarser,' she said. Lucknowites, by contrast, are more into delicacies or nazakat wale khane, and have a predilection for fall-apart-in-the-mouth texture. 'Yahan to bas cheez hothon pe rakhi aur nigal li. Itni zehmat na kare koi ke chabana pade kuch (People in Lucknow like things ultra-soft and can't be bothered making the effort to chew),' joked the epicure.

A diehard fan of Lucknowi shamis for their subtlety and seasonality, Noor loves to serve them at her parties. 'Pudina or chopped mint added to a shami in the hot season gives a burst of freshness in the mouth. It tastes just like a Lucknow summer,' she said, her face lighting up.

The Shamis of Yore with Sufia Kidwai

What was the shami of yesteryears like?

As a translator of old Awadhi tomes, Sufia Kidwai has a clue or two. The retired English professor, who loves geeking out over vintage cookbooks at her Hazratganj home, had volunteered to dig out a few from her collection. 'We could go over them together,' she offered me over a call, and promised a taste of her famed kebabs as a bonus.

When I entered her gate, Sufia was hunched over a stash of newspapers, lost in rumination. Her thriving winter garden, awash with colourful, scented flowers, was a delight for the senses. 'It's been a freezing winter. The world was feeling very grey, but now it's sunny again,' she said brightly, as I paused to admire a cluster of onion-pink dahlias.

Sufia had ferreted out two books for me. The first one, *The Classic Cuisine of Lucknow*, is the culinary memoir of Mirza Jafar Hussain. Translated from Urdu to English by Sufia, it chronicles the dishes the author grew up eating at the house of his grandfather, who was a physician for the last nawab of Lucknow, Wajid Ali Shah.

Brows furrowed in concentration, she read out the recipe for shamis in staccato sentences. Written using antiquated units of measurement like sers and chhataks, it was interesting in the subtle ways in which it differed from the current style of making kebabs. The process called for adding a slice of raw papaya to the keema before boiling. This suggests the technique of adding 'galawat', or tenderizing meat by adding raw papaya, may also have been used to make shamis at the time. Poppy seeds were occasionally used to season the mixture. Also, the filling for the kebabs was more elaborate and included finely shredded boiled egg and paneer.

The second book, *Hareemi Dastarkhan*, belonged to Sufia's mother. Published in 1949, it was authored by a magazine publisher who went by the pseudonym Hareem. Hareem's recipe placed the now-omitted stuffing at the very heart of the kebab. 'Shami kebab tikiyon ke un kababon ko kehte hai jinke andar pyaz katar kar bhari jati hai (A shami is defined as a kebab with a filling of chopped onions),' it said. It called for incorporating yoghurt or lemon juice to the kebab mix, adding fried onions for colour, and dipping the discs in a mixture of beaten eggs and a little saffron before shallow-frying them in ghee.

The session was instructive as it illustrated how dishes change over time. It allowed me a glimpse into the artisanal approach of previous generations towards kebab-making and the meticulous technique that would go into making the perfect shamis.

Sufia believes that shamis get a bad rap due to the mediocrity of the versions served today. 'It's true that most have been dumbed down,' she said. 'Everywhere I eat shamis, I find them tasting different. People skip the stuffing, add too much jeera, bulk up the keema mixture with potatoes, and deep-fry the kebabs.'

The kebabs at Sufia's home, made following the exactitude of her mother's recipe, were delicately spiced, with just-detectable cardamom, black pepper, and cinnamon. Making them the old-fashioned way helped Sufia realize how much pain and sweat her ammi would put into her cooking.

'It makes me feel like she is still around,' Sufia said softly.

Shami Masterclass with Shivraj Singh and Abha Singh at Khajurgaon Palace

If shamis had a culinary ambassador, it would undoubtedly be Shivraj Singh. The son of Raja Amresh Kumar Singh and Rani Abha Singh is a die-hard fan of the kebabs and considers making them from scratch as a dying art kept alive only at a handful of homes, including his own. When I expressed my keenness to learn, he persuaded his mother to unlock the secrets to making crisp, lacy-around-the-edges shamis for me.

Shivraj's residence, the beautiful Khajurgaon Palace, is richly decorated. I couldn't take my eyes off the pink-themed durbar, the Turkish frescoes, the Belgian glass chandeliers, the courtyard with arches. But Abha, who hails from the Kalakankar royal family of Uttar

Pradesh, was already waiting for me in her open, light-filled kitchen.

To make the kebabs, chana dal had been pre-soaked before being boiled along with hand-pounded mince—Abha used one part dal to four parts meat—and spices in a pressure cooker. The mixture had been manually pounded on a stone to achieve the delicate texture that is the hallmark of a good shami.

As she encouraged me to hand-form the kebabs, I eyed the plates of finely chopped onions, green chillies, and coriander leaves placed next to the kebab mixture. 'Should I mix it all in?' I asked.

'No, no. You must always stuff a shami. Most cooks these days mix the ingredients into the kebab mixture, but that's *not* the right way,' she scolded, demonstrating the art of stuffing the onion-and-green-chilli filling into the centre of each patty.

She shallow-fried the kebabs and cooked each patty until it developed a light crust from the griddle yet retained a high amount of juiciness inside. A garnish of coriander leaves was the final fragrant touch.

The end result was a satin-textured kebab with astonishing richness. The stuffing added a noticeable depth of flavour. Gingery and lemony flavours danced in every bite, anchored by the meaty warmth of the mince and lentils. The meaty morsels were paired with yakhni pulao and a runny mutton korma known as suruwa. 'We always end up eating this combination on Holi and Dussehra,' Shivraj revealed between mouthfuls.

The mother–son duo, who regard the shami as the original king of kebabs, were pleased to see me savour their family heirloom. 'If the recipe for shamis is perfectly followed, they turn out to be as soft as galawati kebabs with an additional burst of flavours from the filling. Now you have proof,' Abha said.

Making kebabs the way his ancestors did over two centuries ago is important to Shivraj. Not only is it a vital link to his past, but also an important safeguard against eroding traditions. 'It's at the very heart of being a real Awadhi. It's who we are,' he said passionately.

Breakfast with Sheeba Iqbal Jairajpuri at Azim Ally ki Kothi

For most Indians, shamis are a snack, but in Awadh, they're also a morning treat. Though often served with paranthas or pooris, the pairing of shamis with roghani tikiya, a ghee-enriched flatbread, is considered almost symbiotic in old Lucknow. 'You have to eat a nashta (breakfast) of kebab-tikia at my place before you leave,' trilled my friend Sheeba Iqbal Jairajpuri, who organizes Awadhi-themed culinary pop-ups at venues across India. I landed up the very next morning.

The enticing perfume of madhumalti, a type of lush red Rangoon creeper blooms, engulfed me as I entered Sheeba's quaint 125-year-old haveli at Chowk. She emerged from her spacious courtyard to greet me with a cheery smile. 'Aaiye, aaiye. Your Chowk-style nashta is waiting for you,' she said, guiding me indoors to her dining room with a high ceiling, ornate chandeliers, and arches fitted with multicoloured Belgian glass.

I wasn't expecting such a lavish spread. The table heaved with food—crumbly shamis; warm, flaky roghani tikias; thick-sliced potatoes seasoned with cumin; sweet pickles known as morabba; clotted cream; spicy scrambled eggs; shakkar or crumbled jaggery; hot ginger tea; and khadao ka doodh, or thickened milk lavished with nuts and strands of saffron. A big bowl of sautéed green peas, squirted with a little lemon juice, occupied pride of place at the centre of the spread.

Tucking into the shamis, I was delighted to discover a layer of cream in the filling. The trick, taught to Sheeba by her mother-in-law, gave the kebabs added creaminess and oomph.

The spread had the twin hallmarks of Awadhi food—subtle flavours and tantalizing aromas. But the poetic nomenclature of the dishes intrigued me the most—khagina (scrambled eggs), balai (cream), aloo ke qatle (potato roundels). Even the peas had a fancy name. 'When the season's first crop of peas hits the market, we call them nayi bahar or new glory. Their sweetness is unmatched,' Sheeba said, proudly sharing that she had hit the market early to snag the best bounty.

As she described the food, Sheeba enunciated vividly in Urdu, leaving me spellbound by the way the sounds rolled off her tongue. My own mangled attempts at pronunciation amused her to no end.

'No, no. It's khagina. Say "khh" from the epiglottis. And it's qatle, not katle. Speaking Urdu is not everyone's cup of tea,' she teased me with a cluck of her tongue.

Just when I thought I couldn't eat another morsel, the sharp, sugary smell of jalebis exploded in the room. To sate the sweet tooth, my hostess had called for a fresh batch from the famous Radhey Lal Sweets in Chowk. We crunched into the golden loops, loving the bursts of syrupy sweetness.

The glorious traditional Muslim breakfast sent me off with an entirely new appreciation for the shami as a breakfast star. The combination of textures and flavours awakened me to the richness and beauty of Awadhi morning meals.

As I was leaving, my hostess urged me to pronounce the word 'galawati' correctly. 'Please don't ever say "galoti" or "giloti" like they say in Delhi. It jars the ears and makes me lose my appetite,' she said with an eyeroll.

'Be grateful no one calls it gulati (Hindi word for a flip) kebab!' I joked. Sheeba doubled up with laughter.

Kebab Lunch with Shamona and Ishrat Khan at Nadiya Kinare

Lucknow is synonymous with culinary excess, so it is easy to leave the city without experiencing the flavours of everyday life. I longed to taste the city's daily home dishes.

The fare at Shamona and Ishrat Khan's place at Tilak Marg delivered this simplicity. The Pathan multipreneur called me over for an informal yet elegant lunch of shamis kebabs paired with arhar ki dal (pigeon peas) and matar ka pulao(peas pulao), a beloved winter combination in Lucknow. 'We'll make galawatis too, so make sure you show up hungry,' Shamona urged.

Joining us for lunch were Ishrat's mother Masarat, his maternal aunt Mumtaz, and his part-British uncle Tariq and his wife who were visiting from London. Ishrat's ancestors set up Asgar Ali Mohammad Ali, Lucknow's legendary perfumery known for its exquisite range of attars like kewra, rooh gulab, and amber.

Their heritage home, romantically named Nadiya Kinare, meaning 'by the river', due to its close proximity to the Gomti, is awash in nostalgia. Seated in their cavernous living room, we were surrounded by fragments of family history—the German piano that belonged to Ishrat's grandmother, the English love seat from where his grandfather would read out stories to his wife, a secretly lockable kitchen cabinet, hunting trophies, a vintage wooden knife for carving roasts, and dinner sets of rare porcelain. 'It's like a museum. Everything is ancient here,' Shamona said, grinning.

As lunch was laid out, the sweet, mellow smell of browned onions pervaded the room. There was matar ka pulao and methi aloo (potatoes sautéed with fenugreek), arhar ki dal, shamis, galawatis, aloo gosht ka salan (meat-and-potato curry), and raita. The winter flavours paired with the succulent kebabs was a winning combination. It was the sort of simple but full-flavoured fare impossible to find in restaurants.

We ate with our hands, licking our fingers instead of reaching for napkins. The shamis, stuffed with a delicious filling, gave off the merest fruity-floral whiff of kewra. But it was the galawatis that wowed me. Marinated overnight with raw papaya, fried onions, and the family's secret garam masala blend, they were like velvet down the throat. The kebabs were fragrant, complex, and exquisitely delicate. Well, mea culpa. I admitted reluctantly that the usually overhyped galawati can actually be a superlative kebab.

The recipe for both kinds of kebabs, perfected by their family cook Munna, had been with them for generations. 'We are emotionally very linked to them. They are like family jewels,' said Masarat, as she dug out stories from the family lore.

In this quaint house overlooking the river, Ishrat's high-spirited ancestors would host rollicking feasts. 'Such was the spirit of light-heartedness, that Ishrat's grandfather Abul Qasim Khan, who would entertain his British friends here before Independence, would jokingly ask them, "When do you plan to leave our country?"' Masarat recounted with a chuckle.

Along with banter, Awadh's self-assured cosmopolitanism was in abundant display during these massive gatherings. People of all faiths would laugh, eat, and listen to qawwalis together in keeping with the city's Ganga-Jamuni tehzeeb (high culture underpinned by the amalgamation of different religions). 'It's incredible how much bonding would happen over food in our home. Even the bitterest fights would dissolve over helpings of perfectly made kebabs and korma,' she reminisced fondly.

The carefully preserved legacy continues to be a starring ingredient in the family's annual dastarkhwans. 'On Eid we have around 200 guests visiting us, almost all non-Muslims. They love our kebabs, just as we love playing teen patti or cards with our Hindu friends on Diwali. That, to us, is the true spirit of Awadh,' said Ishrat, though he sadly acknowledged the erosion of this culture in current times.

Masarat viewed the shami as both an edible and a symbol of Awadh's imperilled syncretism. 'If we can save shami, we might just save what is most precious to us—our tehzeeb,' she said, voice heavy with emotion.

Awadhi Feast with Syed Ahmad Bilal at Gomti Nagar

'The whole world seems to think that Lucknowites only know how to make kebabs and pulao. It's time to prove them wrong,' declared my friend Syed Bilal Ahmad in a booming voice, as he invited me to partake of an old-fashioned, no-holds-barred family dawat. To my delight, he also invited our mutual friend Adity Chakravarti, the author of the acclaimed book *Reha'ish: At Home in Lucknow*, along with her son Aaditya.

Bilal, who runs a food and beverage marketing agency in Lucknow, lives in tony Gomti Nagar. As I showed up at his upscale home, he introduced me to his wife Huma, an IT professional; his mother, Doctor Tabinda Khwaja aka Ammi; and his brother Uzair, who runs a chain of cloud kitchens. Bilal's maternal uncle and aunt, who live with the family, joined us too.

The table was loaded even by Lucknow standards. Mutton shamis, kakori kebabs, murgh musallam (whole roasted chicken), mutton do piaza (thick mutton curry with onions), fried quail, maash ki dal (urad lentils), mutton pulao, fish korma, mutton kofte (meatball curry), and raita. The surprise standout was a platter of turai ke shami, made from ridge gourd peels. With a crisp outer texture and soft interior, the vegetarian shamis were a tad spicier than their non-veg counterpart, though no less delectable.[4]

'Ammi took a day off from work to cook everything. She very much loves playing hostess, and we love the fun and chaos of it all,' said Huma, modestly underplaying her own contribution to the effort.

'What, how on Earth did you pull off this feast in a single day?' Adity exclaimed, turning to Ammi, as a chorus of praise erupted for the super-cook.

The food bordered on sublime. I couldn't pick a favourite dish—the thin, tangy fish curry punched up with tamarind, or the deliriously tender mutton do piaza. Finally, my vote went to the murgh musallam. The sumptuous, golden-skinned bird made for a stunning centrepiece and rendered the most divine juices.

The mutton shamis were succulent, moist, and finely wrought. When I praised their smooth texture, Ammi shared her secret sauce—adding a bit of ground poppy seeds and coconut to the kebab for extra softness. I relished the veg variant too, another prized family recipe.

Chatting with my hosts, I discovered that the famous Awadh–Hyderabad culinary rivalry caused the fiercest food debates in their household. Huma, who grew up in Hyderabad, was partial to shikampuri, the Hyderabadi variant of shami, filled with yoghurt, coriander, mint, and chopped onions. 'I'm in the minority, but I don't give up without a fight,' she said.

'That's not fair. Bilal made Hyderabadi biryani and red chicken for you through the pandemic. You forgot that already?' Uzair asked, putting Huma on the backfoot.

'It's true. My husband really pampers me. He is a great cook,' she complimented, making Bilal blush.

When the conversation segued to the declining popularity of shamis, a palpable cloud came over the table. Sensing the dip in the mood, Ammi disappeared for a few moments and returned with platters of gooey shahi tukda (fried bread slices soaked in sweetened milk) and delicate phirni (milk-and-ground-rice pudding). The sweet treats, as delectable as the plates that preceded them, cheered everyone up for another round of banter and fun.

As the plates were cleared, Bilal recited a couplet for the gathering. '"Sar-e-aatish jo ashk rezaan tha, kisi aashiq ki thi kebab mein jaan (No doubt this kebab has a lover's mind. Fire and tears together where else would you find)!"

'These lines from Lucknow's famous poet Ghulam Hamdani Mushafi perfectly sum up the emotion we Lucknow-walas feel for our kebabs,' he said, as the curtain descended on our modern-day dastarkhwan.

Scented Shami with Chef Mohsin Qureshi at Azrak

Shami's glory days as a restaurant star may have passed, but a few worthy spots remain. Along with home-cooks, there is a coterie of chefs who are working to revive the dish.

Mohsin Qureshi, the bearded executive chef of Lucknow's Saraca Hotel, strongly believes that Awadh's closely guarded knowledge of aromatic roots, spices, and essences put its cuisine above others. As we chatted at Saraca's blue-themed restaurant Azrak, he insisted that the key to a great shami is the region's prized khushbu ke masale.

A trayful of jadi bootis (herbs) had been arranged for me to get a whiff. Some were native to Awadh, while others originated from places as far as Spain. Chock-full of medicinal properties, Mohsin traced their popularity back to the hakims (traditional physicians) of Awadh, many of whom turned cooks during the reign of the nawabs.

Mohsin pointed out the ones he used to make shamis—kababa, nagarmotha, kokeela, and jatamasi. I crushed the esoteric seeds and pods with my fingers. Each had a distinctive aroma, pure and intense. 'They impart a lovely finish to the shami. You will be able to taste my kebab two hours after you have eaten it,' Mohsin said.

Along with aromatics, Mohsin likes a bit of fat in there as well. 'Most people use lean meat, but a little charbi (fat) reverses the drying effect of dal and ensures that the kebab stays seductively moist,' he said. A gooey khoa-and-curd filling was yet another inspired touch. 'Try it. You'll know the difference right away,' he said, as he proudly presented his masterpiece garnished with ruby-like kernels of pomegranate.

The kebab was gorgeously fragranced. 'Bottle this scent for me, please,' I said, making him glow with pride. The taste, all silky meat and tantalizing spice notes, was just as elegant. Mining secrets from the era of the nawabs, it epitomized Awadh's flair for layering flavours.

There was a finesse and a kind of ethereal quality to Mohsin's creation. It was proof that the no-frills shami could become an ultra-luxe creation in the hands of a master.

◆

My time in Lucknow was utterly gratifying. Seduced by the city's slow-cooked charm, I wanted to stay forever in this oasis of romance, poetry, and overflowing meals.

I'm happy I tasted the shami in places where people still consider it precious and prepare it with skill, knowledge, passion, and love. It was revelatory that something so familiar could have so many regional and seasonal variations.

The most important lesson I took away from my visit was realizing that things can—and do—go extinct if we don't nurture them. The food world is capricious. Ingredients and tastes change. Not every dish stands the test of time.

Shami kebab represents a whole world of foods from our country's past that is now less ubiquitous, but no less delicious than its more popular counterparts. A masterpiece of the kebab genre, it's a classic worth reviving. The winning combination of dal and meat makes it unique, and also a healthier alternative to meat-only kebabs.

The cyclical nature of human cravings gives me hope. The '20-year Rule', a commonly referenced concept in the fashion industry, states that what's popular now will be popular again in twenty years. It applies equally to the culinary world. Food trends are always on repeat as we are influenced by what previous generations ate. Pretty much everything that's retro is becoming relevant again. If meat loaf and baked Alaska can make a comeback, why not shamis?

Indian Accent's duck shamis, created way back in 2010 by Chef Manish Mehrotra,[5] are proof that the kebabs are indeed fair game for experimentation. Elevating the kebab from its Plain-Jane status, the groundbreaking chef reimagined it as a patty of duck meat crisped with sevia (thin threads) of kataifi pastry and served with a tart barberry chutney. The stunner, paired with a full-bodied malbec, continues to be a bestseller on the restaurant's menu.

Such creativity inspires confidence. Perhaps a chef-y overhaul will reinscribe the classic's place in India's culinary life. Or maybe someone on TikTok or the Gram will take a fancy to the neglected classic and turn it into internet gold.

I hope shami is reborn, more delicious than ever, and becomes the new cult favourite. But even if that doesn't happen, it will remain my favourite kebab.

To me, a shami is forever.

Recipes from My Travels

SHEEBA IQBAL JAIRAJPURI'S SHAMI KEBABS

MAKES: 14–16 KEBABS　　TIME TAKEN: 1 HOUR

INGREDIENTS

Mutton keema	500 gms, hand-pounded
Chana dal	100 gms
Whole red chillies	3
Ginger	1-inch piece, chopped
Garlic	5–6 cloves, chopped
Bay leaves	2
Onions	2, coarsely chopped
Cumin	1 tbsp
Black peppercorns	1 tsp
Green cardamom	5
Black cardamom	3
Nutmeg	¼
Mace	2 flowers
Cinnamon	1 inch
Star anise	1

For filling,

Malai	½ cup
Green coriander	a handful, chopped
Green chillies	1-2, chopped
Onion	½, finely chopped
Mustard oil	3 tbsp

METHOD

Put the ingredients for the kebabs, excluding the ones for the filling, in a pressure cooker along with 1 tbsp water.

Let it cook till the first whistle on a high flame, then reduce the flame and let it cook for 10 minutes.

Switch off the gas and let it cool.

Open the pressure cooker lid and check for any water content. If there is any water remaining, cook the keema on a high flame without stirring so that the excess water dries up.

Once the mixture is cooled, remove the spices. Grind the spices and the keema, each separately, on a silbatta (hand-operated stone grinder) until smooth.

Shape the patties and make an indent at the centre of each.

Put around ½-1 tsp malai along with chopped onions, green chillies, and coriander in the indent. Close the indents and reshape the patties.

Once the patties are shaped and ready to cook, heat 3 tbsp mustard oil on a hot tawa and fry them on both sides until golden-brown.

Serve hot with onion rings, slit green chillies, and green chutney.

Tip: Instead of malai, you could also use good-quality cream cheese or hung curd for the stuffing.

TABINDA KHWAJA'S TURAI KE SHAMI

SERVES: 4 TIME TAKEN: 45 MINUTES

INGREDIENTS

Turai peels	300 gms
Chana dal	125 gms, pre-soaked
Onion	1, chopped
Ginger	2 inch, chopped
Garlic	8–10, chopped
Green chillies	1–2, chopped
Garam masala	¼ tsp
Salt	to taste
Water	100 ml

For the stuffing,

Onion	½, finely chopped
Green chilli	1, chopped
Green coriander	a handful, chopped
Oil	2 tbsp

METHOD

Wash the turai (ridge gourd) peels and cut them into small pieces.

Rinse the chana dal thoroughly.

In a pressure cooker, add the ridge gourd peels, chana dal, chopped onion, ginger, garlic, green chillies, garam masala, and salt.

Add water and pressure-cook for 10-15 minutes until the dal and ridge gourd peels are soft and well cooked.

Once cooked, remove excess water and allow the mixture to cool slightly.

Mince the mixture in a mixer until smooth.

Add finely chopped green coriander, green chillies, and onion to the mixture.

Shape the mixture into kebabs of tikki size.

Heat a nonstick pan with 2 tbsp oil. Shallow-fry the kebabs until golden-brown on both sides.

Serve hot with onion rings and lemon wedges.

INDIAN ACCENT'S DUCK SHAMI, CRISPY SEVIA, BARBERRY CHUTNEY

SERVES: 4 TIME TAKEN: 30 MINUTES PLUS COOLING

INGREDIENTS

For duck shami,

Duck legs	500 gms, cooked and chopped
Ghee	5 tbsp
Ginger	1 tbsp, chopped
Garlic	1½ tbsp, chopped
Deggi mirch powder	1 tsp
Makhani gravy	½ cup or 100 gms
Green chillies	2–3, chopped
Garam masala powder	1 tsp
Chaat masala	2 tbsp
Saunth (tamarind) chutney	5 tbsp
Fresh coriander	a handful, chopped

For barberry chutney,

Mint chutney	3 tbsp
Saunth chutney	5 tbsp
Chaat masala	1 tsp
Barberries	25 gms

For crispy sevia,

Kataifi pastry	30 gms (available frozen in gourmet stores)
Oil	2 cups, for frying

METHOD

For duck shami mixture,

Heat 4 tbsp ghee in a pan, add ginger and garlic and sauté till golden. Add the deggi mirch powder and makhani gravy and let it simmer.

Bhunao (sauté) the mix for 2 minutes; add green chillies, garam masala, chaat masala, and mix well.

Add the chopped cooked duck and saunth chutney. Mix evenly and cook till the mixture is semi-dry and a bit sticky so as to hold its shape.

Sprinkle chopped coriander and allow the mixture to cool.

Make balls of 40 gms each from the mixture, then make them into patties.

Apply 1 tbsp ghee in a griddle or a pan and sear the kebabs on both sides until golden-brown.

For barberry chutney,

Put mint chutney, saunth chutney, chaat masala, and barberries in a blender until smooth.

For crispy sevia,

In hot oil, immerse a metallic tea strainer and swirl kataifi in until crisp.

Drain excess oil with a tea towel and set aside.

Arrange hot seared shamis on a platter and garnish with crispy sevia. Serve with barberry chutney.

Tip: In case you don't find duck legs, you could use cooked chicken mince instead. Cranberries could be used instead of barberry. The chicken keema mixture could be made into a smooth paste in a blender. Instead of kataifi, you could shred spring roll sheets or phyllo pastry sheets and fry them.

For makhani gravy (recipe by Chef Amit Pamnani),

Tomato	200 gms
Garlic	2–3, chopped
Kashmiri chilli powder	1 tsp
Cashew nuts	5–6
Butter	1 tbsp
Honey	1 tsp
Sugar	1 tsp
Green cardamom	1

METHOD

Add all the ingredients, except the butter and the honey, in a vessel.

Cover and cook on a slow flame for 20–25 minutes until the tomatoes are soft.

Switch off the flame, let it cool, and blend the gravy until smooth.

Strain the gravy; add butter and honey and use as required.

Chhole

THE BEAN-EATERS

A plate of chhole gives me a warm, fuzzy feeling. My grandmother would make it for me whenever I visited her in Ghaziabad, as a child.

By the end of the hour-long journey from Delhi to my grandparents' home, my belly would be growling. The entire house would be redolent of Dadima's pot of succulent goodness, which needed nothing but discs of puffed pooris or bhaturas to mop it up.

Chhole masala, a family recipe dating back to pre-Partition times, would be prepared in her trusty iron kadhai. The spicy flavours combined to produce something extraordinary. I adored the slightly fruity, tangy flavour of the anardana, or dried pomegranate seeds which she would use to spike the dark mess.

Chhole was Dadima's favourite too. She had learnt to make it from my great-grandmother as a newlywed in Lahore. My grandfather completed his education and married my grandmother in the city. He shifted to Lucknow before the Partition along with my great-grandfather and started working with a Dutch oil company.

Though my grandparents did not experience the trauma of Partition that millions did, Dadima missed her first home after marriage, which they left behind in Lahore and to which they could never return.

A bowl of chhole always brought with it a bout of storytelling. Dadima would talk of hosting parties for my grandfather's bridge buddies, retail therapy at Lahore's favourite shopping haunt Anarkali Bazaar, and weekend visits to Gujranwala's malta-laden orchards.

Given the proximity between Lahore and Amritsar, Dadima embellished her recipe for chhole and other Punjabi dishes whenever she visited the latter city. Despite a profusion of brilliant chhole-bhature spots in Delhi—including the iconic Kwality founded by Pishori Lal Lamba, who came from Lahore in 1940—she remained partial to the fare of the Golden City. 'You need to go to Amritsar to eat chhole, my child,' she would often say, her deep-set eyes lighting up.

As it happened, I didn't get to Amritsar until nearly two decades after her passing. When I did, I decided to make chhole the focus of my visit.

As you enter Amritsar, the sweet, nutty perfume of boiling chickpeas is everywhere, enveloping the city in a cosy haze. Amritsaris can't get enough of its irresistible chestnut-ish flavour or its dense, velvety texture. The heart-shaped beans are an unavoidable part of day-to-day life in the city. Regardless of time, somewhere in Amritsar, there is a plate of chhole being devoured.

But if Amritsaris are partial to chhole, it is not because the beans were the first kind they ever ate. K. T. Achaya points out, in *Indian Food: A Historical Companion*, that though the Bengal gram or desi kala chana is native to India, the bigger, blond kabuli chana is a fairly recent addition, and probably came to India 'in the eighteenth century CE from the Mediterranean by an overland route'.

Though the white chickpea has its roots in Turkey, Amritsaris have embraced the delicious staple as their own. Chhole in all its guises is the language of comfort and an expression of shared pleasure. Indeed, if one were to think of an Indian equivalent to the white bean-loving Tuscans, who are known as 'mangiafagioli' (bean-eaters in Italian), it would be the Amritsaris.

You could be forgiven for thinking of all Amritsari chickpea dishes as one big homogenous offering. But chhole or chane[1] are more of a genre than a single dish in the Golden City. From crispy, spicy snacks and tangy sides to hearty mains, the legumes show up just about everywhere. There's a chickpea dish to appease the gods, another to cure the sniffles, a third to serve as a party nibble, and a fourth to eat as a gluten-free salad.

Though regarded as the quintessential dhaba dish, there are wonderfully intimate home recipes too, made using simple, fresh ingredients and time-revered techniques.

I craved a taste of both.

DHABA CHHOLE

Chickpea Trail with Gayatri Peshawaria

Amritsar's itinerant food culture stems from an unabashed love for eating out.

At the heart of this fondness are the city's dhabas, the legendary roadside eateries famed for their spanking fresh food, and oceans of ghee and butter. It was these charmingly kitschy joints, first set up by the displaced people of Punjab during the country's Partition that helped spread the gospel of chhole to other parts of India.

Each joint tends to have its own specialties, perfected over years of hard work and reflective of the owner's roots. Many offer a long list of options: chhole masala, palak chhole, aloo chhole, chawal chhole, aloo tikki-chhole, samosa chhole.

Such a wealth of choices can be overwhelming for the first-time visitor. Happily, Gayatri Peshawaria, a consummate content creator and a former food and wine journalist, offered to help me work through this delicious dilemma. 'We're going on a week-long chhole-tasting excursion. And remember, this is Amritsar. Please ignore your belly,' announced the born-and-bred Amritsari in a tone that brooked no further argument.

Right at the outset, my vivacious guide explained the cardinal chickpea rule observed by Amritsaris. Eating the dish, whether at home or at a restaurant, calls for a sacrosanct distinction between the chhole you eat with bhaturas (deep-fried leavened flatbread) and those you eat with kulchas (baked leavened flatbreads). Plain or saade chhole are eaten with kulchas. The chickpeas are simply boiled and lightly flavoured with masalas and don't have any ghee or oil. Bhaturas, pooris, luchis (fried flatbread made from maida), and samosas, on the other hand, are eaten with tadke wale chhole, in which cooked chickpeas get a tempering of tomatoes, onions, ginger-garlic, and spices in pure desi ghee.

As much as cooks like to experiment with more creative takes on chhole, Gayatri revealed, this long-standing distinction is generally honoured. The underlying logic is simple. Bhaturas, being fried, work better with tadke wale chhole, whereas kulchas are baked and pair well with saade chhole. Fried with fried. Baked with non-greasy. Makes sense.

Like most locals, Gayatri has strong opinions about where to eat. 'Amritsaris can be very fussy about where we eat. Tourist traps are a no-no. We are looking for that authentic Amritsari taste with the correct spices,' she said.

A breakfast of kulche with chhole is where the legume truly rules. We started off with Gayatri's favourite, Bahadur Kulcha Corner, a nondescript cubbyhole comprising two tables, a tandoor, and a tiny room the size of a broom closet. The chhole here came paired with thick potato-stuffed Amritsari kulchas and chutney. As I tucked into my meal, I was consumed by the warm gooeyness of the chickpeas and the way they played against the crisp yet moist kulchas.

The next day found us at All India Famous Amritsari Kulcha on Maqbool Road, one of the city's revered breakfast haunts. The late Anthony Bourdain gave it a rave review during his India travels, vaulting the ramshackle shack to global stardom. Seated on rickety plastic chairs, we watched a kulcha specialist stuff a mixture of potato, paneer, and cauliflower mixture into a ball of layered dough, close it up like a dumpling and roll it out. He then tossed the disc, frisbee-like, to his co-worker, who caught it mid-air and plastered it onto the tandoor. The final touch—slathering unreal amounts of butter on the flaky flatbread.

Humidity caused our hair to curl around our faces as we tore pieces of the big fluffy, doughy kulchas. The chhole were plain, but it was the tongue-tingling jolt of the chutney, an electric mix of tamarind water, onions, chopped raw mangoes, green chillies, and spices that made the meal soar. Light, tangy, and packed with flavour, this chhole-and-salsa mix was the ideal dunk for the crispy, buttery flatbread. 'The trick is to give a taste of everything in one bite,' Gayatri said. I did and was rewarded with simultaneous hits of sweet and sour, crisp and buttery, sharp and mild, silky and toothsome.

The following day, we ate breakfast at Kanha Sweets on Lawrence Road, famed for its poori-chana served with aloo launji, a sweet-sour potato preparation laced with fennel and a hint of sugar. The pooris were larger than usual, and crisp with a thin layer of spiced dal stuffing. The combination was inspired, the mellow spiciness of the chhole getting a spike of tanginess from the launji. On Gayatri's suggestion, we amped up the meal with gajar ka achaar (carrot pickle), gur ka halwa (jaggery halwa), and a large glass of sweet lassi. 'It's a carbohydrate and sugar bonanza,' she said brightly, clearly not seeing the formidable portions of food as a problem.

The next evening, Gayatri took me to Basant Avenue for bo wale kulche. A uniquely Amritsari creation, I first read about it in Vikas Khanna's book *Amritsar: Flavours of the Golden City.* The Amritsar-born chef fondly recalled making trips to his father's store in the area, just to eat the 'stinky' kulchas, so called because of the bo, or smell imparted to the baked leavened flatbread by the fermentation of the dough. Made by Himachali cooks from Kangra, the bheege kulche get their distinctive flavour from yeast known as khameer.

The squishy, yeast-risen kulchas were dunked into a drum containing copious amounts of chhole, which were thicker and darker than those served at Kanha. The drenched kulchas were then removed, topped with a couple more ladles of chhole, and wreathed with a garnish of onions, raw mangoes, green chillies, and amla (Indian gooseberry) before being served.

'Why dunk a perfectly crisp kulcha?' I asked, unable to hide my disenchantment at the idea of eating soggy, limp bread.

'Because us Amritsaris swear by it. The kulchas are the perfect foil for the spicy chhole. It's our mac and cheese,' Gayatri scolded gently, explaining that when one eats it, it's not just chhole or kulche one tastes, but the whole gestalt of the dish.

I took more of a shine to the matthi-chana combo, another Amritsari special served at the same joint. Crumbly matthi, a flaky savoury seasoned with cumin seeds, was topped with the same chhole and finished off with mint chutney. The final touch was a sprinkling of raw amla pieces for some punch. The result was crusty yet mushy, tangy yet herby—a genius marriage of textures and flavours.

Gayatri, who had shared a close bond with her late grandfather, revealed that the crispy treat was his favourite as well. 'Dada's evening snack would always be matthi-chana from Basant Avenue. I remember him sitting in his garden on his favourite wrought iron chair. With his glass of masala chai, he would open the humble plastic bag of matthi-chana with the excitement of a kid in a candy store. With great care, he would assemble the matthi on his plate and top it with chana, almost like a crostini, and garnish it with the toppings. Then, with the evening song of the koel on the gulmohar tree and the garden fragrant from a fresh sprinkling of water, he would feast on his favourite snack like a king,' she recounted.

On day five, Gayatri and I woke up early and made a pilgrimage to the gold-and-marble shrine of Shri Harmandir Sahib to offer our prayers (and for the divine ghee-smothered kada prasad). Later, we visited the Partition Museum at the historic Town Hall building. Among the exhibits that caught my eye was a set of utensils—a plate and a bowl made of bronze, and a brass lassi glass, owned by one Kamal Bammi's family before Partition. These, as per the museum caption, were 'brought across from their house by a Muslim friend of the family, when he travelled from Pakistan to visit them in Delhi in 1949'. Preserved as a result of tragedy, the relics were shot through with heart-wrenching pathos.

Lunch was at the nearby Bharawan Da Dhaba. More a full-scale restaurant than a dhaba, the atmosphere here was busy and the crowd diverse—everyone from moustache-twirling truck drivers to suit-clad bankers. T-shirt-clad waiters navigated the large, packed-to-the-rafters space with an air of brusque efficiency. 'Don't expect politeness,' Gayatri said, winking at me as we settled on a lunch of chana masala with lachha (ringed) parathas. Within minutes we were served plates of piping hot chickpeas softened in a braise of onions, ginger-garlic, anardana, and spices. The cooked beans, I noticed, had retained their shape perfectly, unlike the mushy saade chane served with kulchas.

The dhaba's owner, Subhash Vij, who joined us as we ate, told us that his grandfather Diwan Chand Vij had started the eatery from a tent when he emigrated to Amritsar from Pakistan's Sialkot in 1912. 'In those days, the trend of going out to eat at restaurants wasn't there.

People would just come and buy chhole or dal to take home. Things were so cheap. You could buy a good quantity of chhole for as little as 25 paise! Today, they sell for ₹100-150 a kilo, but at that time you could get a whole bori (sack) for ₹50!' he said.

At Subhash's insistence, we also got a second course of bharta (grilled eggplant mash), palak paneer (paneer braised with spinach), and malai kofta (paneer and potato balls in a creamy gravy). Everything was first-rate, creating the quintessential dhaba experience—hearty, unpretentious, and reasonably priced. I fell hard for their doodh-chawal ki kheer (milk-and-rice pudding)—creamy yet light as a dream, a testament to the superlative quality of dairy in Amritsar.

On day six, Gayatri took me to Namak Mandi. Crowds swirled noisily around us as we made our way to meet the fourth-generation owner of the legendary Dharam Pal Sethi (DPS) Chholeya Wale, Akash Sethi, in the old city. Seating us inside his tiny open kitchen, he ordered a plate of their famous chana masala. Seasoned impeccably, the mushy stew of chocolate-coloured chickpeas was medium spicy, and came with tamarind chutney, chopped green coriander, and coils of green chillies.

Akash, who wholeheartedly celebrated his pre-Partition roots, proudly shared that DPS got its start way back in 1895 when his great-grandfather Kahan Chand Sethi began making chhole to eke out a living. After moving to Amritsar post Partition, three generations of the family had transformed their small business into a local landmark known as much for its soulful renderings of chhole as for its chana masala powder. The proprietary spice blend, first created by Akash's great-grandfather, is a rage among Amritsaris. I bought some on my way out.

Kesar Da Dhaba, regarded as the gastronomic touchstone of the city, was impossible to bypass. Its velvety dal fry, slow-cooked overnight and tempered freshly before being served, is legendary, but the revered eatery also cooks superb chhole. A ten-minute rickshaw ride through the Old City alleyway of Chowk Passian got us to the icon. As we claimed a side table, its current owner, Ramesh Kumar Mehra, greeted us cheerfully.

Justifiably proud of his family's four-generation reputation for quality, Ramesh recounted how his great-grandfather, Lala Kesar Mal, started Kesar from Sheikhpura, a small town near Lahore, in 1916. After moving to Amritsar during the Partition, he restarted the business and carefully built up a menu of Punjabi staples like dal fry, palak paneer, and kadhi chawal (curd-and-besan dish with steamed rice). 'He started with dal fry and laccha paratha. My great-grandmother, Paarvati Devi, joined him. At that time, freedom fighters used to have meals at our place. It was just a small place. When the dhaba started running well, he added chhole to the menu, which became a roaring success. It's been 109 years and dal fry and chhole fry are still the most popular dishes at Kesar.'

Ramesh suggested we get the chhole fry with rice. What made the chhole remarkable (apart from the mandatory 'secret' spice blend) was the process of cooking them over a low flame over coals in copper vessels, which enhanced the taste. Plump from slowly absorbing the aromatic spices in which they were cooked, and punctuated by gulps of sweet lassi capped with a dense layer of white butter, they made for hearty country fare designed to fill the belly.

After finishing my meal, we lingered for a while at Kesar. Draining the last drops of lassi from my glass, I looked back at the week gone by with a sense of satisfaction. My dhaba-crawl had been illuminating. Devouring the city's best with Gayatri had made me appreciate how varied and creative Amritsari chhole are.

Every dhaba was an adventure unto itself, with its own special vibe. But it was Kesar, with a strong flavour of its pre-Partition history, that I found the most compelling. Maybe it was the picturesquely distressed setting, or the gentle whirring of air coolers, but just crossing the threshold of this colourfully chaotic wonderland had made me deeply nostalgic.

It was easy to imagine how refugees from Pakistan, upon first arriving in India, would have transformed a thrifty pot of chhole into a dish that is so much more than the sum of its parts.

Scrambling to survive, these modest, self-taught cooks would have burnished the golden beans to start their makeshift businesses.

Making a pot of chhole would have brought them hope, a cure for homesickness, financial empowerment, and a sense of starting over.

The subtext made me acutely conscious of my surroundings. Here in this bastion, built upon hard-won dreams, I could appreciate my grandmother's favourite comfort food at its most soul-stirring, steeped in remembrance.

HOMEMADE CHHOLE

Amritsar's home-cooks are just as besotted with chickpeas as its dhabas. It's a favourite dish they love to make and eat at home on a regular basis—and not just when they are entertaining.

I was craving a taste of these family dishes, synonymous with cosiness and joy. Fortunately, Abhimanyu Rattan Mehra stepped in and invited me to his boutique hotel and offered to host a weekend of home-cooking.

The hotel, called Ranjit's SVAASA, is a 200-year-old red-sandstone haveli steeped in history. Old-school charm pervades the historic mango-tree-lined property. The stately kothi is Abhimanyu's home. It's where his forefathers lived and where he and his brothers played as children. The original structure of the building has been retained and looks much the same as it did two centuries ago.

Abhimanyu comes from a long line of luminaries. The rooms of the property are named after his ancestors—Rattan Chand, Raja Singh, Kalyan Singh, Lal Chand. Originally from Peshawar, they had come and settled in the walled city and served as the sarvarah (the management team of the Golden Temple before the formation of the Shiromani Gurdwara Parbandhak Committee) during the late 1800s. His grandfather, Dev Chand Mehra, started the Ritz Hotel and brought in the first international airline, Ariana Afghan Airlines, into Amritsar.

SVAASA, curated by Abhimanyu's mother Rama Ranjit Mehra, was a tribute to his father Ranjit Rattan Mehra, a well-known hotelier, whom the family tragically lost to cancer. 'Svaas means breath in Sanskrit. We believe dad's breath and blessings still pervade this place,' he said softly.

The scion showed me around with pride, pointing out framed photos of his forebearers, a beautiful Persian carpet gifted to his father by an Afghan (who got stranded in Amritsar and eventually got back home thanks to his father's intervention), and the sprawling courtyard, once a massive kitchen where a line of cooks would sit, chopping vegetables and grinding fresh spices to make his grandfather's beloved dishes.

Like the haveli, the diverse dishes that made up our lunch were a part of family lore. Amritsari chhole masala, gobi (cauliflower) pulao, beetroot raita, and the piece de resistance, a whole tandoori singhara (catfish) encased in a metal grill and basted over fire. 'They are all my grandfather's favourites, passed down to mum, and then to me. Dada ji wasn't a cook as much as a lover and connoisseur of good food, poetry, and music. He loved to entertain. Though he never touched alcohol, he was always the life of the party,' Abhimanyu shared.

The chhole, spiced with amchur, onion, and ginger slivers, and darkened with tea leaves, formed an integral part of the menu at SVAASA, especially for vegetarian diners. 'At home, we always make it for parties and enjoy it with pooris or laccha parathas. It's my favorite, and even more mouth-watering when we add a bit of puréed spinach sautéd with kasuri methi. The colour does not change, but the texture makes it dribble a bit. It just blows me away.'

As we ate, Abimanyu attempted to trace the white chickpea's roots in Amritsar. Kabuli chana, which originated in the Mediterranean, came to the city when undivided Punjab extended all the way to current-day Pakistan, he said. 'Amritsar was a very important city on the ancient Great Silk Road, which connected the East and the West. Being a dry port, it was the hub of trade. Green and black tea would come in from Darjeeling to Amritsar and be sent to Afghanistan in exchange for dry fruits. My guess is that white chickpeas came in that way too, as part of trade, en route from Afghanistan via Lahore. I assume this is also how tea leaves must have, through experimentation, found their way as an ingredient in the Amritsari chhole masala.'

The hotelier attributed the popularity of chhole in Amritsar to two main reasons. First, the mineral-rich, sweet water of the city (Amritsar is located between the rivers Ravi and Beas) made the otherwise hard to digest bean a lot easier on the stomach. Second, the combination of the fibre- and protein-rich dish eaten with carbs made it a cheap yet complete meal for all.[2] The different communities living in the city—Sikhs, Marwaris, Jains, Muslims, and others—have all adapted chhole as per their own tastes, which reflects in the widely varied approaches to making the dish.

The chickpea's creamy texture not only pairs well with heavy spices, it is also an ideal match with all kinds of breads. 'Thanks to our unique brand of Amritsari fusion, we love to eat chhole with just about anything—bhaturas, pooris, tandoori kulchas, bheege kulche, buns, even samosas and aloo tikkis,' he said.

As the conversation turned more personal, my host delved into his own memories. He vividly recalled how his mother's chhole-poori would be waiting for him and his brothers Vishal and Iqbal when they returned from school on Monday afternoons. After a quick shower, the trio would sit on the carpet, covered with a white cloth to protect it from stains, and eat out of thalis. 'The noisy window AC would be on, and my mother, dashing in and out of the kitchen, would be breathless as she fed three hungry boys,' he recounted.

The simple meal was always followed by slices of fresh, sweet watermelon. But the most special part of the meal would come in just before that, as the brothers split up a final poori to mop up any leftover masala or chana from the bowl. 'It was similar to the way you would use your fingers to lick off leftover chocolate cake batter,' Abhimanyu recounted.

To date, it was this image that came to his mind every time he ate chhole at home. 'It's a dish I eat with my entire being,' he said. 'If I close my eyes, I can still taste that shared bowl of deliciousness.'

The Lahore Connection

The next day, Abhimanyu introduced me to his friend Navneet Singh, who was visiting from the UK. A psychotherapist specializing in addictions, he has a past in hospitality as well. His family owned the now-closed Hotel Astoria. Along with his father, he formerly ran two restaurants, Astoria Food Pavilion and Oka café, on Amritsar's Ranjit Avenue, before relocating to London in 2022.

For Navneet, who grew up here, chhole was a long-established tradition, to be honoured with friends and family. He has his own take on the craze for the dish in the city. 'The recipe for plain or saade chhole does not include the use of any root vegetables and is therefore acceptable across religions. Also, it can be eaten boiled without any oil or ghee, which makes it very economical for all sections of society.' Navneet likes eating them in all forms, including besan or chickpea flour. 'Just on this trip I must have eaten varieties of chickpeas at least ten times in 21 days,' he said. 'You can take the man out of Amritsar but you can never take chhole out of an Amritsari!'

Interestingly, he has a Lahore link (his great-grandfather owned farm land on the outskirts of Lahore before Partition) and was able to point out the key differences between the chhole of the Twin Cities.[3] 'Chhole in Lahore is more of a breakfast item as opposed to the all-day sport it is here in Amritsar. There, it is often enjoyed with soft naans and cooked along with meats of different kinds, including the famous Lahori murgh chhole, a spicy chickpea and chicken dish. The range varies from shorba or soupy dishes to thicker gravies. Traditionally, rogan or fat would be added as the meal was meant to fuel you up for a day of hard work.'

More Lahore talk happened with Manpreet Sidhu, an Amritsar-based producer, actor, and entrepreneur, who has worked on major films like the Dev Patel-starrer *The Wedding Guest* and Aamir Khan's *Laal Singh Chaddha*. Manpreet told me that his grandfather, who was a farmer, would go to Lahore daily to sell his chhole and other produce. 'The largest mandi was in Lahore, and people would travel to and from the city all the time,' he added.

Though the border is no longer fluid, Manpreet believes that the bond between the Twin Cities remains strong seventy-eight years after the Partition. 'Amritsar and Lahore have a lot in common, from our dialect and humour to our love for food. Lahore was the biggest cultural centre of north India, and the old-timers in Amritsar still say,

"Jinne Lahore nahin vekhya o jamiya hi nahin (If you have not seen Lahore, you haven't been born yet).'"

Expressing a strong desire to see the 'Paris of the East', Manpreet spoke longingly of a time when Amritsaris would be able to drive down to Lahore in their cars, have lunch, and drive back the same day. 'It's what people in most major international border cities do. But the politicians on this side and the Pakistani Army on the other side will never let this happen,' he said sadly.

Palak Chane with Saroj Kapoor

Another bout of stellar home-cooking was in store the following day at SVAASA, with Abhimanyu's aunt Saroj Kapoor. An avid home-cook and erstwhile caterer, she offered to teach me how to make palak methi chane (chickpeas cooked with fenugreek and spinach), a recipe she learned from her mother. The light was streaming through the kitchen windows as I watched her fry the onions, garlic, and ginger along with tomatoes; then add ground methi and palak; followed by boiled chickpeas and masalas. Next went in whole coriander and cumin seeds and CTC tea (black tea processed with the 'crush, tear, curl' method) roasted on a tawa. Large chunks of fried paneer finished the dish.

Simmered slowly and gently with greens and spices, the chickpeas took on a velvety, creamy consistency. Resting in a glossy glaze, they looked almost too pretty to eat, but Abhimanyu and I polished them off quickly with hot methi pooris and glasses of punchy jaljeera, a cooling digestive drink. Saroj, whose family came to Amritsar from Pakistan's Sahiwal (formerly Montogomery) during the Partition, had a gentle demeanour, and talked about food with great precision. 'The dish must be flawless,' she said. 'The key is to taste as you cook. I do that at every stage.'

As we ate, she pointed out other chhole preparations in Amritsar. A popular variety, she said, was the red chana. This easy-peasy version calls for nothing but boiling chickpeas along with some baking soda and red chilies and adding some red colour. 'I don't much care for it. It's not very tasty,' she said, grimacing.

Then there is the restaurant-style 'Kwality' chane she makes with bhaturas. 'I put a tadka of ghee and spices like jeera, dhania (coriander) powder, amchur, ground anardana, salt, red chilli powder on top of boiled chanas,' she said, adding that the anardana acts as a digestive.

Pindi chhole, though popular in Delhi, wasn't much sought after in Amritsar. 'It's dry and blackish (from the addition of tea leaves or amla water) in colour, seasoned with cumin and anardana and made without onions and tomatoes. Amritsari chhole are a bit runny, lighter in colour, and made with a tomato-onion gravy. The combination of masalas for the two dishes is also different,' Saroj explained.

Her own favourite, chickpeas with paneer, was an 'it' combination with Amritsaris. 'We love our chickpeas. We love our paneer. Give us a dish with both and we're twice as happy,' she said with childlike glee.

Kala Chana Shorba and Hara Chholia

Brown chickpeas or kale chane, which have a dry, wrinkly, and slightly harder texture than the larger and creamier kabuli variety, are also popular in Amritsar, especially as the first meal of the day. Before the arrival of safed chane or white chickpeas, it was this bean that was primarily consumed as breakfast food by field-hands. A serving of the nutritious bean (indigenous to India, unlike kabuli), supplied farmers with the energy crucial to their labour.[4]

The pulse is considered auspicious, which helps explain why kala chana with amchur is a Navratri staple. It is served as prasad along with halwa-poori or luchi on Ashtami, the eighth day of Navratri, when the kanjaka puja is held.

The tonic effect of the legume is also well-established. When boiled, its flavour intensifies, transforming it into a rich and flavourful broth. Abhimanyu's chef served me this elixir, flavoured with ginger, garlic, tomatoes, and onions, credited with magical restorative properties. 'It's guaranteed to give you an iron kick, especially when you are sick,' he said. It was filling and soothing.

I also lucked out in being in the city during the season of chholia or fresh green chickpeas, which you can shell and cook, much like fava beans or peas. As lovely to look at as they are to eat, they go into everything from pulao to aloo-wadi (potato-and-lentil dumpling curry). The offering I tried at SVAASA was fabulously simple—a plate of steamed green beans with a tempering of ginger, salt, and black pepper, and served, but naturally, with Amritsar's mandatory knob of butter.

CHHOLE WITH A TWIST

Though traditions continue to hold strong in Amritsar, change is afoot. Most would regard as blasphemous the idea of a health food wave in the land of ghee and butter, but as everywhere else in the country, lighter food is fast gaining ground.

Traditional versions of Amritsari chhole were created for Punjab's farmers who needed the carbs and fat to labour in the fields. Today, locals have made subtle changes to the calorific food, like not dousing the dish with ghee, or eating it with a wheat flour (instead of maida) kulcha. These slimmed-down versions speak to a new way of living and working. 'We are eating healthier and having a bit of everything,' Gayatri said, as we caught up once more on my last evening in the city.

She also attributed this change to international television shows like *MasterChef* and celebrity chef culture. With the likes of Nigella Lawson and Gordon Ramsay emerging as household names, many of the younger generation home-cooks are taking the comfort food their grandparents made and adding their own creative flourishes.

'Across generations, Amritsaris have always loved to entertain. It's in our nature. But nowadays, with everyone being so well-travelled and knowledgeable about global food, the way we entertain is changing. Like, if I were hosting a get-together for my girlfriends, I would rustle up bite-sized snacks like chhole masala hummus with lavash or chhole crostini.'

For me, Gayatri had made an updated version of her granny's chhole. The original called for tossing boiled chickpeas in ghee in an iron kadhai along with spices. 'Onions and garlic would be sautéed in a separate pan. Once transparent, Dadima would add the chhole in batches, half a cup at a time, so each bean would be coated evenly.

After the addition of amchur and coriander powder, a final chheenta (sprinkle) of water would be added to prevent the dish from sticking to the pan,' she said.

Gayatri had tweaked the classic by skipping the onions, glazing her chhole with white wine instead of water, and adding a dollop of mascarpone. Finally, instead of fresh coriander as a garnish, she used basil and topped it up with cherry tomatoes.

It was a great dish, inventive and zesty. But after a few spoonfuls, I found myself longing for the original. Reading my expression, Gayatri burst out laughing. 'I always come back to the old recipe too. It's hard not to,' she said, confessing that the best dishes often don't need updating.

As my ten-day-long party came to an end, I felt pleased. Digging into the city's storied chickpea dishes, I had squeezed out every last bit of deliciousness from my visit. To have tasted the must-have comfort foods of dhabas as well as beloved family recipes, and to have celebrated the contexts in which they were created, was a rare adventure.

I left Amritsar with at least five or six packets of the crunchy anardana-crusted papad I so adored, as well as the elation of having experienced the city's soul through a beloved classic.

◆

During my travels across the globe, I have relished a range of chickpea treats, from an outstanding homemade hummus in Tel Aviv to a rustic pasta e ceci in Puglia. But Amritsar has a chickpea culture unlike any other. The versatile repetition of the beans is something I love about the city's cooking—simply boiled, bolstered with paneer, tweaked with an international flair, and best of all, laden with spices and slowly simmered.

The magic of eating chhole in Amritsar comes not merely from the pleasure of the food. Zeroing in on specific historical aspects, like ancient trade routes and cataclysmic migrations, enabled me to appreciate how dishes and ingredients travel, get locally riffed, and become a part of a city's identity.

There is a certain poignancy to experiencing the dish in

the Golden City. The simple, intimate meals I savoured were extraordinarily evocative, equally about the mise-en-scène as they were about food. They made me realize how seamlessly the cuisine of this city, a short drive from the Pakistan border, and still bearing the echoes of a bygone era, blends together time and space.

Film director and screenwriter Akira Kurosawa once said, 'It is the power of memory that gives rise to the power of imagination.' To me, chhole became a taste of undivided Punjab, of a homeland before it was torn apart by the Partition. The dish conjured Punjab's syncretic, multicultural, and multireligious traditions, and all the centuries and regions the lush state used to rest on.

Though none of the plates I ate in Amritsar tasted quite like my grandmother's chhole, I felt more connected to her than ever. I could see why this dish made her so emotional. Scattered all over Amritsar are fragments of the rich and diverse culture destroyed by the Partition. There's so much of the past bubbling away under the surface of the present.

Chhole elicited a sentimental response from me. The joie de vivre of Amritsar, combined with the potency of its history, opened up my senses like never before.

It felt just like a hug from Dadima.

Recipes from My Travels

RANJIT'S SVAASA'S AMRITSARI CHHOLE

SERVES: 4 TIME TAKEN: 1 HOUR PLUS OVERNIGHT SOAKING

INGREDIENTS

Kabuli chana	1 cup
Water	2 cups
Tea bags	2
Bay leaves	4
Cloves	4–5
Black cardamom	1

Ghee	50 gms
Tomatoes	300 gms, chopped
Kashmiri chilli powder	1 tsp
Turmeric powder	¼ tsp
Garam masala	1 tsp
Coriander powder	1 tbsp
Cumin powder	½ tsp
Spinach puree	1 cup (200 gms spinach, boiled and blended)
Amchur powder	1 tsp
Kasuri methi	1 tsp, crushed
Salt	to taste

METHOD

Put 1 cup of chickpeas in a large bowl and rinse well. Pour 3–4 cups of water and soak them overnight or for at least 8 hours.

Drain the water and rinse well.

Put the soaked chana in a pressure cooker along with 2 cups water, tea bags, bay leaves, cloves, cardamom, and salt.

Cook for 2–3 whistles on medium heat.

Test if the chana is cooked; it should mash but still hold its shape.

Heat 50 gms ghee in a pot and add the tomatoes with a little salt. Cover and cook the tomatoes for 10 minutes until they break down and turn soft and mushy.

Add kashmiri chilli powder, turmeric powder, garam masala, coriander powder, and cumin powder. Cook for 5 minutes.

Add the boiled chana along with its water and mix well.

Cover and let it simmer for 15 minutes.

Add the spinach purée, amchur powder, and crushed kasuri methi powder.

Mix well and check for seasoning.

Serve hot with rice, naan, roti, paratha, or poori.

RANJIT'S SVAASA'S AMCHUR WALE SUKHE CHANE

SERVES: 4 TIME TAKEN: 20 MINUTES PLUS OVERNIGHT SOAKING

INGREDIENTS

Kabuli chana	2 cups
Water	1½ cups
Ghee	1 tbsp
Coriander seeds	1 tsp, roasted and crushed
Cumin seeds	1 tsp, roasted and crushed
Red chilli powder	1 tsp
Turmeric powder	1 tsp
Garam masala	1 tsp
Fresh coriander leaves	a handful, chopped
Kasuri methi	1 tsp, crushed
Ginger	1 tbsp, cut into thin strips
Amchur	1 tsp
Salt	to taste

METHOD

Wash the chana in lots of water and soak them in 6–8 cups of water overnight or for at least 8 hours.

Rinse the chana and put it in a pressure cooker along with 1½ cup of fresh water and 1 tbsp salt.

Cook it for 5–6 whistles on medium heat. Switch off the flame and let it cool.

Test the chana for its doneness. It should mash easily when pressed but still hold its shape.

Heat 1 tbsp of ghee in a deep pan. Put the crushed cumin and coriander seeds in it to crackle.

Add the boiled chana, turmeric powder, chilli powder, and garam masala. Cook for 5 minutes on a low flame.

Add kasuri methi, fresh green coriander, ginger strips, and amchur. Mix well and cook on a low flame for 3 minutes.

Serve hot.

Tip: For a darker colour, you can put a tea bag in the pressure cooker while cooking the chana. The chana will turn a nice deep-brown colour.

Smoked Pork

BAPTISM BY SMOKE

The cuisine of the northeast was terra incognita to me. Having never visited the region before, I was wondering how to navigate this fascinating world. Which iconic food best represented the culinary culture of the eight northeastern states?

When I posed the question to my friend Roopa Barua, a documentary filmmaker who grew up in Jorhat, she deemed it a no-brainer. 'Smoked meat, particularly pork,' she said.

Though misconceptions about the region's food abound (such as momo being the emblematic dish of these parts), it is this elemental ingredient and the dishes around it, Roopa opined, that truly represent the cooking of the northeast. In all its iterations across the area, the lusty, meaty flavour of smoked pork epitomizes comfort. 'It is to us what the tandoor is to Punjab,' she revealed.

Roopa associated the beloved staple with winter picnics and campfires. The subject conjured memories of freshly smoked skewers of pork—hot, juicy, and infused with the flavour of smouldering logs. She recalled the sound of popping fat, and the pleasure of gnawing endlessly on the meaty chunks. 'I can still feel my hands greasy with crackling,' she said gleefully.

The transformative power of smoking had always intrigued me.[1] Now, listening to Roopa's rhapsodies, I needed no further convincing. As I began planning my sojourn, she introduced me to Geeta Dutta, an Assamese doctor[2] who moonlights as a food blogger and influencer. A promoter of indigenous northeastern cuisines, Geeta has been documenting the foodways of the tribals for years and gets a lot of love on social media.

Loquacious and open-hearted, Geeta has deep knowledge of

Assamese cuisine and a ready willingness to share it. We instantly hit it off. As we brainstormed, she named a slew of memorable dishes from the region—smoked pork with wild foraged greens from Assam; wahan mosdeng, a smoked pork salad from Tripura; smoked pork with axone from Nagaland; vawksa rep leh antam, or smoked pork with mustard leaves, from Mizoram.

Before long, I was dreaming of these delicacies. I longed to visit every state and taste each dish Geeta had described. Sadly, that wasn't possible. So we narrowed down my adventures to three states—Nagaland, Assam, and Meghalaya.

As we connected over a last telecon before my trip, Geeta had just one piece of heartfelt advice for me: 'Discover the northeast with an open heart, and a curious palate.'

MUMBAI

Smoked Pork with Lai Haak with Gitika Saikia

While still in Mumbai, I decided to get a primer from the city's pop-up queen, Gitika Saikia. Long before northeastern food became trendy, the pioneer of Assamese food (both tribal and urban) in Mumbai, was singing praises of indigenous ingredients like elephant yam and fermented bamboo shoots and showcasing them in her meals.

Gitika invited me to watch her prepare smoked pork with mustard leaves in her Juhu kitchen. Cooked with an Assamese flair for simplicity, it was made without a drop of oil. She parboiled the pork to jumpstart the tenderizing process and rendered out some of the fat in a pressure cooker along with garlic and chillies, before seasoning with coarse-textured Assamese mustard leaves known as lai haak.

She had whipped up an array of sides too—dried fish chutney; fragrant steamed joha rice; and kosu pitika, a mash of boiled taro, sliced onions, and fermented local fish sharpened with raw mustard oil; and bhut jolokia or ghost peppers.

Smoking meat in the northeast, she explained, has a history dating back millennia. Though fish is at the core of Assamese cooking, smoked pork traces its ancestry to the tribal communities that entered Assam from China, Bhutan, Myanmar, and other Southeast Asian countries.

The tribals were hunter-gatherers and the last to take to agriculture. When they killed a large animal like a water buffalo or a wild boar, the only way to keep the surplus meat from going bad was to smoke it over the jui-haal or chaang, the hanging structure atop a chulha. The preservation hack ensured a ready supply of meat to be used through the year. As smoking imparted a moreish flavour to the meat, it became the starring ingredient of a host of beloved dishes.

The simple partnership of smoked pork and mustard leaves had seen families through winters for as long as Gitika could remember. 'Its beauty lies in its simplicity, how we marry a high-quality protein with greens from the regional pantry to create magic,' she said.

The coming together of three beloved ingredients—nose-tingling lai haak, silky smoked pork, and tongue-searing bhut jolokia—makes for a sublimely satisfying blend. As I dug in, the sharpness of the chilli hit me with its intensity before yielding to the meat's slow-cooked moistness.

I couldn't have hoped for a more sumptuous start to my adventures.

DIMAPUR

Smoked Pork and Axone with Joel Basumatari

As my plane touched down in Dimapur, I felt a rush of excitement. Joel Basumatari, a master of haute Naga cuisine, was at the airport to receive me along with his little boy Aiden. The chef, who has been racking up awards for his work on slow food and tribal cuisines, had promised me a taste of his cooking. But first, he whisked me off to the local market to give me a crash course in Naga ingredients.

With its endless pyramids of exotic herbs, wild edibles, and creepy-crawlies, Super Market (named so) feels like a brave new world to the newcomer. I could barely recognize anything. 'Welcome to Nagaland,' Joel teased, noting the lost look on my face.

Strolling around the stalls, he pointed out the aromatic local ginger—smaller, spicier, and sharper than its regular counterpart—slender green stalks of wild Naga garlic, fire-engine-red tree tomatoes, and hillocks of raja mircha or ghost peppers, responsible for the fireworks of Naga cooking.

On our way out, Joel stopped to buy parcels of axone, the traditional fermented soybean cake beloved to Nagas. The umami bomb, which speaks more of Southeast Asia than the Indian subcontinent, was displayed in two versions—a wet one wrapped in banana leaves, and a dry one encased in yam leaves. 'Depending on the type you use, you will get a totally different version of the same dish,' Joel told me, snagging the solid variant for our session that afternoon.

Joel, who supplies smoked meats and Naga sauces commercially from his backyard, had a state-of-the-art three-tiered smoker. When we entered his sprawling home, a few chunks of pork and beef were slowly smoking on the side, bathed in beautiful wood smoke.

A bout of frenzied cooking ensued. Joel, who is part Sema, part Angami, and part Kachari, was making awoshi kipiki ngo axone, or smoked pork with axone. A specialty of the Sema tribe, the Naga delicacy makes a mandatory appearance on Christmas and on weddings. 'It's the heart and soul of Naga cooking,' Joel said, attributing the iconic status of the dish to its native ingredients and big flavours.

The sultry afternoon unfolded to the sounds of chopping and blending. To make the axone, Joel put a block of fermented beans in a pot of boiling water and left it to slowly cook for an hour. The pungent fragrance of the beans seemed to magnify manifold as they simmered, suffusing the kitchen with an earthy, funky aroma. When the water had evaporated, Joel added bite-sized pieces of smoked pork and local Naga chillies to the blend.

As the flavours melded and intensified, Joel rustled up a Naga chutney known as tathu by charring piquant tree tomatoes on the fire and blending them with green chillies, onions, Naga garlic, and shredded buffalo meat. 'It's my favourite,' he smiled, proceeding to make a Naga 'boil' of mustard leaves and pumpkin.

When the axone was ready, Joel elevated the classic by adding lightly toasted majenga (*Zanthoxylum oxyphyllum*, a type of Szechuan pepper used widely in Naga cuisine) seeds to add a fruity, peppery bite. The final chef-inspired touch was a garnish of majenga leaves, fried to a crisp on slow flame. 'They add a lovely crisp contrast to the tenderness of the pork,' Joel said.

Robust, pungent, and complex, the dish was unlike anything I had ever tasted. It featured just a few ingredients, but the flavour-hit was massive. I found it remarkable that fermentation and smoking (as opposed to spices) could coax such depth of flavour out of a dish.

The interplay of salty, umami, funky, and savoury was a curious flavour spectrum for me. My palate struggled with the newness and strangeness of it all. Thankfully, Joel wasn't the least bit offended. 'Naga food is acquired taste. Not everyone loves it at first bite, but once you have tasted it, you will feel like eating it again,' he said encouragingly.

The chef stressed that notions of 'good' and 'bad' in food are often cultural and rooted in upbringing. 'The smell of axone is something I grew up with, so it doesn't offend me. People in the mainland may dislike it, but to understand a new food, you need to accept its different-ness. You need to give it time,' he said.

It was a powerful lesson. Rare delicacies and less familiar foods—blue cheese, oysters, caviar, century eggs—often demand a sense of commitment and perseverance to become pleasurable.

I didn't fall in love with smoked pork and axone right away. Yet that first taste marked a watershed. The dish challenged my senses, jolting me out of my comfort zone.

That's what made it great.

Naga Smoking Techniques with Toshi and Annie Jamir

What alchemy of fire and wood turns a portly pig into silken-fleshed deliciousness?

I was hoping Annie Jamir, the owner of Longchen homestay, would detail out the processes, but she directed me to her husband. 'Talk to Toshi. He's a smoking hound. He's hardcore,' she said.

Clad in a black hat, white polo tee, and khaki shorts, Toshi joined us at the machang, an alfresco bamboo platform where breakfast was served the next morning. A purist at heart, he regards smoking as a true labour of love. 'You gotta slog to get it right. There are no shortcuts,' he said, his passion for the art reflecting in the seriousness of his expression.

The rituals of cleaning, curing, and smoking were muscle memory to the aficionado, who credited his early training to his mother. 'Mum was a Khasi from Shillong, but more Naga in her ways than dad. She taught me to use every last morsel of the animal, including the hide,' he shared.

Later, as an officer in the Assam Regiment, Toshi upped his smoking game by observing his batchmates. 'The regiment was a mix of people from different northeastern tribes—Kukis, Khasis, Bodos, Jaintias, Nagas, Mizos, and others. Each had his own technique and process, and we learnt constantly from one another,' he recounted.

Thrown on the frontlines for months on end, smoking meat meant survival. 'Wild boar, deer, jungle fowl, monkeys—we hunted and smoked it all. We had such a gala time, we even forgot our families!' he said, guffawing.

The retired military man makes the most out of the working farm around their homestay—from the hogs penned in the woods to the open outer kitchen where he smokes meat throughout the year.

Though smoking techniques vary across the sixteen Naga tribes, the tried and tested method followed by Toshi is broadly representative. Sourcing his pork from the neighbourhood butcher, he insists on cleaning and cutting the carcass himself. Salting, which dehydrates the meat and serves an essential anti-microbial function, is the crucial next step. Toshi also uses a coarse, dry rub of cracked pepper mixed with red chillies or dried lemon leaves to flavour the meat. 'You can use any spice you like. Just keep it simple,' he said, adding that the flavour of the meat must not be overwhelmed.

Smoking organically over traditional bamboo racks, Toshi likes to build and tend his fires manually. The charred appeal of smoked meat, he explained, derives in large part from the chemical properties of hardwood. Cellulose and lignin, present in the cells of wood, yield aromatic compounds during combustion, imparting a toasty scent. The Maillard reaction, responsible for the browning of meat, does the rest, imbuing the flesh with subtle savoury, sweet, and bitter flavour notes.

The end result—a preserved, flavoured, and partially cooked hunk of meat—is used by each of the Naga tribes differently. Toshi swore by his signature dish, a searingly pungent smoked pork and bamboo shoot curry. 'It's sure to make you sweat,' he promised.

Luckily, tamoming, the Changki delicacy the couple fed me, was anything but lethal. Made from smoked pork cooked with mashed potatoes, tomatoes, and dried chillies, its taste was mellow, with the subtle spiciness from the herbs gently seasoning the dish.

My session with the Jamirs was revelatory. When Nagas smoke meat, they keep alive the most ancient method of preserving food known to mankind. Transcending mere utility, the ritual channels a primitive, almost atavistic, desire to connect with our prehistoric past.

Eons ago, someone put some flesh over flame and turned it into a piece of smoky scrumptiousness.

It must have felt like abracadabra then. To me, it still does.

GUWAHATI

Oma Narzi and Sobai with Nayana Swargiary Phangsho

Driving from Dimapur through verdant swaths of forested hills, I reached Guwahati at dusk. Geeta, clad in blue jeans and a navy-blue kurta, picked me up from my hotel the following morning. Petite and bespectacled, she had the frenetic energy of a teen.

'You're finally *here*!' she trilled, making me feel like we had known each other forever.

We were driving down to an area called Koinadhara Hill, close to the Meghalaya border, to meet Geeta's friend Nayana. Nayana is a Bodo,[3] married to a Karbi. The Karbis are an ethnic community concentrated around the Karbi-Anglong district of Assam and a few other regions. The couple has a traditional smoking platform called dhowasang ('dhowa' means smoke and 'sang' means a raised platform in Assamese) where I could watch their ancestral process of smoking. Nayana had also promised to cook us a grand lunch featuring two iconic Assamese dishes—oma narzi or smoked pork with jute leaves; and sobai, or smoked pork with black lentils.

Chatting on the way, Geeta shared that her passion for promoting native foodways was spurred by a concern for the steady erosion of indigenous Assamese food traditions. 'Communities like the Karbis have traditionally been oppressed by upper classes. Even now they continue to be told that they are inferior and irrelevant. I work with people like Nayana to ensure that their precious culture and food traditions don't fade,' she said.

Resplendent in a canary-yellow mekhela sador, Nayana was standing in the doorway when we reached. She greeted me with a warm hug. 'I'm *so* happy to see you,' she said, as she introduced me to her husband Nipul and brought out a ceremonial platter of tamul (betelnut leaves) to welcome us. Minutes later, her eight-year-old daughter Anushka appeared, cradling a duckling.

Nayana has a homestead garden. We walked around for a bit, picking native leaves and herbs. I nibbled randomly on a few, just for the thrill of it.

The dhowasang was housed in Nayana's outer kitchen. Entirely made of bamboo, it was storehouse, place of worship, and smoking cabin all rolled into one. 'Karbis believe in animism and still worship their forest gods. For them, cooking a meal is as much about spirituality as about nourishment,' Geeta explained, pointing out the stump or zongora khuta on the left, where the family made its offerings to the forefathers as a mark of respect before eating.

In the centre of the kitchen was a bamboo shelf for storage, with an array of neatly arranged items—a Karbi rice wine dispenser known as titalao; bamboo hollows; dried bogori or ber, used as a souring agent in dals and curries; and a basket of dried fish.

At the far right of the kitchen, chunks of pork belly lay on the bamboo rack suspended over glowing embers. Slowly smoked over four days, they had become meltingly tender. The pig, reared in the house itself, had been slaughtered for Bihu. 'Tribals usually kill a pig for occasions like marriages, festivals, or death. It's a way for the community to come together in a gesture of goodwill and sharing. No part of the carcass is wasted. It's our way of showing respect to the animal,' Geeta said.

Watching Nayana cook in her zero-tech kitchen was a learning experience. Squatting over logs of burning wood, she seemed to move to a rhythm of her own. To make the oma narzi, a Bodo dish, she dry-roasted jute leaves to rid them of moisture before boiling them with water, rice flour, and smoked pork. For the sobai, a Bodo specialty, black lentils were simmered atop a fire along with khar.[4] When done, fried smoked pork was added along with ginger and garlic. The blend was then mashed with a churner until it acquired a sticky, porridge-like consistency.

The charming meal served with moringa khar and sticky rice, laid out on the floor over bamboo mats, epitomized respect for native ingredients. A subtle smokiness emerged at the back of my palate as I tucked into the oma narzi. The bitterness of the jute leaves, tamed considerably from cooking, played as an earthy counter to the sweetness of the pork. The taste was interesting and alluring and peculiar, all at once.

I relished the sobai too. Having absorbed massive amounts of porky flavour as they cooked, the black lentils had a nutty creaminess, which complemented the rice perfectly. 'In Bodo villages, eating sobai means you're feeling happy. Are you happy?' Nayana asked.

Of course I was. Rich yet balanced, these dishes were unlike anything I had ever tasted. Most of the world may not have heard about these nutritious indigenous foods, but unhealthy city diets could certainly take a leaf out of their book.

After lunch, Geeta pounded some kon jolokia or bird's eye chillies, with ginger and salt, and served it along with glasses of freshly brewed rice beer known as harlong. 'You've had tequila shots. Now try this. Cheeeers!' she cried, raising a raucous toast. I took a fiery bite followed by a swig. It was dynamite. Moments later, Nayana delivered a batch of smoked pork skewers on our plates.

I decided to loosen my belt and surrender.

Brahmaputra Cruise with Runa Rafique and Geeta Dutta

The following day, Geeta was supposed to take me to meet piggery entrepreneur Runa Rafique at her farm. But the plan had gone up in smoke as a storm had hit the previous week, destroying the sitting area and drenching the field.

Hungover from the previous day's excesses, I was secretly relieved to get a morning in bed. But when Geeta suggested cruising down the Brahmaputra with Runa, my inner tourist was tickled. The idea of a leisurely drift down one of India's longest rivers seemed just the ticket to squeeze some sightseeing into an otherwise crammed itinerary.

We took the time to amble along the bucolic river as we waited for Runa. 'Runa ba was the first Muslim lady in Assam to get into pig farming. She is highly educated and very cool. You will love her,' Geeta said.

Runa arrived minutes later. Clad in a black cotton sari, she was urbane, elegant, and sophisticated. Geeta's fondness for her friend was evident as she excitedly showed her photos of our previous day's Karbi revelry. 'What, you all had rice beer? No wonder you look so jolly!' Runa said, visibly amused.

Geeta had managed to get upper-deck tickets. Under a blue sky smeared with white clouds, *Alfresco Grand* announced its departure with a loud blast of its horn. As the vessel set sail, the crowd cheered with gusto.

Onboard, the vibe was relaxed, eased by rounds of beer and munchies and the balmy evening breeze. Sailing along, we were treated to a spectacular sunset the colour of golden wine.

Chatting with Runa, I discovered that she had worked with medical NGOs before switching to pig farming. It wasn't a difficult transition. 'Seventy per cent of pork consumption in India happens in the northeast. So I had a ready market. Farmers were sitting on my doorstep to buy livestock,' she said.

Did her religion come in the way of her plans? 'This is the northeast, my dear. We are cool with such things,' Runa said breezily, sharing that she was raised in a progressive family in Upper Assam, where attitudes are a lot more liberal. It wasn't all smooth sailing, though. 'When I started the pig farm, some people stopped saying hello to me. All of a sudden, I wasn't getting so many wedding invitations.'

After losing her piggery to African Swine Fever (ASF), Runa got into chicken farming. To make things more interesting, she started DhowaSang,[5] an artisanal brand that offered smoked versions of pork, chicken, fish, and duck.

The venture filled a yawning gap in the market. Smoked pork, traditionally a country dish, was not commercially available in cities when she launched her brand. Runa's product stood out as she offered meat slow-smoked on a traditional dhowasang using time-honoured Naga techniques. 'There's no soot on the flesh with this gentle method, which indicates minimal exposure to carcinogens. This gave us a leg up over industrial smoked meat,' she said.[6]

Runa produced a packet of smoked pork from her bag to show me. It was a deep shade of red, looked well-marbled, and was insulated by a layer of firm, creamy fat.

Most states outside of the northeast didn't yet care about this prized hunk of meat, but Runa was determined to change that. The stigma around pork, she believes, has much to do with the perception of pigs as filthy, excreta-eating animals. But those days are long gone. 'Farmed pigs are hygienic; fed a clean, wholesome diet; and vaccinated every month. Once people see how our animals are raised, their perceptions will change.'

An uncommon choice on Indian menus, Runa believes pork deserves a chance. With a taste that's superior to chicken, a lower carbon footprint than mutton and buffalo meat, and a slew of nutritional benefits—it's a rich source of B vitamins, iron, and minerals—a well-raised, hygienically fed pig is among the most sustainable meat options out there, she opined.

Smoking notches up the appeal manifold. 'Smoked pork is fast, healthy, and seriously delicious. Being 60–70 per cent pre-cooked meat, it shortens cooking time by half. And unlike fresh meat, it can be preserved for up to three months in the deep freezer without any loss in taste. What's not to love?'

As we approached terra firma, Runa expressed hope that meat-eaters across India would come to appreciate the delicacy as much as they did. 'Smoked pork's time is just around the corner. Who knows, it might even earn our region a GI tag,' she said wistfully.

Geeta, who was on a mission to broad-base the appeal of her friend's product, had developed a bunch of recipes featuring the meat. Cooks could choose from traditional options like smoked pork with bamboo shoots or Western preparations like smoked pork with red wine.

'Whatever floats their boat,' she shrugged.

SHILLONG

Meghalayan Pork Basics with William Diengdoh

Leaving behind the urban cacophony of Guwahati, I drove down to Shillong the next day. Connected by a 100-kilometre stretch of lush scenery, the scenic road hugging Lake Umiam had lookout points at every turn of the wheel. I paused more than once to fill my lungs with the woody, minty smell of pine leaves.

It was late evening when I reached. As darkness swaddled the mountains, I decided to step into Cafe Shillong in Laitumkhrah for a bite. When I entered, Leonard Cohen crooned from a speaker somewhere.

Gerald Samuel Duia, a popular local tour operator who was showing me around Shillong for a couple of days, had promised to meet me at the restaurant. He was nowhere to be seen, but chatting with the waitress, I serendipitously discovered that the owner of Cafe Shillong was into producing cold-cuts. She pointed him out to me. Clad in a white shirt and faded blue jeans, William Diengdoh was sitting just two tables away from me, in the smoking zone.

He joined me for a comforting bowl of pork thukpa (Tibetan noodle soup). The entrepreneur told me that he ran a brand called Regetta Farms-Meat Treat and had spent a decade breeding local pigs. He was pleased when I told him about the focus of my visit. 'You've come to the right place. Eating good smoked pork is a birthright in Shillong. We are hardcore carnivores,' he said, grinning.

Due to the preponderance of meat in the state, Meghalayan smoked pork traditions are unique, diverse, and delicious. The three major tribes of the state—the Garos, the Khasis, and the Jaintias—

all make it differently. 'Khasis like subtlety and mild flavours,' William said. 'We cook in bamboo hollows and add our own spices, like the pebble-sized ginger known as ing-khmoh, our native turmeric known as lakadong, and of course, bamboo shoots.'

Popular Khasi dishes include the likes of smoked pork fried in its own fat along with some onions, smoked pork stew thickened with potatoes and paired with tungtap or dried fish chutney, some curries, and the region's pride— doh nei iong, or smoked pork with black sesame. William also told me about the local bamboo shoot-harvesting festival known as por pdem lund rachong, held from October through November, in which a ten-foot bamboo basket is used to gather bamboo shoots. Fresh pork is added to the basket and left to ferment for three months. 'When you open the basket, the flavour of bamboo shoot has infused the pork so deeply that you don't need any other seasoning. Just cut the pork into cubes and cook. It's sensational,' he said.

The genetics of the pig is a crucial component in influencing the taste of the meat, William pointed out. Praising the unique flavour profile of Meghalayan pork, he pointed out that the local pig, Ñiang Megha, a registered genetic profile, has more of a pygmy or wild boar characteristic. 'It's not a taste you could ever get from a typical Yorkshire or Hampshire pig. The rind is tender, thin, and succulent. It binds beautifully with the bite, bursting with natural flavours of the meat and smokiness, leaving behind an unforgettable aftertaste.'

William is convinced that the charcuterie made from locally raised pigs from Meghalaya could be at par with the finest in the world. 'At its best, it's as good as Spanish Serrano ham and prosciutto,' he said. Sadly, local varieties have all but disappeared, owing to deadly diseases like ASF and the government's failure to conserve indigenous breeds.[7]

Meghalayan smoked pork, William believes, has serious global potential as a niche, high-end product. 'But to get there, we need to develop a food production system that insists on rearing indigenous pig breeds like Ñiang Megha.' After losing his pigs to ASF in 2021, the farmer-entrepreneur was already working on restarting his breeding program to revive local breeds. 'The idea is to have a highly precise selection of the carcass. Only then can we produce a gourmet product that stands out,' he said passionately.

As we ended our session, William suggested visiting Mylliem village, the commercial swine hub of Meghalaya. 'Travel with a local. It will be easier,' he advised. A moment later, Gerald appeared magically and revealed that the next day's plan included a halt at Mylliem, followed by a home-cooked meal at a village in Ri Bhoi.

My perch, the venerable Pine Wood Hotel, had an idyllic view of the mountains. I fell asleep watching the stars and the flickering glow-worms, and visualizing the feasts that lay ahead.

Pork Fry at Mylliem Village

An hour's drive through pine-blanketed hills got us to Mylliem. The superlative smoked pork here is sold at tiny kong shops, so called because they are run by women ('kong' means 'sister' or 'madam' in Khasi).

Gerald took me to one called Nongsteng, named after its owner Nita Nongsteng. Cranking out local delicacies since the early 2000s, it had long tables and benches, and rows of pickles and condiments.

He pointed out the array of Khasi staples displayed inside—pig innards, pork doh khlieh or diced pork salad made with pig's brains, doh masi or beef roast, doh shain or meat balls, jadoh (Khasi-style pulao), smoked pork fried with tomato and onions, and a rustic salad of tomatoes and local jatira leaves.

Nita, standing behind the counter, was every bit the no-nonsense matriarch, her hands deeply callused from years of working. For some reason, she was deeply suspicious of me, and demanded I produce my passport. 'She's a tough cookie,' I remarked. Gerald laughed. 'Khasi ladies are like this. We are a matrilinear society. She knows she's boss,' he said.

Nita seemed to thaw a little when I praised her gleaming utensils, and even managed to crack a half-smile. Gerald approved of my icebreaker. 'No Khasi lady can resist that compliment. They take great pride in keeping everything shining and clean,' he said, laughing.

Most kong shops smoke their own meat. At Nonsgteng, much of the process was directed by Nita's son Batyngshain. The hoodie-clad youngster took us on his bike to his smokery, known in Khasi as sem thad doh. Pulled into thick, meaty garlands, hunks of pork and beef were slowly smoking on a rack when we entered. 'They're almost done,' Batyngshain said, as we posed for a selfie or two.

The process of smoking was more or less the same as what I had witnessed elsewhere—make a fire from hardwood; cut, salt, and smoke the meat; and, finally, stitch the pieces together with bamboo thread. Batyngshain emphasized that only meat from local breeds of pig and buffalo was used. 'No one really cares for chicken around here,' Gerald piped in.

Back at the shop, Gerald and I ordered the day's smoked pork special, which arrived on the table along with rice flatbreads known as putharo, a fermented soybean relish called tungrymbai, and cups of red tea.

The dish featured freshly smoked pork belly and streaky shoulder cooked in a simple masala of tomatoes, onions, garlic, and salt. With a mellow umami and buttery texture, the pork was absolutely addictive. The warm unctuous morsels melted as they hit my mouth. It was lust at first bite.

The rustic meal embodied the Khasi ability to seemingly effortlessly extract the best out of local pork and simple ingredients. I couldn't help but notice the contrast between the humble setting and the rich, voluptuous flavours.

The kong shop was delicious proof, yet again, that the best food comes from simple places, and that you don't need a bottomless wallet to eat well.

Smoked Pork with Black Sesame at Khweng Village

As the afternoon sun peaked, we left Mylliem behind, heading north towards the district of Ri Bhoi. Gerald, who believes that Khasi cuisine is at its least adulterated in home kitchens, was taking me to his native village for a Bhoi meal. The countryside was quiet and idyllic, with patches of rectangular neon-green grass fields framed by thick forests of pine and bamboo.

The Bhois, a sub-group of the Khasi tribe, are famed for their vibrant meat dishes, including pork with black sesame, the region's unrivalled favourite. 'Bhoi food is fantastic. I haven't had a single guest who hasn't licked the plate clean,' Gerald boasted.

A quiet hamlet of around 100 households, Khweng is an active weaving village producing Eri silk, also known as Ahimsa silk (because the silkworm is not killed during the production process). Gerald's friend Rikynti Syiem, our host for the afternoon, worked at the Eri factory. We passed it on the way to her residence. The cute little red-and-white house was perched on an incline with sweeping views of the green foothills in the distance.

A serene woman with a low bun of black hair and gleaming white teeth, Rikynti was tending to a patch of wild pink roses in her garden when we arrived. Clad in a fuchsia pink dress with a jainkyrshah (traditional Meghalayan apron) and bright purple flip-flops, she greeted me with an awkward handshake as she led us inside a cosy bamboo gazebo. Two golden Lhasa apsos darted around our feet as we settled into well-worn cane chairs. Moments later, a furry feline settled itself on my lap.

Speaking in her native Bhoi, which Gerald translated into English, Rikynti held forth on the culinary philosophy of the Bhois, which is all about immersion in nature. Like Karbis, Bhois are keen foragers and love to incorporate wild herbs and edibles into their meals.

Walking into her backyard, she showed me bitter sohngnang or small pea brinjals; jatira or water celery, often made into salads or cooked with yam; dark green jajew or roselle leaves; jarain or buckwheat, used to flavour pork or dry fish; and jaralud, which has a bitter taste. 'Everything you see here goes into my food,' she said.

Back at the gazebo, the round bamboo table was already mosaicked with bowls of food. Our feast comprised smoked pork with black sesame and bamboo shoots; tungtap or dried fish with fermented taro leaves; and smoked beef with taro yam, all served with khao khasi or local red Khasi rice, bitter brinjals, and platters of rustic leafy salad.

'How do you say bon appetit in Khasi?' I asked Gerald.

'Bam bha shibun!' Gerald said. 'It means, "Eat lots!"' As I echoed the words, Rikynti broke into a grin.

The dishes were typical of Bhoi food: hearty, folksy, and rooted in ancestral cooking. Treasured like family heirlooms, they were symbols of cultural pride for Rikynty. It was easy to see why doh nei iong was the go-to pork dish in Meghalaya. The slightly oily character of black sesame seeds worked magic in the staple, giving it a tahini-like creaminess and nutty flavour along with a striking dark colouring. The smoked beef, lean and gamey, was nicely set off by the sludgy sweetness of the taro root. Faintly redolent of smoke, it was seasoned with fresh lakadong from Rikynti's garden.

Taro featured in a different form in the fish dish. Dried local fish known as tungtap were mixed together with fermented taro leaves, garlic, black sesame, and jaralud, and punched up with local small chillies. 'It's the same fish used in the spicy fermented dried fish chutney known as tungtap made in homes,' Gerald explained.

As always, I was struck by how easy it is to make food taste good in the northeast. Everything was seasoned delicately; there was a subtle balanced taste to the meat, and the greens shone.

'How do I tell her I love the food?' I asked Gerald.

'We say bang bha,' he said. I repeated after him.

'A bit louder. Baaang bhaaaa!' he said.

Rikynti was amused. We all laughed.

The sumptuous feast in this picture-perfect part of Meghalaya was unforgettable. Though language was a barrier, my tomfoolery and appreciation for Rikynti's cooking and culture had made her drop her guard. We lingered long after the bountiful meal, chewing on bits of ginger candy, talking of this and that.

When I got up to leave, my hostess hugged me goodbye, this time with a familiar, easy warmth. 'Come back soon. You're our friend now,' she said.

It's the best thing a rookie could hope to hear.

◆

My first visit to the northeast left a lasting impression on me.

I was fortunate enough to savour an eclectic assemblage of meat-focussed dishes from a mosaic of topographies.[8] They showed me that the region is a wonderfully diverse carnivore-haven with rich food traditions.

I'm not a big pork-eater. Fish and goat-meat are my proteins of choice. But the porky delights I savoured in the northeast enthralled me. The lusciousness of the meat seasoned with just-picked greens made me a fan.

The unusual character of the dishes added to their appeal. Each introduced me to a world of native produce and flavours. Primal yet Noma-esque, these unsung treasures deserve to be savoured by the world.

As an ingredient, smoked pork has earned a permanent spot in the northeastern pantry—I see no reason why it shouldn't in ours too. It's a meat of character and interest, and definitely worth exploring. Distinct from its global brethren, it is praise-worthy for its unique flavour and texture.

But there was more to my visit than taste. Throughout my travels, what came across the strongest was my hosts' love for preserving their food culture and centuries-old traditions. The native farmers, producers, and home-cooks I met were custodians of a venerable food system rooted in hyperlocal farming, short supply chains, zero carbon footprints, and strong social bonds.

I was struck by the spirit of self-sufficiency I witnessed everywhere I went—people living off the bounty of the land, growing their own produce, rearing their own livestock, and incorporating hyperlocal herbs and plants into their diets, just as their ancestors had done. Not only were they keeping alive precious relics of the ancient world, they were upholding the highest ideals of food sovereignty.

Discovering these lively worlds led to being initiated, albeit slowly, into a new way of experiencing food. The adventure seemed a bit overwhelming at first, but it ultimately won me over.

Back in Mumbai, my smoked pork cravings are sated thanks to resources like Manxho and Pigzees. Geeta, who continues to exhibit unflagging zest for my porcine education, sounded characteristically chipper when I told her about my discoveries.

'Welcome to the tribe,' she said.

GITIKA SAIKIA'S SMOKED PORK WITH LAI HAAK

SERVES: 4 TIME TAKEN: 40 MINUTES

INGREDIENTS

Smoked pork	500 gms, cut into cubes
Garlic	5–6 cloves, crushed
Lai haak	1 bunch, washed, cleaned and roughly torn
Salt	to taste
Bhut jolokia/green chillies	1–2, chopped
Tomatoes	2–3, sliced

METHOD

Heat 1 cup of water in a pan.

Add the smoked pork cubes with a little salt. Cover and cook for 15 minutes, stirring occasionally.

Add crushed garlic, chillies, and sliced tomatoes.

Cover and cook for another 10 minutes or till the water has been absorbed.

Add the lai haak and cook without the lid on till everything is mixed well with pork oil and spices.

Serve hot with steamed rice.

GITIKA SAIKIA'S DRY FISH AND BOILED TARO CHUTNEY

MAKES: 300 GMS TIME TAKEN: 20 MINUTES

INGREDIENTS

Taro tuber	250 gms
Dry fish	2–3, preferably fermented
Bhut jolokia	1, grilled
Tomato	1, chargrilled

Garlic	3 cloves, chargrilled and peeled
Salt	to taste
Mustard oil	2 tsp
Maan dhoniya (broad leaf cilantro)	a handful, chopped
Heart leaves (mosundari)	a handful, chopped

METHOD

Boil and clean the taro.

Mash it and set aside.

Clean the fish in water, dry roast and coarsely pound it with bhut jolokia, garlic, and tomato.

Mix everything with salt and a dash of raw mustard oil.

Add all the leaves and serve immediately.

JOEL BASUMATARI'S SMOKED PORK WITH AXONE

SERVES: 6 TIME TAKEN: 1.5 HOURS

INGREDIENTS

Smoked pork	1 kg
Fermented soybeans (axone, use Sema variety)	200 gms
Dried red chillies	15
Majenga (*Zanthoxylum*) seeds	2 tbsp, broiled and crushed
Local Naga ginger	10 gms
Local Naga garlic	10 gms
Majenga leaves	a handful, for garnish
Tomato (optional)	1, chopped
Salt	to taste

METHOD

Wash smoked pork with hot water and cut into big pieces. Set aside.

Add fermented soybeans (axone), dried chillies, and tomato, in sufficient water, and continue to boil until the soybeans have developed flavour.

Remove the whole red chillies and grind them along with salt, using a mortar and pestle.

Cook the dish for an hour until the gravy thickens.

Add the smoked meat to the gravy and let it cook for another 30 minutes. When the meat is well-cooked and tender, add the chilli paste and cook for 5 minutes.

Crush ginger and garlic and add to the dish.

Add the broiled and crushed majenga seeds and boil the gravy for a few more minutes.

Garnish with fried majenga leaves.

Serve with steamed rice and chutney.

RIKYNTI SYIEM'S SMOKED PORK WITH BAMBOO SHOOTS

SERVES: 4 TIME TAKEN: 1–1.5 HOURS

INGREDIENTS:

Smoked pork	½ kg
Garlic	6–8 cloves
Black sesame	Roasted and pounded, 1 tbsp
Bamboo shoots	4 tbsp, chopped
Green/red chillies	3–4
Salt	to taste

METHOD

Wash the smoked pork and boil in water.

After boiling for about 30 minutes, add bamboo shoots. Boil for some more time.

Add crushed garlic cloves or garlic paste.

Add black sesame seed paste.

Add some chillies and salt and cook till the bamboo shoots become tender.

Serve hot.

Rasgulla

BALL OF FAME

I'm in awe of the rasgulla.[1]

Each time I witness a ball of cottage cheese puff up in a pool of sugar syrup, I'm dazzled. From its ethereal looks to its honeycomb-like texture, rasgulla is an incredibly sophisticated sweet. It's nothing short of a marvel that curdled milk can transform into something so utterly delectable.

Indians are among the few people in the world who combine cottage cheese with sugar. What leap of imagination led to this ingenious take on the centuries-old practice of curdling milk? How and when did cheese get transmuted so ingeniously in the hands of Indian sweet-makers?

The war over the GI tag that erupted in 2015 offered two very different answers to such questions. With both West Bengal and Odisha staking a claim over rasgulla's origins, the battle between the neighbouring states got fiercely territorial. Odias traced the sweet's origins to the age-old ritual of giving it as bhog (sacred offering) at the Jagannath Temple on Niladri Bije, the last ritual of Rath Yatra. Bengalis, on the other hand, insisted that it was invented by Nobin Chandra Das, the 'Columbus of rosogolla', in 1868.

At the heart of the skirmish was the practice of making chhena (also known as chhana) or cottage cheese, the pillowy dairy derivative that forms the base of the puffy sweet. Many believe that the practice of making chhena was introduced by the Portuguese during the seventeenth century when they had settled in the Hooghly district of West Bengal.[2] Made from acidified milk, traditionally regarded as taboo by the adherents of Hinduism,[3] it could not have been used to make sweets at the Jagannath Temple in preceding centuries as claimed by the Odias, others argued.

The bitter war of words eventually settled with both West Bengal and Odisha being granted the GI status for their respective versions, based on their ingredients, texture, and taste.

The controversy piqued my curiosity for reasons other than the sweet's origins. For years, I'd dreamt of exploring Kolkata's rasgulla scene, wanting to get as close as possible to the mindboggling diversity offered by Bengali sweet-makers, known as moiras. Now, I also wanted to taste the sweet's iterations in Odisha, which don't get enough play outside the state.

To fully appreciate the magic and scope of the sugary confection, I had to eat it in both states. A pilgrimage for rasgullas—what could be sweeter?

BANGLAR ROSOGOLLA

Warm Rosogollas at Jamuna Sweets with Poorna Banerjee

My mishti ('sweet' in Bengali) adventure began with Kolkata food wiz Poorna Banerjee, who took me to a sweet shop at her para (neighbourhood) in Kolkata's Phoolbagan for warm rosogollas. 'Gorom (warm) rosogolla is a Bengali obsession. You can't not want one,' dished the curly-haired blogger, who has been chronicling the arc of Bengali food and cooking for years.

Clad in a billowing white maxi dress, Poorna spoke with tireless gusto about Kolkata's favourite sweet. Not only are rosogollas considered the most satisfying when enjoyed hot off the kadhai, she told me, the sugared tonic is the go-to comfort food when you are down with a bout of 'pet kharap' or diarrhoea. 'A warm rosogolla is the purest form of protein, carbs, fat, and sugar in digestible form. When your body can't retain anything else, the simple food gets easily absorbed and gives you instant energy,' she explained, as we drove down the lanes of north Kolkata for our session.

The idea of taking me to a corner shop was not just to introduce me to this beloved local tradition but also to immerse me in the authentic culture of rosogollas. 'In Kolkata, everybody goes to the local mishti shop, as chhena is highly perishable. It's in these tiny joints that you see traditional sweet-making practices still thriving. And it is here that the poor queue up to get leftover "ros" or syrup to enjoy with their rotis,' she said.

Jamuna Sweets is an unprepossessing shop with a small storefront. When we arrived, a fresh batch of rosogollas was being turned out. Seeking shade from the heat under the spreading branches of a jacaranda tree, we grabbed a couple right away. The warm dumpling bounced slightly in my mouth as I took my first creamy-sweet bite. Habituated to eating stiff, refrigerated rosogollas, I was struck by how much the experience of eating the sweet changed at a higher temperature. It felt softer and utterly comforting, like the culinary equivalent of soaking in a hot tub.

Pleasantly sweet, it did not have the saccharine quality usually associated with mass-produced mithai. As I swallowed one round of sweets after another, Poorna chortled. 'I told you,' she said. 'When it comes to rosogollas, enough is never enough.'

Chatting with my companion, I learnt that rosogollas show up at virtually every special occasion in Kolkata. They are a festival staple, a rite of childhood, a party-circuit stalwart, an excuse for rosogolla-eating competitions and addas, and even bring a smile at funerals. 'Oh, and they taste amazing when you're high,' Poorna said, recalling her university binges.

It's the precise method of cooking the sweet that renders Banglar (Bengali) rosogolla a standout, she stressed. To demonstrate her point, she squeezed one out until it became a fraction of its size. 'This sponginess is a defining feature of Bengal's rosogolla. The Odia rasagola is firmer, almost crunchy in texture and has an inelastic structure, whereas our spongy version has a stretchy, flexible texture that only cow milk can achieve.'

The single-string consistency of the ros or sugar syrup makes the Bengali variant lighter. And the precise syrup-to-chhena ratio gives the delicacy a flavour that's sweet without being cloying. 'A Bengali rosogolla is an exercise in restraint. In this sense, we are a lot like the Japanese,' Poorna opined.

It's no surprise that the carefully calibrated confection marked a culinary milestone when it was first devised. The orb struck a chord not just with its simplicity, but also for its pearly hue. Before the arrival of rosogollas, Poorna revealed, chhena was mainly used to make sondesh, a dry Bengali sweet made from mashed cottage cheese. Learning the art of boiling chhena balls in sugar syrup enabled sweet-makers to create a whole new genre of syrup-based sweets known as rosher mishti.

Some of the latter category was displayed in the shop counter—rosomalai or rosogollas soaked in sweetened milk; malai chop or rosogolla discs slathered with thick cream; cham cham, or elongated, squeezed-out rosogollas with a creamy khoa core; rajbhog, or large, stuffed rosogollas flavoured with saffron and cardamom; and kheer kadam, or rosogollas enrobed in a thick layer of khoa. 'All are versions of rosogolla, so you can see how Bengalis perfected the art of making this sweet. We made so many things out of it and gave it a strong identity. That's why we can proudly claim it as our own,' she said.

Sated on sweetness, we got a shingara (West Bengal's version of the samosa) each. The savoury was tiny in size, with a thinner crust than the Punjabi samosa. The potatoes were finely diced instead of mashed, and seasoned with just a hint of panch phoron (blend of five spices used in eastern India). Two bites and it was over.

I was grateful to Poorna for starting my education at Jamuna Sweets. It was so much more interesting than the slick predictability of the sweet available at factory-run big brands. Not only did I understand better what rosogolla means to Kolkata, I came away with a newfound respect for Kolkata's independent sweet shops and stalls. A source of joy to millions, these unassuming haunts democratize access to the city's favourite sweets by making them affordable.

They are the real heroes of the mishti world.

Spongy Rosogollas at K. C. Das and Rosogolla Bhaban

Any rosogolla trail that skips K. C. Das, the birthplace of the Banglar rosogolla, would feel as sacrilegious as visiting the Vatican City without a stop at the Sistine Chapel.

Old-world craftsmanship reigns supreme at this legacy sweet shop. It was here that Nobin Chandra Das first transformed chhena into the spongy, spherical sweet we adore and revere. In the first stage of the trial in 1866, the young sweet-maker took fragmented clumps of boiled, mashed chhena; added raisins, pistachios, and saffron; and shaped them into balls to make a sweetmeat called baikuntha bhog. Two years later, after more trial and error, he mastered the technique of boiling the sugar syrup in a way that the cottage cheese balls didn't disintegrate, and the rosogolla was born.[4] In 1930, the legend's son, Krishna Chandra Das, helped spread the sweet outside its native home by creating a canned variant that lasted longer. The first major tweak on rosogolla, the rosomalai (or ras malai), was also invented here,[5] as were many subsequent iterations like ras madhuri (oval or rectangular rosogollas dipped in sweetened milk and decorated with sondesh cream) and prabhu bhog (rajbhog covered with grated khoa and garnished with pistachios).

Ritajit Chatterjee, the quality-control executive at the K. C. Das factory at the time,[6] had agreed to give me a tour and greeted me at the entrance. The automation of the unit, tucked away in the historic quarter of Bagbazar, felt like a world away from the roadside mishti shop I had visited the previous day. When I entered, 1,000 litres of milk had just arrived and was being boiled and curdled into chhena in batches.

As we entered the hall where the sweets were made, the steam from boiling rosogollas hit my face. Machines whirred and bleeped and the fresh, earthy smell of chhena hung in the air. 'The rosogolla you make is only as good as the chhena you use,'[7] Ritajit said, as he handed me a small ball of the soft cheese. It was smooth, cool, and slightly bouncy.

Ritajit described the steps involved in making the rosogollas, honed to a precise science over the decades. First, boiled milk is curdled by mixing with whey water to extract chhena. A quick dip in water purifies the precipitate, ridding it of the acidic taste. After being drained in a centrifuge, the chhena is kneaded into a smooth paste. The soft cheese is then rolled into balls, boiled in sugar syrup until plump, and dropped in a lighter syrup to soak.

The sponginess of the rosogolla, Ritajit pointed out, boils down to a bit of chemistry. The chhena has to be processed from raw cow milk with a precise fat content of 3.5 to 4 per cent. The whey has to mix with the milk at a particular temperature (85°C). The thickness of the sugar syrup has to be maintained at 30 to 40 per cent. Brix and boiling time must be closely monitored. 'In short, it's the most temperamental sweet you can possibly make,' he said.

Sponginess is symbolic too, as Dhiman Das, the director of K. C. Das, told me during our meeting at his historic home, Rosogolla Bhaban, on Rabindra Sarani. Dhiman da, as he is fondly known, regards the rosogolla as a metaphor for the quintessentially inclusive nature of Bengalis. 'The porosity of rosogolla, much like the city of Kolkata, absorbs people of all classes, castes, creed, and colour. Its sweetness unites all,' he said.

What about the acrimony that ensued from the GI war, I asked. 'Oh, that had its good side too. After all, had it not been for the controversy, this issue would never have come up, and we wouldn't have got our GI tag,' said Dhiman, whohad led the battle to protect the legacy of his ancestors.

With the issue settled, he was excited about his latest innovation—vegan rosogollas. After months of experiments with different concentrations of non-dairy milk, trials were in their final stages. 'Soymilk has too strong a taste, so we have been trying out almond milk. We'll get there with a few more attempts,' said Ritajit.

The Art of Rosogolla-tasting with Nitai Ghosh at Chittaranjan Mistanna Bhandar

To enjoy the sweet's legacy more fully, I stepped into another north Kolkata rosogolla shrine, the pocket-sized Chittaranjan Mistanna Bhandar dating back to 1907. Often regarded as the finest rosogolla shop in all of Kolkata, the icon is helmed by the ebullient Nitai Ghosh.

Hailed as the master of the sponge rosogolla and known for the years of scientific research he has put into perfecting the sweet, the doyen had invited me to learn the art of rosogolla-tasting. I had no idea such a thing existed, but the notion of savouring the sweet like a fine wine intrigued me.

An earthen pot or khuri with two snowy rosogollas nestled in a pool of syrup was waiting for my tasting tutorial. My teacher's opening instructions made it clear that he regarded the rosogolla not as an intellectual but a visceral pleasure. 'Don't use your head, use your heart. You need to taste a rosogolla with all your five senses. Only then will its character unfold,' he said.

As I gingerly picked up the khuri, Nitai told me to bend and really get my nose inside to experience the bouquet more profoundly. I closed my eyes and inhaled, allowing myself to be enveloped by the mellow, milky smell. 'Now take a bite, and roll it over your tongue,' he instructed. The sweet sloshed with juice as I bit into it. It was a little chewy with just a hum of sweetness, and especially delicate—among the finest I had eaten.

A creature of habit, I unwittingly squeezed out the second rosogolla before biting into it. This did not go down well with my mentor. 'Oh no! You just killed the rosogolla!' Nitai cried. 'The extra syrup should automatically get out with each bite. If you squeeze the sweet, the aroma goes out with the syrup. Remember, rosogolla is ros first, then golla. You cannot get rid of the syrup. It's the soul and body of a rosogolla.'

Cooling down a bit, he explained, 'Don't pinch a rosogolla. Love it, touch it, hug it. Make love to a rosogulla. Don't murder it. If you squeeze it, you only get the dead body.' A second round of rosogollas was ordered followed by a third. With each attempt, I learnt to eat more slowly, mindfully, and appreciatively. The class set off a sensorial journey like no other. It made me see the sweet as a gourmet food in the same league as the fussiest French confections.

Spending time with Nitai at the shop, I discovered that his approach to rosogolla-making was as intuitive as his appreciation of its taste. Despite mechanization having come to the brand, the crafting of rosogollas at Chittaranjan continues to be understood sensorily, in terms of touch, smell, sight, and feel.

'The karigars here still shape the rosogolla balls by hand and boil them manually. They know just from a glance or a sniff whether they have turned out right. Now that's true love,' he murmured.

Baked Rosogollas with Sudip Mullick at Balaram Mullick & Radharaman Mulllick

A man of limitless imagination, Sudip Mullick, the scion of Balaram Mullick & Radharaman Mullick, culls boldly from a global repertoire, presenting Bengali sweets in a modish way.

His baked rosogollas,[8] blanketed in creamy layers of sondesh and rabri (dried top layers of milk dipped in condensed milk), and browned to a golden crisp, have been hailed as a modern classic. Curious to learn about the trailblazing confection, I stepped into their Jadu Babu Bazaar outlet in Bhawanipur.

The shop, with its colourful displays, wooden floors and panelling, and sweet aromas, was a bit like the mishti equivalent of Willy Wonka's chocolate factory.

Trim and lithe, Sudip showed up directly from the gym. Chatting in his office, he shared that the baked treat was created over a month of trials in 2004, when he was fresh out of catering college. Intrigued by the international baked dishes like au gratin, baked Alaska, and tetrazzini, he wanted to apply similar techniques to mishti.

The first attempt involved covering rosogollas with shredded Amul cheese and baking them in his trusty OTG. The result was too salty. The second trial, this time with mozzarella, made for a meltier finish, but saltiness remained an issue. By the third attempt, he had figured that the complex, aromatic sweetness of nolen gur (date palm jaggery) rosogollas—the kind that's made by boiling chhena balls in jaggery syrup—worked better for the baked version. The final masterstroke was to bake the sweet with rabri.

The experiment yielded an exceptional sweet. Until then, Kolkata moiras knew only steaming, boiling, and deep-frying. They had never baked. The new sensation took the city by storm. 'Kolkatans had never seen anything like it. People were attracted to the shine, the glaze, the smokiness, the decadent burnt-top look of a baked rosogolla. They loved it,' he said.

Sudip's playful spirit had spawned several other rosogolla creations, including his truffle rosogollas that come in an assortment of flavours. For sheer spectacle, nothing matches his flambéed rosogollas, which he loves to make for weddings. 'I shallow-fry the rosogollas till they become a little reddish in colour, then pour rum and ignite them, and finish with some nolen gur cream. People go crazy,' he shared.

The latest ace up his sleeve is an air-fried rosogolla, a concept that has not hit the market yet. The idea is to dehydrate a rosogolla to preserve it. 'When you add warm water and re-hydrate it, it becomes fresh again.' Though it's still a work in progress, Sudip has experimented enough with the innovation to know it will work.

By the end of our conversation, several trays of mishti had done the rounds—chocolate sondesh with a swirl of ganache, creamy madhuparka made from yoghurt and khoa, blueberry doi (curd) with real fruit pulp, daab (tender coconut) sondesh, and of course, baked rosogollas.

'How on earth do you remain so fit amid so much decadence?' I asked Sudip as we were about to say goodbye.

'That's why I hit the gym,' he said, grinning. 'So I can eat more mishti.'

Kamala Bhog with Oiendrila Ray Kapur

When I entered Oiendrila Ray Kapur's sprawling penthouse in Ballygunge, there were spectacular blooms bursting out of pots and vases from virtually every corner of her living room—pristine white jasmines; plump, pink-tinged lotus buds; and a blaze of coral ixoras.

'The flowers are for you,' said the entrepreneur, welcoming me with a warm hug. The co-founder of KOI Worldwide, a Kolkata-based luxury travel company, had invited me over for a homemade Bengali meal alongside the rosogollas that she grew up eating in her native village in Bengal's Malda district. 'The variety you get in the Bengali countryside is quite different from the spongy ones we have in Kolkata. They're smaller and disappear in your mouth,' she said.

We sat down at the ornate table, laid out with a starched linen tablecloth, embroidered napkins, and heirloom silverware, with food to match. The gleaming silver thalas (platters) were a wedding gift from Oi's parents. 'Most people keep these things under lock and key, but I believe in laying it all out. It instantly makes any occasion special!' she said.

The multi-round meal, served in true-blue Bengali style, was designed to showcase the individual flavours of each combination. It kicked off with chholar dal (Bengal gram) and aloo posto, the quintessential Bengali potato dish made with poppy seeds. The second course comprised chingrir malaikari, a creamy prawn curry made with coconut milk and spices. Next came slow-cooked mutton or kosha mangsho, another Bong favourite, followed by a round of plum chutney with papad.

To my amusement, Gagan, Oi's Punjabi husband, opted to have everything served together. 'I don't have the patience for all these courses,' he said. 'Give me all the good stuff already.'

As we ate, Oi recounted vignettes from her fairytale childhood in Malda. Life in her village was full of traditions and festivals, and rosogollas invariably starred in these celebrations. 'I can still see myself standing outside the bharar ghor (pantry), waiting for the aunt-in-charge to hand me a couple extra rosogollas. The syrup running down my hands, the bliss of engulfing those tiny balls one after the other! Damn! I wish I could be that child again, even if it's for a day!'

It wasn't white rosogollas but sunny yellow ones that festooned the table at the end of the meal. Oi, who considered classic rosogollas a tad plain for special occasions, had got their family cook to make kamala bhog, a sophisticated version of the original, enlivened with orange zest. The treat was rich and silky, proof that the classic only gets better with a whispery touch of citrus. The colour reminded me of Van Gogh's sunflowers.

Oiendrila had chosen to serve the sweet as a homage to her late grandmother, who would pour her being into making delicious mishti for the family when she was alive. 'I called her Dida, though the rest of the house called her mejo ma. I always associate the texture and flavour of kamala bhog with her,' she shared.

Two distinct memories of the matriarch stood out for Oiendrila. The first was from her childhood, during her doll's wedding to her cousin's doll. 'We were all of five or six, and those were the kinds of games we played in a tech-free world,' she said, laughing. The ever-indulgent Dida had decided to play along with the idea and made miniature mishti for the imaginary nuptials!

The second memory was of Dida making sweets again, this time for Oiendrila's (real) wedding. 'With over 2,000 guests attending, the tenacious lady at the ripe old age of eighty-four, made chhanar jilipi (fried chhena and khoa spirals in syrup) and kamala bhog for everyone, with just one assistant. That, for me, was the biggest gift I received at my wedding,' she said emotionally.

We sat around long after the meal, chatting and reminiscing. With her finely honed aesthetics, my hostess had managed to recreate the sort of elaborate meals once served in aristocratic homes, presenting dishes like rare works of art. I will never forget the display of finely chosen tableware, Oi's warm hospitality, and her love for good food.

Assembly Desserts and Innovations

The rosogolla, being a ubiquitous sweet in Kolkata, is the star ingredient of a host of assembly dishes.

I tasted a delicious version, courtesy of art collector Bomti Iyengar, whose charming home offers sweeping views of the Eden Gardens, the Shaheed Minar, and the Howrah Bridge. The rosogolla payesh he fed me was the recreation of a beloved dessert he would eat as a kid. I watched it being made in his kitchen by his cook Shankar, who added squeezed-out rosogollas bought from the corner shop to thickened milk. The slight chewiness of the rosogollas offered a delicious contrast to the smooth creaminess of the base. The taste was very subtle, and not too heavy or sweet. I reached for seconds and thirds.

Kewpie's restaurant owner Rakhi Purnima Dasgupta[9] called me over for an interesting savoury twist on the classic. A bowl of pre-bought rosogollas and warm water was set down before me on a table as I watched Rakhi's Man Friday squeeze out each sweet thrice—twice in warm water and then in cold water. He then made a regular curry base of ginger, garlic, onions, and tomatoes, and simply added the squeezed rosogollas to it.

I didn't much care for it on the first bite, but by the third I found it oddly interesting. The dish worked because of its unexpectedness—the novelty of a rosogolla being served as a savoury. The combination of tomato-onion curry masala and rosogolla hugged the line between savoury and sweet, making it impossible to tell one from the other.

For foodpreneur Swati Saraf, the rosogolla is a magical medium for endless riffs on flavours. Ranging from quirky to downright outrageous, no pairing is taboo for the 'flavour queen of rosogollas'. Swati took to experimenting with rosogollas after walking out of an abusive marriage. She had her thunderclap moment when a handi of rosogollas arrived on her father's birthday and no one was interested in eating them. Realizing that the allure of the confection had weakened over time, the nonconformist devised flavours like paan, green chilli, alphonso, muskmelon, litchi, even vodka and bhang (hemp).

The idea of a Maggi rosogolla made me blanch, but the whacky creation had earned her a huge fan following among kids. In the purist mishti circles of Kolkata, these whimsical creations may be frowned upon, but all Swati needs is her market. Three-hundred-and-fifty flavours later, she is unstoppable. 'It worked out nicely in the end,' she said. 'The rosogolla gave me a new life. And I gave new life to it.'

Echoing Swati, Lahana Ghosh, the outspoken scion of Jugal's, a leading mishti brand in Kolkata, conceded that the iconic sweet had fallen out of favour, elbowed aside by a pantheon of trendier confections. 'You don't see kids hanging out at mishti shops anymore. They find pastries sexier than rosogollas,' she rued, as we met over coffee at the historic Calcutta South Club.

Her approach to making mishti cool, though, was not by creating modern variants or new flavours, but shining the spotlight back on legacy. 'I don't want to innovate. I want to celebrate what we have,' she said.

Lahana, who grew up watching rosogollas being made in the first-floor karkhana (factory) of her Sealdah home in central Kolkata, considers the sweet a one-of-a-kind handmade artifact. Its future, and that of all mishti, she believes, lies in preserving age-old artisan traditions of sweet-making and advocating a better life for the karigars or sweet-makers. 'Karigars are the DNA of mishti. Their understanding of milk and sugar is unparalleled. If we lose them, we lose everything. For our sweets to flourish, we need to pay them well, train them, bring them forward with us,' she said passionately.

Unlike the much-touted French pastry traditions, she argued, Bengali mishti has yet to be projected as the exceptional product it is. The old practice of making rosogollas with nokuldana (mimosa sugar balls) exemplifies the sophistication of the sweet. 'When chhena balls are first cooked in syrup, the nokuldana inside them melts, creating a network of sugar-syrup channels. This web, flexible after being soaked again in sweet syrup, gives the rosogolla its soft, sponge-like texture. Designed to trap syrup in its crevices, the structure ensures that squeezing it releases the syrup, while dipping it again soaks it back up, allowing for a delightful experience of absorbing and releasing flavours,' she explained.

Showcasing these artisanal methods of making rosogollas through viral social media reels and organizing The Jugal's Literature Festival in 2023, the first of its kind devoted to Bengali mishti, are some of the steps that she has taken to mine her legacy with an eye to the future.

Later that evening, Lahana sent some rosogollas over to my hotel. As I gently pulled one apart to admire its filigreed interior, I could feel the passion of the karigar who had honed it. Its scent, stamped with the provenance of its ingredients, took me to another time and place.

I took a bite and braced for heaven.

ODIA RASAGOLA

Pahala Rasagolas and Khirmohan with Sweta Biswal

Rasgulla arouses as much frenzy in Odisha as it does in the neighbouring state. And it's no Betty to West Bengal's Veronica. Here, the soft, non-spongy avatar is the star of the show. It's even spelt differently. 'R-a-s-a-g-o-l-a. Don't say "rasgulla" or "rosogolla" here, or you'll get into a lot of trouble,' warned Odia food expert Sweta Biswal, cocking an eyebrow. Sweta, who has a legion of fans on Instagram and recently authored her first book *Beyond Dalma*, had agreed to be my culinary guide in Odisha.

We were on our way to Pahala, where a stretch of 100-odd shops along the Bhubaneswar–Cuttack Highway produce the gold standard of Odisha's rasagolas. The kiosks draw visitors from across the country to savour their famously delicate light-brown rasagola. Sweta promised that it would be the softest rasagola I would ever eat. 'You'll fall in love,' she said, smile widening to a grin as she told me about her rasagola-crazed twelve-year-old. 'He won't let me enter the house if I don't take some back for him today.'

Sweta has an openness that makes her easy to be around. Like most Odias, she believes that rasagolas have existed in Odisha for centuries. The tradition, she pointed out, is well documented in Balarama Dasa's Dandi Ramayana, written in the fifteenth century.[10] Several other sources bear out the lineage of the sweet, confirming that chhena was extensively in use in medieval India.[11]

'Odias created the rasagola. Bengalis put it into a can,' Sweta quipped.

'But if Odia rasagolas are so old, how come they are not as famous as the Bengali ones?' I asked.

'Oh, that's just because us Odias don't shout about our talent. There's a lot of incredible food in Odisha. People just don't know about it,' she said with a shrug.

Veering the conversation to less murky waters, I enquired about the Pahala rasagola's origins. Admitting that they were nebulous at best, Sweta said that as per popular belief, a priest from the Jagannath Temple had taught the people of Gobindpur, a nearby village, the art of making rasagolas. 'The sweet would be made and sold in the village, till some enterprising guy thought of opening a shop next to the highway. It caught on and now most shops have shifted to Pahala.'

Crossing chhena suppliers on motorcycles making their way through the traffic, we reached our destination. With sweet shops as far as the eye could see, Pahala is one ginormous pot of rasagolas. Scouring the kiosks, we saw the sweet displayed in a gamut of browns running from barely beige to golden-brown and toffee. There were different sizes too, for different prices.

We stopped to talk to Sanjay, owner of the eponymous shop, which he has been running for over two decades. The supersized rasagola he treated us to was moist, dripping, and so light that it was like biting into sweet air. The wispy confection hummed with the faintest whiff of cardamom. I couldn't think of a more delectable way to savour the fresh, dairy flavour of chhena.

The brown colouring and slightly toasty taste, Sweta told me, comes from cooking the rasagolas longer than their Bengali counterparts, causing the syrup to caramelize. Also, unlike the spongy Bengali rosogolla, where no binder is used, the Pahala karigars use a bit of semolina to bind the mixture.

Moving on from Pahala, an hour's drive got us to Salepur, a town famed for another landmark sweet shop, Bikalananda Kar's Rasagola. Regarded as an icon of Odia mithai, it is to Odisha what K. C. Das is to West Bengal. The 100-year-old brand, started by its eponymous owner, is famed for its khirmohan, a brown rasagola with thicker, sweeter syrup.

Chatting with Saipriya, the granddaughter of the founder, who manages the brand along with her family, I learnt that the difference in formulation between the Pahala and the Bikalananda Kar rasagola lies in the sugar-to-water ratio of the syrup and the longer boiling time of the latter confection.

The first bite made me wince. Intensely sweet, it was like sucking on a piece of candy. Cooked for a longer time, its sugars and milk solids had caramelized more, imbuing the sweet with a rich butterscotch-like flavour. With its assertive sweetness and graininess, the tawny confection had the depth of a recipe handed down generations.

To preserve this precious legacy and pass on the knowledge needed for local sweet traditions to survive, the Kar family had opened India's first culinary college dedicated to Odia sweet-making. The institution teaches students how to make over 500 varieties of sweets from Odisha, using both modern and traditional techniques.

'We encourage students to learn and then work for us. The only way forward is education. The fate of our sweets hinges on this,' Saipriya said, ending our meeting on a note of promise.

White Rasagolas at Jagannath Temple, Puri

Rasagolas have deep religious significance across Odisha, but it is in Puri, home to the venerated Jagannath Temple, that this faith reaches its crescendo. The apocryphal story goes that Lord Jagannath, on returning from his nine-day Rath Yatra, pacified his wife Lakshmi by offering her rasagolas when she blocked his entry into the temple. The goddess was angry with him for taking his siblings Balaram and Subhadra on the yatra instead of her. The resolution of the lovers' tiff, known as Rasagola Puja, is performed each year on Niladri Bije, the final ritual of the Rath Yatra.

Though I couldn't time my visit for the festival, chief servitor of the Jagannath Temple, Badagrahi Jagannath Swain Mohapatra aka Guru ji, who ties the marriage knot between Jagannath and Lakshmi during the rasagola ceremony, had agreed to meet me at his home. The Badagrahis are tribals and considered close relatives of Lord Jagannath.

Guru ji was in the cowshed. Clad in a dhoti and a vest, a gold chain and rudraksh mala adorning his neck, he looked content with his herd of bovine friends. 'I feel at peace here,' he said.

The vexed issue of origins seemed to matter little to the priest, who views rasagola as an expression and extension of the divine, fashioned from the shape of Lord Jagannath's eyes. 'Jab se Jagannath hai, tab se rasagola hai (Rasagola is as old as Jagannath himself),' he said.

He believes that the superior quality of milk yielded by the local cows is the reason the deity chose to live in Puri. 'Our chhena is the best because of the local water and the fresh cow's milk brought in from the countryside,' he said. His son Raja, also a priest, concurred. 'Puri rasagolas have no cardamom flavouring or caramelization of sugar. Only the purest white rasagola is offered as bhog during the Rath Yatra.'

I tried one on my way to the temple. The puffy, ivory dumpling was a straight shot to the soul. It was firm yet ultra-soft with pristine milky notes and a lingering, creamy finish.

Inside the temple complex, falling under the spiritual spell of Puri's life seemed like the most natural thing amid the colour and pageantry of traditions observed over centuries, the throngs of devotees, the layers of faith. Everything there was tied to Jagannath, regarded as more of a living deity than a god. 'Jagannath and I have a very informal relationship. I talk to him like I would talk to my elder brother,' Raja da said affectionately.

Later, as the priest drove me to Chandrabhaga beach, the sunset took on a magical quality. Watching the sky change from burnt marmalade to dusky lavender, he turned thoughtful. 'Rasagola encourages us to look inward,' he said. 'Think about it. Just two ingredients—milk and sugar—come together to create something so perfect. It's a mantra to live by. Just work with what you have, and you can be happy.'

His words resonated profoundly with me. I felt soothed, anchored, nourished. As I was leaving for Bhubaneswar, Raja got me a fresh batch of rasagolas from a roadside shop to recharge my sweet tooth for the journey back. Cupping the clay handi, I felt the heat of the freshly made sweets.

It made me smile. I was ending where I started. With a treat of warm rasgullas.

My circle of sweetness was complete.

◆

My visit let me look at a familiar sweet with new eyes. I tasted some extraordinary versions and met some wonderful people. The best part—I could justify gorging on sweets round the clock.

So who makes the better rasgulla?

It's tough to choose. If I had to distil my trip into one thought, I would say that the sweet rises above any state or individual and refuses to be classified by GI tags. The ultimate pacifist, its persuasive powers are legendary. It soothes the tummy, makes peace between Lord Jagannath and his missus, and bridges social divides. Give peace a chance, the rasgulla says in Satyajit Ray's classic *Goopy Gyne Bagha Byne*, which has the spongy orbs falling from the sky and bringing an end to war.

The origin of the confection is a culinary mystery that is unlikely to be solved. As Ishita Dey, co-author of *Beyond Kolkata: Rajarhat and the Dystopia of Urban Imagination*, pointed out, the GI tag war, while reiterating how food and place are entangled, also exposed its limits. 'Places are made of people, especially migrants. In that sense there is no single story of origins and multiple legends of origins point to different foodways. There is a lot of intermingling of cultures between Odisha and West Bengal, and with constant cross-fertilization of influences, the boundaries have blurred,' she said.

I was intrigued by the tapestry of styles I tasted in both states, which, for all their differences, shared many elements: the mastery over milk and sugar, the love of old-world traditions and the emphasis on sensory craftsmanship. The cerebral, elegant approach of the Bengalis was in stark contrast to the folkloric approach of the Odias. The former saw it as a tightrope-walk of technique, while the latter regarded it as an embodiment of faith, ritual, and continuity. This duality makes the rasgulla one of India's most fascinating sweets.

In an increasingly interconnected world, inspiration is more important than origins. Rather than politicizing the confection, we should harness its vast global potential. Indian cheese desserts, led by rasgulla and its variants[12] and would benefit from building an even stronger brand identity. The sweets are lighter and healthier and deliver that creamy mouthfeel without being heavy.

There is so much going for the rasgulla—its sensual charisma, its universal ingredients, its pop-culture appeal. Refusing to be static, the sweet can be baked, flavoured, and refashioned into different forms. And with modern iterations popping up all over the place, the possibilities are endless.

Let us celebrate laudable initiatives like The Jugal's Literature Festival and the Bikalananda Kar Industrial Training Centre, on both sides of the state border. Could such worthy efforts provide a roadmap for the future of Indian sweets?

As a mithai lover, I can say, we should only be so lucky.

OIENDRILA RAY KAPUR'S KAMALA BHOG

MAKES: 24 TIME TAKEN: 1 HOUR

INGREDIENTS

Cow milk	1 l (try Amul)
Lemon juice/vinegar	2 tsp
Water	2 tsp
Corn flour	1 tbsp
Fresh orange rind	2 inches
Orange food colour	a few drops
Orange essence (optional)	a few drops
Sugar	2 cups
Water	5 cups

METHOD

Put the milk in a large saucepan and bring to a boil. Once boiled, let it simmer for 5 minutes.

Mix 2 tsp lemon juice or 2 tsp vinegar mixed with 2 tsp water and add to the milk. Stir it continuously.

The milk will start to curdle and separate the solids from the liquids.

Take a muslin cloth and hang it over a large vessel. Strain the curdled milk over it and tie the cloth over a tap for 15 minutes until all the excess water has drained away.

Remove this cottage cheese and put on a clean tabletop. Mash it nicely. Add 1 tbsp corn flour and mix it well. Take the 2-inch orange rind and make it into a paste or grate it finely. Add to the cottage cheese.

Add a pinch of orange food colour. Knead it well for 10 minutes until smooth.

Make it into round balls of desired size and keep aside.

Heat 2 cups of sugar with 5 cups of water in a kadhai along with a few drops of orange food colour and orange food essence. Bring the mixture to a boil and then add the cottage cheese balls in the boiling syrup. Let them cook covered for 15 minutes.

Switch off the gas, hold the vessel on both sides, and shake it mildly for 2–3 minutes.

Let the cottage cheese balls stay in the syrup.

Serve warm.

Tip: In case cow milk is not available, you could use fresh full-fat buffalo milk. But do not use milk from tetra packs.

SUDIP MULLICK'S BAKED ROSOGOLLAS

SERVES: 4 TIME TAKEN: 2 HOURS PLUS COOLING

INGREDIENTS

For rosogollas,

Milk	2 l
Vinegar	4 tbsp
Water	4 tbsp
Sugar	2 cups
Water	4 cups

For sondesh,

Chhena	200 gms
Nolen gur	200 gms

For rabri,

Milk	300 ml
Condensed milk	150 gms

METHOD

For rosogollas,

Boil 2 litres of milk in a pan.

Once the milk comes to a boil, switch off the gas, add 4 tbsp vinegar mixed with 4 tbsp water to the milk, and let it split.

Stir the milk slowly, so as to curdle it nicely and let the solids and liquids separate.

Take a muslin cloth and put it over a strainer.

Pour the curdled milk over the muslin cloth so as to drain off the excess liquid.

Hang the cloth over the sink for 10 minutes to remove excess water to form chhena.

Reserve 200 gms of chhena for the sondesh.

Knead the remaining chhena with your palm for 10 minutes until it is smooth and doughy in texture.

Make roundels from this smooth chhena into desired sizes, making sure there are no cracks on the surface.

Heat 2 cups of sugar along with 4 cups of water and bring it to a boil.

Gently put these round chenna balls in the sugar syrup, cover the vessel and let them cook for 15 minutes.

The rosogollas will have doubled in size. Switch off the flame.

Pour 1 cup water to the rosogolla syrup to lighten it and let them cool in it. Chill once they are cooled for a couple of hours.

For sondesh,

Heat a pan with 200 gms of chhena and 200 gms of nolen gur and cook for 10 minutes on a slow flame until it starts to leave the sides of the pan.

Remove the mixture on a plate and let it cool.

For rabri,

Boil 300 ml milk and let it simmer for 15 minutes until it is reduced to half.

Add 150 gms condensed milk to the milk and reserve.

For baked rosogollas,

Put a layer of sondesh mixture on the base of a baking dish.

Squeeze the rosogollas to get rid of excess syrup and arrange on top of the sondesh layer.

Pour the rabri mixture on top of the rosogollas and bake in a hot oven at 200°C for 15–20 minutes until golden-brown on top.

Serve hot.

Tip: For a quick version of this dessert, you could use shop-bought rosogollas, sondesh, and rabri, and layer them and bake in a hot oven.

SWETA BISWAL'S PAHALA RASAGOLAS

MAKES: 10 TIME TAKEN: 1 HOUR 30 MINUTES

INGREDIENTS

Whole cow milk	½ l
Maida/suji	1 tsp
Caramelized sugar	powdered
Cardamom powder	a pinch
Citric acid crystals	½ tsp
Or	
Vinegar	2 tbsp
Sugar	½ cup
Water	2½ cups

METHOD

Bring the milk to a boil on a medium flame in a thick-bottomed vessel.

Once it gets to a rolling boil, keep on the flame for another 2–3 minutes.

Dissolve the citric acid crystals in 1 cup hot water, or vinegar in a cup of room-temperature water.

Remove the milk from the flame and keep aside for 4–5 minutes.

Add the citric acid in one corner of the vessel till the milk shows signs of curdling. Using a spatula, mix the milk thoroughly till the greenish water (whey) and milk solids (chhena) get completely separated.

Place a thin cloth over a metal strainer. Pour the contents of the vessel over it. Wash the chhena under running water to remove all traces of citric acid. Bundle the corners of the cloth and squeeze out all the water (do not squeeze too hard) to make it completely dry.

Hang the chenna for 20 minutes.

Remove the chhena from the cloth and place it on a clean kitchen counter.

Knead the chhena for 10 minutes until it is smooth.

Sprinkle the suji and caramelized sugar over the chhena and continue kneading until it is smooth.

Cover the chhena with a moist cloth and keep aside.

Meanwhile, mix ½ cup sugar with 2½ cups of water and cardamom powder and bring it to a boil.

Pinch small balls out of the chhena dough and roll them into smooth balls between your palms making sure there are no cracks on the balls.

Put these balls in the boiling sugar syrup. Cover with a lid and cook for 30 minutes on a low flame.

Switch off the flame and let them rest for 5 minutes.

Meanwhile, boil 2 cups of water in a saucepan and switch off the flame.

Remove the chhena balls and put them in the hot water for 5 minutes.

Transfer the balls back into the syrup and let it stand for 15 minutes.

Serve immediately (they are best enjoyed warm) or keep in the fridge for a few hours and then serve chilled.

Tip: To make caramelized powdered sugar, heat 100 gms of sugar in a pan with 1 tbsp water until it starts to caramelize. Once caramelized, pour it on an oiled steel plate and let it cool. Once cooled, break into pieces and then powder it in a mixer. Use as required and store the rest.

Acknowledgements

This book represents the confluence of a lot of wonderful people. Many hands held me up along this long journey.

I'm thankful to all the brilliant chefs, home-cooks, bloggers, food historians, and others I met during my travels, for sharing their expertise. I feel beholden to them and hope I have done right by them. Those who have passed away are honoured in these pages. I am lucky and privileged to have known them.

I owe a debt of gratitude to my editor Aienla Ozukum for her infinite patience and many perceptive comments, and to Shaoni Sarkar for her detailed copy-editing. Appreciation is also due to Simar Puneet, a former commissioning editor at Aleph Book Company, who first approached me to write this book.

My father Narendra Kumar Sabharwal read every chapter, and made many useful suggestions. I'm also grateful to Murzban F Shroff, Karan Bali, Dhiman Das, Vikas Khanna, Manish Mehrotra, Ranveer Brar, Colleen Taylor Sen, Hansel Vaz, Rohinton Mehta, Meher Marfatia, Perzen Patel, Srikanth Sheshagiri, Ishita Dey, Geeta Dutta, Manpreet Sidhu, my cook Nargis, and all those who extended their time, support, and insights.

Special thanks are due to Chef Amit Pamnani, my former colleague at *BBC Good Food*, for testing the recipes I have included in this book. His tips, after trying out each dish in his kitchen, have been added to the recipes.

I appreciate the efforts of Yasmin Khambatta for shooting several of the beautiful photos included in this book. A big thank you is due to my friend Pervez Rustomkhan, who helped me with more things than I can list here.

Finally, this book, like anything good in my life, would not have been possible without my mother Promila Sabharwal's blessings.

Notes

Introduction: A Lot on My Plate

1. Arjun Appadurai, 'How to make a National Cuisine: Cookbooks in Contemporary India', *Comparative Studies in Sociology and History*, Vol. 30 No. 1, 1988.

Biryani: Making Rice Dance

1. Abdul Halim Sharar, *Lucknow: The Last Phase of an Oriental Culture*, Delhi: Oxford University Press, 1989, p. 157.
2. Mirza Jafar Hussain, *The Classic Cuisine of Lucknow: A Food Memoir,* Lucknow: Sanatkada Publications, 2016, pp. 128 –129.
3. Author Tarana Husain Khan dwells on the subject in her excellent essay, 'Narrating Rampur's Cuisine: Cookbooks, Forgotten Foods and Culinary Memories', in *Global Food History*, Vol. 9 Issue 2, 2023. She points out that that though the mutiny of 1857 catalysed the refinement of Rampuri cuisine, the nawabs of Rampur had become keen gourmets even earlier. This is evident from the fact that the cookbooks at the Raza Library date back to the early nineteenth century.
4. Tarana has succeeded in reviving nearly fifty old Rampuri recipes. A collection of these will be published in her forthcoming cookbook.
5. The dish was recreated at Jashn-e-Rampur at IIC Delhi, and at Rivaayat Rampur Food Festival at Jeha Numa Palace Hotel, Bhopal.
6. This is noted by food historian Pritha Sen though she adds that potatoes were chosen because they were regarded as exotic. (Nilofer Sen, 'Wajid Ali Shah and the birth of Awadhi Cuisine in Bengal', 7 October 2021, <https://www.goya.in/blog/wjid-ali-shah-and-the-birth-of-awadhi-cuisine-in-bengal>.)
7. Food historian K. T. Achaya notes that, 'by 1780, potatoes, peas and beans, according to an 1860 report, were in high repute as foods in Kolkata…' (*The Illustrated Foods of India A-Z,* New Delhi: Oxford University Press, 2009, p. 210.)
8. Toshita Sahni, 'Swiggy Clocked 83 Million Biryani Orders In India This Year: Report Reveals', *NDTV*, 23 December 2024.

Dosai: Love (and a Little Chemistry)

1. K. T. Achaya, *Indian Food: A Historical Companion*, New Delhi: Oxford University Press, 1994, p. 127.

2. Ibid., p. 46.
3. According to K. T. Achaya, dosai, first mentioned in Tamil Sangam literature of the sixth century CE, existed in ancient Tamil country in the first century CE. Malayali historian P. Thankappan Nair, on the other hand, claimed that the food originated in Udupi in present-day Karnataka. Rice, according to Achaya, was integrated with lentils to make idli batter only after 1250 CE. (*A Historical Dictionary of Indian Food*, New Delhi, Oxford University Press, 2001, p. 104–5).
4. As per Achaya, 'The cooks who accompanied the Hindu kings of Indonesia during their visits home (often to look for brides) between the eighth and twelfth centuries AD, brought innovative fermentation techniques to south India.' (Ibid., p. 105.)
5. In a Tamil Brahmin home, brunch refers to a 9–10 a.m. meal, and tiffin refers to an early-evening 'dinner'. As per Viji, small towns in Tamil Nadu still follow this.
6. According to Krishnamoorthi, thinai (foxtail millet) flour and honey, mixed into a laddoo, is a part of Tamil Nadu's ancient folklore. 'I believe it is mentioned in *Tolkappiyam* that when Lord Muruga (Karthikeya) was courting Valli, a tribal girl, she gave him this laddoo to eat,' he told me.
7. 'Lauric Acid – an overview', sciencedirect.com, <https://www.sciencedirect.com/topics/agricultural-and-biological-sciences/lauric-acid>.
8. Chef Vijay Kumar's south Indian restaurant Semma in New York was awarded a Michelin star in 2024 for the third consecutive year. It is known for its mini kal dosais and gunpowder dosais.

Butter Chicken: The Burden of the Bird

1. Khoa, also known as khoya, khowa, and mawa, is evaporated milk solids.
2. The two parties are currently fighting out a case in court to settle who the real inventor of butter chicken and dal makhani is.
3. When I called up Monish Gujral to fact-check my piece, he claimed that butter chicken was not invented in Delhi, but in Peshawar between 1930 and 1940 by his grandfather Kundan Lal Gujral.
4. Ashish Chopra passed away in 2023.
5. Both Tanzore and The Pink Poppadom closed down a while ago. Gautam Chaudhary currently runs a gourmet consultancy called Demiurgic Hospitality. His most recent reimagining of the dish, 'Butter Chicken Mashtini', is served in a martini glass. To make it, creamy butter chicken curry is ladled over a bed of fluffy mashed potatoes, creating a harmonious blend of savoury and comforting textures, topped with a sprinkling of fresh coriander and a crisp papadum roll to finish.

6. The dhungar process is a traditional north Indian technique used to add a rich, smoky flavour to dishes. To perform it, a piece of hot charcoal is placed in a small bowl within the cooked dish and ghee drizzled over the charcoal to create smoke. The dish is immediately covered to trap the smoky aroma.
7. Malcolm Gladwell, 'The Ketchup Conundrum', *The New Yorker*, 29 August 2004.
8. Jay Rayner, 'The cliche is French food is better than ours. The trouble is, it's true', *The Guardian*, 13 September 2018.

Vada Pav: One for the Road

1. Author Suketu Mehta famously wrote, 'Whose city is Bombay? Bombay is the vadapav eaters' city.... It is the lunch of the chawl dwellers, the cart pullers, the street urchins, the clerks, the cops and the gangsters.' (*Maximum City: Bombay Lost and Found*, New Delhi: Penguin Books India, 2004.)
2. The late chef, writer, and travel documentarian Anthony Bourdain referred to vada pav as the 'Bombay burger' when he tasted the snack in Mumbai.
3. Ashok runs the stall along with his younger brother Ajay.
4. Author Colleen Taylor Sen notes that this became possible due to the Columbian Exchange, or the period of global trade that took place following the 1492 voyage of Christopher Columbus to the Americas. 'The far-flung trading posts of the Portuguese and Spanish empires…became the hubs of a global exchange of fruits, vegetables, nuts and other plants…. To India, the Portuguese introduced potatoes, chillies, okra, papayas, pineapples…and tobacco.' (*Feasts and Fasts: A History of Food in India,* London: Reaktion Books, 2014, p. 212.)
5. The origin of pav is detailed by Lizzie Collingham, who points out that when the Portuguese landed in India, they missed their leavened wheat bread. As yeast was unavailable, the 'ingenious Goan cooks used toddy… to ferment the dough,' resulting in the creation of pav and other breads. (*Curry: A Tale of Cooks and Conquerors,* London: Vintage Books, 2005, p. 60–1)
   Subsequently, Goan immigrants brought the fluffy bread to Mumbai.
6. Khidki Vada is the oldest trademark registered vada pav brand of India, and is available at franchisee shops in Kalyan, Thane, Pune, Indore, and other cities across India. The founder, Yeshwant Vaze, passed away in 2023.
7. Dishoom, owned by Shamil Thakrar, is another popular London eatery that sells vada pav along with other dishes from Mumbai. I got in touch with the brand's Sara Stork, who shared that one of their regular customers would travel all the way from the Isle of Wight once a week just to eat vada pav at their café.
8. Vada pav was ranked thirty-ninth by the experiential food guide TasteAtlas in its 'Top 100 Sandwiches in the World' list in 2025.

9. The latest challenge to the legacy of vada pav has come from the BMC's order calling for Mumbai's traditional brick-oven bakeries, which make the laadi pav used for vada pav, to switch to eco-friendly electric ovens. Baking in a wood-fired oven contributes to the taste and texture of the crusty bread.
10. 'Hawker Culture in Singapore', nhb.gov.sg, < https://www.nhb.gov.sg/what-we-do/our-work/sector-development/unesco/hawker-culture-in-singapore>.
11. 'Hawkers Succession Scheme', nea.gov.sg, https://www.nea.gov.sg/our-services/hawker-management/programmes-and-grants/hawkers-succession-scheme>
12. In recent years, a few schemes have been launched to help hawkers, such as the PM Street Vendor's AtmaNirbhar Nidhi (PMSVANidhi) scheme launched in 2020 to provide capital access to street vendors after the Covid-19 pandemic. The Street Vendors Act, 2014, was introduced to protect the rights of hawkers and regulate vending. However, there has been continued lack of clarity over the act. (Richa Pinto, 'BMC Cracks Down On 20k Hawkers In 2 Months, Residents Say Not Enough', *Times of India*, 22 December 2024.)

Dhansak: An Invitation to Gluttony

1. Parsi kavabs are slightly different from the regular flat kebabs. They are shaped into balls, and usually have a bit of mashed potato along with minced meat in the patty mix.
2. Hormazdyar Dastur Kayoji Mirza writes, 'various theories have been propounded, and various years have been proposed' about the arrival of Parsis in India, ranging from the traditional 716 CE to 936 CE. (*Outlines of Parsi History*, Mumbai: Mirza, 1987, p. 231.)
3. K. T. Achaya, *Indian Food: A Historical Companion*, Delhi: Oxford University Press, 1994, p. 75. Achaya references Santha Rama Rao, *The Cooking of India*, New York: Time-Life Books, 1969, p. 152.
4. I met Keki Umrigar in 2019. He passed away in 2020 during the Covid-19 pandemic. In 2023, Mumbai Parsi Punchayet, in remembrance of Keki's contribution towards maintaining Fire Temple wells, placed a plaque with his name on the well in Godavara Gamadia Agiary in Fort, where he spent his life. The Umrigar Masala business continues as part of the family legacy and is now looked after by Farida Umrigar.
5. Nargis Mistry was the caterer of Ripon Club when I interviewed her. She was replaced by Tehemtan Dumasia. I tried Tehemtan's dhansak at the club recently. It was delicious.
6. Mehroo Kadkhodai passed away in 2024.

7. Hormazdyar Dastur Kayoji Mirza, *Outlines in Parsi History*, Mumbai: Mirza, 1987, p. 231.

Goan Fish Curry: Being Hooman

1. Hansel Vaz pointed out that kokum, the fruit of the *Garcinia indica* tree, is commonly known as 'bhinda' or 'bhinna' in Goa.
2. Teflam is sourced from the Indian Prickly Ash (*Zanthoxylum rhetsa*), a forest tree common in Goa's Western Ghats as well as many other parts of the Indian subcontinent.
3. Nostalgia re-opened with a new team in 2024 but has now closed.
4. Francisco passed away in 2022 from a post-Covid respiratory complication. I regret not being able to meet him after our memorable first meeting.

Undhiyu: Rooting for Change

1. The ingredients and spices for making undhiyu vary widely. This combination is used by Gaurang Sukhadia.
2. Parsis have a dish similar to umbadiyu, known as umbario, made with chicken and vegetables. It features an earthen pot of fire-roasted vegetables and chicken. Alibaug in coastal Maharashtra also has an umbadiyu counterpart known as popti. The non-vegetarian delicacy is made with minimal spices, field beans, onions, potatoes, whole eggs, and chicken. Everything is packed with bhamrut leaves, which have a minty, wild marjoram-like flavour.
3. Chef Varun Inamdar educated me on the many variations of undhiyu. Unlike the Surti version made with green masala, the Kathiawadi undhiyu features a red masala. Then there is chapdi nu undhiyu from Rajkot, a curried version, which comes with chapdi, a wheat flour dumpling; Palanpuri undhiyu, made with mustard oil; Bohri undhiyu, similar to Surti Undhiyu, but made with mutton and jowar muthia; ghada, a spicy Pathare Prabhu variant that includes carrots, eggplants, beetroots, and other vegetables; and ukad handi from Maharashtra's Palghar.
4. Sushila Subodh wrote the bestselling book *Vegetarian Cooking Delights*. She passed away in 2023.
5. Matla nu undhiyu is very similar to umbadiyu but not the same. According to Sushila's daughter-in-law Sharmila Shah, the main difference is in the spicing. Umbadiyu, seasoned with a ground black masala has a dark brown colour, whereas matla nu undhiyu is green, with the natural colour of each vegetable visible.
6. 'Crop biodiversity: use it or lose it', fao.org, <https://www.fao.org/newsroom/detail/Crop-biodiversity-use-it-or-lose-it/>.

7. 'Staple foods: What do people eat?', fao.org, <https://www.fao.org/4/u8480e/u8480e07.htm>.

Shami Kebabs: The Kebab Whisperers

1. Colleen Taylor Sen, *Feasts and Fasts: A History of Food in India*, London: Reaktion Books, 2014, p. 158.
2. Jafar Mir Abdullah passed away in 2023.
3. Abdul Halim Sharar, *Lucknow, The Last Phase of an Oriental Culture*, Delhi: Oxford India Paperbacks, p. 164.
4. Shamis lend themselves beautifully to making a host of vegetarian kebabs including kathal (jackfruit) ke shami, chuqundar (beetroot) ke shami, and arvi (colocasia) ke shami. I also tried a delectable plate of khumb (mushroom) ke shami at Oudhyana, the Awadh-themed restaurant of Taj Mahal hotel in Gomti Nagar.
5. Chef Manish Mehrotra left Indian Accent in 2024.

Chhole: The Bean-eaters

1. Chhole or the pale kabuli variety of chickpeas are also known as chane in Punjab. I have used the terms interchangeably. However, the smaller dark brown variant of chickpeas called kale chane are never referred to as chhole.
2. The protein-rich chickpea, or garbanzo bean, is often called the poor man's meat. It belongs to the category of pulses, which was recognized as 'climate-smart' by the Food and Agriculture Organization.
3. Author Pran Nevile offers an intimate first-person account of pre-Independence Lahore in his 1993 book *Lahore: A Sentimental Journey* (New Delhi: HarperCollins Publishers India). It includes a chapter on the vibrant food culture of the city in the 1930s and 40s.
4. The two main domestic chickpea variants look strikingly different but belong to the same species: *Cicer arietinum*. India is the largest producer of chickpeas internationally, and the top growing regions are Madhya Pradesh, Gujarat, Maharashtra, and Andhra Pradesh.

Smoked Pork: Baptism by Smoke

1. Korean-American chef Edward Lee writes in his 2013 cookbook, *Smoke & Pickles* (Artisan, a division of Workman Publishing), 'Some say umami is the fifth flavor, in addition to salty, sweet, sour, and bitter….I say smoke is the sixth.'
2. Geeta Dutta is a general physician and currently works as Additional CMO of Panipat Refinery.

3. The Bodo (also known as Boro) are the largest ethno-linguistic group in Assam.
4. Khar is an alkaline extract prepared by filtering water through burnt banana peels.
5. This interview happened in 2022. Runa has since closed down her smoked meat business. 'I'm taking a break from it for some time,' she told me, when we connected over the phone earlier this year.
6. It is believed that regularly consuming smoked meats and fish may increase the risk of several types of cancer and cardiovascular diseases. However, the people I spoke with (including Geeta, a doctor herself), opined that the traditional slow-smoking method ensures the meat is exposed to minimal or no carcinogens. I cannot vouch for the authenticity of either claim.
7. As per Runa Rafique, this occurred due to overzealous efforts to promote pig farming in the northeast by introducing exotic pig varieties from states like Punjab, Haryana, and Rajasthan without a strict breeding policy in place to protect the indigenous varieties.
8. Before flying back to Mumbai, I made a pit stop in Delhi, where I tasted a delectable salad of boiled smoked pork enlivened with fresh Burmese coriander at Assamese at-home dining host Sneha Saikia's table. Author and northeast expert Hoihnu Hauzel cooked for me too, giving me a taste of her native Paite community from Manipur. The smoked pork with fermented taro leaves she fed me was full of satisfying bits of fat. 'As kids, we would treat pork fat like ghee. We would just spoon it on the rice, let it melt, and lap it up!' she said.

Rasgulla: Ball of Fame

1. I have used 'rasgulla' as the generic spelling of the sweet. Bengalis use 'rosogolla', 'rossogolla', and 'rasogolla'. Odias use 'rasagola'.
2. Colleen Taylor Sen mentions this in her note on chhena. However, she also adds that 'the early twelfth-century text Manasollasa describes a similar process used to make small balls that were fried.' (Colleen Taylor Sen, Sourish Bhattacharyya, Helen Saberi [eds.], *The Bloomsbury Handbook of Indian Cuisine*, London: Bloomsbury Academic, 2023, p. 77.)
3. The term chhana is derived from the Sanskrit term 'chhinna' or torn, and indicates the texture of the milk when it curdles. As per K. T. Achaya, 'the Aryan taboo on the deliberate "breaking of milk" meant that it was not a favoured item.' (*A Historical Dictionary of Indian Food*, p. 41.) Bengali scholar Haripada Bhowmick expresses a similar view in his book *Rasogolla: Banglar Jogot Matano Abiskar* published in 2015.
4. K. C. Das uses the spelling 'rossogolla'.

5. Along with K. C. Das, the Sen brothers of Matri Bhandar in Comila district in Bangladesh, have claimed to be the original makers of the dessert.
6. Ritajit is no longer working with K. C. Das.
7. Lahana Ghosh of Jugal's reiterated that when it comes to producing the finest chhena, the quality of dairy plays a pivotal role. 'The Doodh Bajar, nestled in Kolkata's iconic Burrabazar, operates much like a commodities exchange, where daily rates are determined. Additionally, the mishtiwalas (sweet shop owners) engage in bidding at the start of the fiscal year, securing "call options" for milk at predetermined prices. It's a fascinating process. Remarkably, milk prices can soar to ₹100 per litre,' she told me.
8. The rosogollas sold at Balaram Mullick (and many other shops in Kolkata) are not spongy in texture.
9. Rakhi Purnima Dasgupta succumbed to a heart attack in 2023.
10. Asit Mohanty, Supriya Kar (tr.), 'Rasagola: The Ritual Offering of Odisha', *Odisha Review*, April 2017.
11. Odia scholar Asit Mohanty has pointed out that there are several descriptions of chhena and chhena products in Balarama Das's Odia Ramayana known as Dandi Ramayana. He writes, 'literature on rasagola has not been compiled systematically in Odisha. Starting from *Sarala Mahabharata* to *Dandi Ramayana*, *Ambika Bilasa*, and *Bidagdha Chintamani*, Odishan food culture is amply described in all these books.' ('Rasagola: The Ritual Offering of Odisha', *Odisha Review*, April 2017.)
12. Ras malai (known as rossomalai and roshmalai in West Bengal) was ranked second amongst the world's top cheese desserts in a list released by TasteAtlas in 2024.

Index

Beans

Chicken

Chickpeas

Coconut

Dal

Eggplants

Eggs

Fish and seafood

Milk

Mutton

Yoghurt and curd